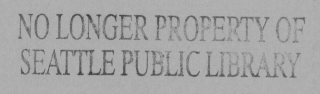

AN IMMOVABLE FEAST

TYLER BLANSKI

An Immovable Feast

*How I Gave Up Spirituality for
a Life of Religious Abundance*

IGNATIUS PRESS   SAN FRANCISCO

Cover photograph:
Church on the island at Bled, Slovenia by Franc Ferjan

Cover design by Tyler Blanski/John Herreid

© 2018 by Ignatius Press, San Francisco
All rights reserved
ISBN 978-1-62164-233-6
Library of Congress Control Number 2017949608
Printed in the United States of America ∞

For Brittany

Yours I am, O Lord, and born for you.
What do you ask of me?

—Saint Teresa of Ávila

CONTENTS

I

MCMLXXXIV

If you're thirsty, you may drink.

—Aslan

Help me to spread your fragrance everywhere I go;
let me preach you without preaching,
not by words but by my example
by the catching force, the sympathetic influence of what I do,
the evident fullness of the love my heart bears to you.

—John Henry Newman[1]

I was born in the middle of a freezing winter, under a moon more than half-lit but less than full. Outside the hospital window the sun would not rise for several hours still. It was the twelfth day of 1984, the year of Tetris, *Purple Rain*, and *This Is Spinal Tap*. My mother and father drove me home in a yellow Chevy Chevette, the hatchback they bought just before they married, and my mother cried because I would not suckle. I was loved and given every comfort, but I don't think a day has gone by that I have not felt something like longing.

Since I am a slow learner, I tried to fill that longing with romance. When I was very young, my heart was brimful of the Wild West, chivalry and knighthood, poetry and wilderness and adventure. Perhaps this is why pastors and therapists said I resisted authority and convention. I cried at the airport when I had to stow my tooled leather gun belt with matching holsters and toy peacemaker pistols. I said that I hated Christianity when my third-grade teacher at Calvin Christian School handed me a football and told me I was too old to play in the woods. I quit piano lessons when my tutor was caught having an affair with the church choir director. I posted a Declaration of Independence on my bedroom door when my parents wouldn't let me cut my hair in the Mohawk fashion and, much to the consternation of churchgoers at the Baptist church we attended, promptly grew a mullet. All in all, it's safe to say that before my eleventh birthday I felt very much at odds with the world.

My parents were rebels in their own way. At the age of fourteen my mother rebelled against the American Dream with that most terrible act of open resistance to the establishment and became a Christian. At sixteen, having been raised by chain-smoking Catholics, my father rebelled himself into becoming an Evangelical Christian. They smashed their Beatles records and evangelized and lived an audacious prayer, and then with the utmost lack of summer of '69 propriety married young and started a family. I was raised on Larry Norman and Keith Green, as well as good home cooking. My first memory of dancing is to Michael W. Smith's 1990 hit *Go West Young Man*. We did not listen to secular music, we did not drink alcohol, and we never missed church on Sundays. Before anything else we were Christians, and I knew that my family was different, strange, and at variance with the prevailing social norms.

Yet, I was never really alone, for I grew up under God-filled skies and my parents spoke of angels. When I was two years old, they dedicated me to the Lord in the presence of many witnesses, and always a sense of the holy compelled my germinating and half-conscious religious life. My toy box was well stocked, my bookshelf boasted a small collection of boyhood classics, and my summers were spent climbing trees or running through the sprinkler with my brother and sister. Our father wrestled and built forts and read aloud from stories by George MacDonald and J.R.R. Tolkien and C.S. Lewis. Our mother listened to her children when we came home from school, asking questions and letting us lick the cookie batter off the spoon. I drew pictures and tried my hand at watercolors, invented alphabets and worlds, and my fifth-grade teacher encouraged me to write poetry, even though I had a mullet.

My earliest memory of my father is when we took the training wheels off my bike. He held my seat and helped me balance as I pedaled, and suddenly I was racing down the sidewalk and he was far behind. In that moment, with the wind in my face and the sun shining bright, I was overcome by the horrible realization that I was on my own. As my father cheered and shouted instructions, I cannot now recall whether I managed to turn around or if I flew over the handlebars; but looking back I consider that first moment of independence, that first moment of responsibility for my own fate, with neither training wheels nor a hand to guide me, the beginning of the end.

One afternoon, I wandered into the backyard feeling bored. I lined up my toy soldiers and then knocked them down. I ate a pear and buried the seeds. I watered the soil and waited to see if a tree would grow. When I grew weary of this, I walked back into the kitchen and sighed, "I'm not even five and I'm tired of living."

"Take a nap," said my mother.

"Can I watch television?"

"No."

So, the days passed, one very much like the other. Not being allowed to watch television, I was forced to press through those moments when we are unable to think of what to do or how to proceed and to fall in love with the world. We all can play, if only we find something to love. I loved brooks and meadows, butterfly nets and old boxes, backyards and kitchens, saddles and hammers. I loved rain, springtime, fall. I loved castles, treasure maps, bullets, and killing the bad guys.

Stapled in the pages of my scrapbook, a scribbled note from my mother pulls back the curtains of my childhood to what I was too young to remember:

I've tried quite a few times to start this, but as typical, there are many interruptions. My pants have wet spots from many tears, and mud from the dirty little hands that wanted a hug. I sit in front of a table with markers, playdough, paint, water, "tools," cowboy hat, papers, crumbs, and a measure (otherwise known as a gun). The bedrooms are a mess, as is the bathroom, living room, and dining room, but somehow today it doesn't matter.

What matters is that I got to read a story while a hot-headed 4-year-old fell asleep while touching my cheek and holding my hand. What matters is that I had two little helpers who got the broom, dustpan, and "helped" fertilize the lawn, edge the sidewalk, and "clean up" the trimmings. What matters is that I got up this morning, made bacon, eggs, muffins to feed

my family and they gobbled it all up and as trusting can be, they expect
more the next meal—even though I haven't thought of what it will be!
I can do the dishes and wash the clothes of the boys in the house and
as I do each I'm reminded that there were lots of games in the dirt,
worms to look at, weeds that were picked, balls bounced, pants pooped
in, cowboys and policemen and dirty faces and sticky fingers and pleases
and thank yous and *who-hoos*!! that went with every piece.

So I feel far behind in all the things that could be done (or that I think
should be done) and I don't think it's so important, because I'm supposed
to be a cowboy right now, or a princess that needs to be rescued, and
I realize there's one character that needs development more than those
cowboys. After all, when Tyler says, "Mommy, did you pray for me
last night while I was sleeping?" I *know*, as long as God wills, I wouldn't
change jobs for anything!

* * * * *

"How do you spell 'handsome'?" said the teacher.

"H-a-n-s-u-m," I replied, haltingly.

The class giggled. I hung my head.

"Special" was a word used to describe me. Teachers said I lived in
La La Land; and, like the Queen of Hearts, some days I believed as
many as six impossible things before breakfast. I dreaded being sent
to a special room during math class to play with colored blocks, but
I was a slow learner. Every spelling bee, students won seashells with
which to decorate their desks. My desk was always empty.

I was also sentimental and headstrong, and I held to my beliefs with
inviolable but often short-lived conviction. One day, I was probably nine or ten, I announced that I was going to run away. I filled
a large red handkerchief with an apple and a sandwich, and tied the
contents to the end of a long stick. I marched around the block with
pride. Not knowing what else to do, I sat on the curb across the street
from my home and I ate my sandwich. And as I was biting into my
apple, I remember seeing my family sit down to dinner through the
dining-room window, and suddenly I felt foolish. Maybe I thought
the world would sputter to a stop in my absence, that my family
would be beside themselves with worry, but there they were eating
dinner, as if nothing had changed. Flabbergasted, I shelved my pride
and went home, and as I entered the dining room my mother cried

and my father laughed and I sat down to a feast. This memory has become for me more than mere history; it is parable.

It wasn't until I was twelve years old that I accepted Jesus Christ as my personal Lord and Savior at a church camp in the woods. I sat with the other campers in a chapel of rough-hewn pine to sing worship songs and listen to different speakers. Eventually, a camp leader in a Hawaiian T-shirt told the story of an Israelite soldier named Achan. Because Achan had taken some of the plunder of Jericho for himself, God allowed the Israelites to be routed in battle and many soldiers died. Then God revealed to the people Achan's sin, and so they stoned Achan, along with his wife, children, and livestock. Then they set them on fire and heaped stones on their charred bodies. Only then did God turn from his anger.

I got a sick feeling. It bothered me that the other soldiers, family members, and animals were killed too. What had they done to deserve death?

"Many were killed," said the camp leader, "and that's the moral of the story. You see, just one man sinned, but many died."

Campers shifted uncomfortably in their chairs.

"What if *we* sin? Does God punish us like Achan? Does anyone else get punished too? Or has God come up with a way to punish sin that has a better ending than this?"

I wasn't so sure.

"With Achan, one man sinned and many died. What if later in the Bible there is one man who *never* sinned, but was still punished? What if this one man died so that many could live? Jesus is not guilty, so God picked him to die. For us. Your sin is very bad, but God poured out his wrath on Jesus instead of you. Jesus took the punishment you deserve. God loves you so much that he sent his Son, Jesus, to die for your sin. And because Jesus took your punishment, if you belong to him, God becomes your Father. You have a home in God. Do you want to belong to Jesus?"

I was "special" and I didn't have any seashells on my desk, but I didn't care. I wanted to belong to Jesus. When the camp leader called anyone who wanted to say the believer's prayer to come up to the front, I leaped to my feet.

In those days I often wondered, am I saved? The question is like asking, "Am I in love?" There is no magic trick, no standardized test. Saying the believer's prayer was neither the beginning nor the end, but it was a turn in the road. It was what any conversion is: the (hopefully) daily turning away from sin and toward God. All I know is that if we give God a minute—and if we never stop giving him a minute—he will turn our minutes into an hour, a life, maybe even an eternity. I am early in my story, but I believe that when it comes to love, God cannot be fooled. He does his part; the question is, Will we do ours?

That night in the chapel, the Holy Spirit's aim was sure, even if the camp leader's telling of the Gospel was not. Did the Father really *punish* Jesus instead of us, and is this an accurate picture of the life of the Trinity? How can the Father regard his all-holy Son as anything other than all-holy? Or could it be that the Cross is a *Trinitarian event* in which Jesus allowed himself to be killed by men so that he could offer himself in the bond of the Holy Spirit as a sacrifice of love to the Father? And could it be that the Father accepts this sacrifice as making satisfaction for the sins of the world precisely because it is the same offering his all-holy Son makes from all eternity, except now in the flesh? It seems that one can only say that Jesus "took our punishment" in a poetic rather than in a literal sense. I was too young to take it in any sense except that I was loved by God, and I wanted to love him back.

And quite without realizing it, I had arrived at the beginning of religion.

* * * * *

"Where's Dad going with Jake?" I asked, feigning ignorance as my mother prepared dinner.

"We talked about this yesterday," she replied softly. "That dog can't stay here."

"*That dog?*" I cried. "You mean *our* dog, Jake."

"He pees on the carpet and he's too old to be trained. We have decided to send him back."

"Send him back?" I shouted. "You mean *abandon* him? Just because he pees?"

"Don't yell, Tyler."

I stomped down the hallway to my room and slammed the door, tears running down my cheeks. It was more than unfair: the idea that someone, anyone, could be *sent back* broke my heart.

Second only to a soul that will not repent, I wonder if the scariest thing in the world is a heart that will not break. I first learned how to harden my heart on the first day of school in the fifth grade, when I told Lucy that I would not play with her anymore. The previous year we had spent recess playing imagination games in the forest, but now I wanted to play with the cool kids.

"You're embarrassed by me, aren't you?" Lucy stood at the foot of the lunch table where I was trying to look cool. "You don't want to be seen talking to a girl."

Ashamed of betraying a friend and embarrassed that the other boys were watching, I decided to look at the ceiling. I spent the rest of the year beneath the monkey bars mindlessly running around with the cool kids and stealing glances at the forest. Looking back, I can see now that I had been foolish and mean—but I was not heartless.

My youth was shot through with wonder. Having neither money nor influence nor power, as vulnerable as any human child, I set forth into the world with eyes wide open and a heart with violin strings attached. Huddled on the floor over a Bible at a children's summer camp, I sobbed uncontrollably in front of my peers when a camper confessed that he had never loved anyone, and he meant it.

"Not even your mom?" I asked.

"No one," he said, and a gargoyle seemed almost to writhe behind his boyish face.

I ran out of the cabin and down the thickly wooded path to the lake. Never being loved is one thing, I thought, but never to love— that was entirely different! Without love there is no world, no other, only the tired clamp of a soul turned in on itself, like a metal folding chair. I stood on the shoreline and shivered at the possibility that it could be better to love than to be loved, that no matter how much God loves us he cannot make us love him back, and that the difference between heaven and hell is Jesus' one simple question: "Do you love me?" (Jn 21:15–17). I listened as the wind knocked the branches of lonely pines against one another and looked up into the night sky. The stars flickered in the vaulted blackness, like votive candles still burning from prayers said in another age. I spread my arms out as far as I could and swore to God that I would never stop loving.

But by the seventh grade, the sadness of the world clenched around my heart. I had a radio and a five-disc CD player, and the

same powers that inspired Snoop Dogg and The Offspring were able
to sow their seeds unhindered in the childish mind of my parents'
firstborn son. I grew my hair out like Kurt Cobain, wore a chain wallet, and pretended to walk with a limp for no reason at all. I blamed
church and my innocent siblings for my insecurities. I scorned con-
formity. Above all, I disdained religion. I had made the easy mistake
of thinking religion was pretense, and that anyone who was pious was
automatically a big phony. That anyone should regard this proposition as not self-evident astonished me.

As I earnestly sought true spirituality, anti-religious sentiment was
at once tacit and axiomatic. I recoiled at the word "religion" just as
I recoiled from the words "institution", "preacher", and "pew". I
wanted nothing to do with a meaningless ritualism that congratulates
itself for going through the motions. Saved by faith alone and not by
works, even to try to keep God's laws was to be guilty of haggling:
"If I behave on the outside, then I will win God's blessing on the
inside." At its best, I believed, organized religion tried to work from
the outside in; but the Gospel worked from the inside out. Jesus
cared about faith, not works. And because I didn't really *do* anything
when it came to Jesus, and because my chain wallet jingled when I
walked, I knew my faith was authentic.

I dreaded those Sundays when my family visited my grandparents'
Catholic parish. The ugly crucifix and the fat priest and the old lady
yodeling on her out-of-tune guitar made me claustrophobic. The
sanctuary reminded me of the public school building in which I was
compelled to spend most of my days, a building reminiscent of a
Soviet Russian experiment. The Mass seemed to leave no scope for
the imagination, which is just as well since my imagination had taken
a turn for the worse. Like so many young people, I thought darkness
was more interesting than light.

* * * * *

I've often wondered if a voice was speaking to me in the battles and
rock music and sunsets. *There is something missing in your life*, it seemed
to whisper. *There is something more.* The voice often came when I
flipped through an outdoor catalogue, resolved to learn a new song
on the guitar, or fell in love. At first, I mistook the source of this

voice to be an invitation to become spiritual or to make memories. For fun, I worked at a church camp and went on mission trips and drank wheatgrass juice. I wrote prayers in my journal and wished I had the guts to ask Molly out on a date. When I was sixteen, I went skinny-dipping and hung fuzzy dice from my review mirror. I climbed mountains and jumped cliffs and raced down the freeway blasting Tupac Shakur and was incorrigibly romantic.

My favorite childhood movies were *The Lone Ranger*, *The Last of the Mohicans*, and *Dances with Wolves*, but by the time I was fifteen years old I was watching *You've Got Mail* over and over again, wishing I owned a little bookshop and drank coffee and generally wallowing in my boyhood crush on Meg Ryan. At night I snuck out with friends and we would skateboard and TP the lawns of girls we liked, and occasionally I would wake up early to read the Bible. Above all, I longed for transformation through contemporary worship music, to lift my hands in praise and to feel the waves of God's love crash against me and have my love return in the undertow. In an unfortunate instance of throwing the baby out with the bathwater, this season of praise would come shuddering to a halt when one of my youth ministers assured us that no matter how horrible we were during the week, God was always happy when we came together to sing worship songs on Sunday.

"But if we don't honor God on the weekdays, why would he want our worship on Sundays?" I asked, hardly grasping the implications of my question.

"That's the great thing about God," my youth minister said. "No matter what we do during the week, we can always worship him on Sunday."

I had been guilty of living one way during the week but worshiping God on Sundays, even believing against Saint Paul's better judgment that the whole situation made grace abound even more, but it wasn't until I heard someone actually say it out loud that I realized how strongly I disagreed with it on principle. Before the end of my sophomore year, I spurned what I called "suburban Christianity", a therapeutic deism in pursuit of the American Dream, and I eventually left the youth group altogether in the heat of self-righteousness. It would be more than a decade before I finally stopped trying to make memories or be spiritual, a whole decade before I got down to the serious business of heaven; but I had heard a voice. *There is something more*, it whispered in the cool of the evening. *Something is missing.*

But what could it be? I had already accepted Jesus Christ as my personal Lord and Savior at a church camp when I was twelve years old. So I had everything.

Looking back, I can see that even in the midst of so many contradictions and confusion that tiny Yes to God imbued my adolescence with hope. I'll never forget coming home from church camp and pulling my mother aside to whisper with joy, "I'm a Christian." She smiled and said she already knew. In 1998, a few years after the believer's prayer, when I had a crush on a girl who loved the outdoors and Jesus and had even been baptized, I wrote in my journal that someday "I'm going to get baptized."

More than Baptism, though, I wanted the girl. I wanted to find someone who was on the same secret road, someone who would say, "What! You too? I thought I was the only one!" She would be drop-dead gorgeous and would love to hike and sit in Adirondack chairs reading poetry. As I put it in a journal entry entitled "A Poem for the One I Do Not Know Yet" on March 30, 1998: "Your body may be beautiful, but your heart must be radiant: a sparkling jewel that has the Lord's light shining out of it." A year later, I declared to God on the pages of my journal: "I want to get married.... We'd play checkers, Monopoly, and then sit by the fire and talk about God."

I wanted the girl, and a part of me also wanted God. In the eighth grade, I read a book called *Intimacy with the Almighty* and was discouraged that the other boys in my youth group neither appreciated its embossed, antique-looking cover nor shared my desire to escape all the noise that makes us numb to the still, small voice. I judged them mightily from the great Olympian heights of my bedroom, where I turned up Green Day and Rage against the Machine and tore pages out of the skateboarding magazine *Thrasher* and read *Intimacy with the Almighty*. Days, weeks, even years would go by and the voice would speak to me again: *Aren't you hungry? There is something missing.*

I listened, and I heard echoes of a summons. And by the time I graduated high school, I began to suspect that the devotions by the lake and the paperback books, the girls and the long walks, the weathered blue jeans and faded ball caps and all the poetry—they were not the thing itself. They were only a clue. The call wasn't to collect tattoos, photo albums, and mystical experiences. What was it? Something *behind* the beauty and the sadness summoned me. I might not have been able to name the voice, but I knew one thing: it was terrifying.

2

Makeshift Sacraments

Where were you when I laid the foundations of the earth ...
when the morning stars sang together,
and all the sons of God shouted for joy?

—Job 38:4, 7

And I pray that you will lead me, a sinner,
to the banquet where you,
with your Son and Holy Spirit, are true and
perfect light, total fulfillment,
everlasting joy, gladness without end,
and perfect happiness to your saints.

—Saint Thomas Aquinas[1]

There is a place in the north country where the road ends in a thick patchwork of pines and birch copses. You will turn left into a gravel drive that pushes through the trees for three miles until, at last, it opens to a lake as beautiful and vast as any sea. You will crank the dial on an antique phone, and twenty minutes later a boat will dock at the landing. Hiding behind a distant peninsula ahead there is a cluster of cabins you cannot get to by car, only by boat, and the cabins stand sentinel over the bay on the far side of the lake. You will be on the edge of wilderness, and there will be no way back except across the water. Here is the resort on the bay, owned and operated by my extended family, and it is the geography I have always loved best.

As a child I absorbed the whole landscape: the sparse topsoil, the white-knuckle roots of the pines as they grip the granite rock, the rivers and lakes, the eerie call of the loon regally patterned in black and white as he makes his territorial claim. I worked at the resort when I was sixteen and learned to revere the tackle and know-how of the trade. In particular, I looked up to my older cousin Jay with an adoration not unlike hyperdulia and second only to latria. He lived in an old trapper shack surrounded by tall pines and wore long, curly black hair and flannels. He played guitar and listened to the forest, walking his trap lines in the winter and tending to the boats in the summer, always smoking hand-rolled cigarettes. Jay spoke of a Great Spirit that you could swim in like water and smell in the cedars. Birds followed him, flying from branch to branch and singing, and I saw them eat from his hand. One day while shingling a cabin roof we agreed that if a man could marry any woman on earth—any one woman at all—it would have to be Anne of Green Gables.

"I wouldn't even touch her," Jay said. "I would only lie awake and listen to her talk."

That summer my jobs included trail maintenance, wood splitting, and ensuring that guests had everything they needed to fish. Every morning I swept out the Finnish sauna, cleaned the old fish house, and dumped the bucket of fish guts on an island across the lake so the bears would stay away from our camp. One morning I packed my Bible and a thermos of coffee with the bucket of fish guts and drove the boat across the lake through a dense fog. I stopped in the middle of the lake as the sun rose to pray and revel in the pink mists, and I *loved* God in the splendors of his creation.

It has never ceased to be just a little frightening that a man can *love* God, but I remember loving him in that boat on the water. A few days later, I was clearing a trail on a high rock face when I saw a storm on the other side of the lake fast approaching. It came rumbling across the water and the rain pummeled me. As the storm blotted out the sun and dispersed every bird, I dropped my axe and stood there on the edge of the cliff in a posture of worship free of all artifice. The storm passed, and the sunlight shone through the birch trees and warmed the forest floor, and my heart was full.

All of this is to say that when I was young there were two primary sacraments: romance and wilderness. As far as I was concerned, the Shekinah glory of God had condescended to dwell somewhere in the wild places of the north, and for me the long drive to the resort was a kind of approach, an opportunity to come clean and to receive absolution from the pines before the moment of encounter.

By the weather vane that was my adolescence, anyone could see my heart was spinning every direction between hymning praises and a pagan poetry. To my credit, even though I tried to fill my deepest longings with romance and received every wild place as an outward sign of an inward grace, above all I sought God in his holy Word. The red letters seemed to be another kind of sacrament, a live conduit of God's power. And so I suppose that in addition to the rude sacraments of romance and wilderness there was also the sacrament of Sacred Scripture. In fact, now that I think of it, I can remember no less than seven makeshift sacraments in my youth. Each one is a clue, or perhaps a cairn easily seen from a distance, enabling me to make sense of those difficult years.

* * * * *

"What is this?" I sassed. "A labor camp?"

"Well, it's certainly not a hotel," said my mother, handing me the trash.

For me, work was a sacrament of initiation. Although I resented chores, I was keenly aware that I came from a long line of men who worked. My grandfather's life was one of hard work. Growing up poor and marrying young, serving in the army and paying his way through university, all the while providing for a family of nine, he worked. My father also worked. As a boy he had a daily paper route, and he worked through high school, buying his own car and saving for college. He also married young and worked multiple jobs in college, and eventually Yale, and supported his growing family of five. My parents always said, "People are more important than things." Our couches were threadbare, we never ate brand-name cereal, and our clothes were from Goodwill, but we were far from poor. Looking back, I am thankful for my father's adeptness at leaving work at the office. He would come home and drop his briefcase and sing our mother's praises before playing with us kids and gathering everyone around the table to pray and eat.

I knew that I was different from my father and grandfather, born in a different time, born into a world with more comforts and distractions. But I *wanted* to work. I had a paper route for a few years and I mowed lawns for cash, but I was keenly aware that someday I would need to get a job. One can be employed at the age of fourteen in Minnesota, and this inspired and terrified me. On my fourteenth birthday I wrote: "I'm nervous, excited, and dreading the fact that I'm going to be able to work this summer." I was hired on as a barista at a local coffee shop, and at the age of fifteen learned how to pull espresso shots and steam milk and manage a till. The café not only opened up to me the world of coffee, but its north-woods, log-cabin motif provided scope for the imagination. In my mind, coffee symbolized the kind of life I wanted, a life of books and quiet reflection.

Passing from one runic stone to the next, I eventually worked at the local organic co-op as a cashier. While the work of a barista was varied and involved technical skill, no inward grace came to me through the outward signs of swiping credit cards and punching SKU numbers. I handed in my two weeks' notice with an essay entitled "Why I Am Not a Machine".

And so in the summer of 2002, at the age of eighteen, I was hired on at an exterior house-painting company that still painted by hand, and not sprayers.

"Wait, you're a virgin?" a painter asked on my first day.

The crew dissolved into laughter. I clutched the high ladder and tried not to look down.

A grab bag of high school dropouts, potheads, and old men who spoke loudly of their adulterous exploits, I found house painters to be an exotic bunch. But the work was honest, and I came home sunburned, exhausted, and happy. By the end of the summer, the others seemed almost to enjoy having me on board, even though I was a "good boy".

There was another work I took very seriously, and that was the business of rocking out. After I quit piano lessons, I angrily grabbed my mother's classical guitar and wouldn't stop pounding on it. I longed for the transcendence that peeked out from behind the iconostasis of rock music, veiled in all her splendor, the queen of all sacraments and the pearl without a price. Before long I had my hands on a steel-stringed dreadnought acoustic guitar and was signed up for weekly lessons. Sensing my resistance to authority, my tutor wisely avoided sheet music and taught me to play by ear. And when I eventually discovered the Dave Matthews and Tim Reynolds album *Live at Luther College*, my passion for acoustic guitar billowed to the heavens.

I remember listening to records with my uncle Tim at his cabin of logs in Wisconsin. "Sometimes a man needs to rock out," he said, then turned up Led Zeppelin. The setting sun pressed through the thick trees and humidity, filling the living room with July. We decided that all rock music was born in July. Uncle Tim paced from the kitchen to the living room to the kitchen to the deck, staring off in a happy haze. That night, after a long day of splitting firewood and gardening, Aunt Lisa joined us, and we stayed outside late in broken lawn chairs and watched the fireflies under a loud and fearless anti-establishment sky.

When I was accepted into a high school for artists, my parents generously gave me an acoustic guitar made of Indian rosewood and cedar and mahogany. I practiced for hours every day, running through scales and learning new songs. Every Saturday I cleaned my guitar in ritualistic fashion while listening to *Live at Luther College*. At the arts school, I connected with another guitarist whose jazz influence and edgy leads complemented my folk songs.

"What's your name?" I asked.

"Dude," he said, beating his guitar furiously, "my name is Nate."

"You're pretty good."

"Yeah man, I'm just jamming," said Nate. "You play?"

We produced our first album by the end of our junior year, performed in coffee houses and on street corners, and dreamed of changing the world with music. The summer before my senior year I wrote:

Nate and I were playing on the corner of Lake and Hennepin with a hat out for money. Many rich, fancy people walked by with icy stares and only a poor, crippled man in a wheelchair and a homeless man with one arm stopped to listen and even dropped cash in the hat. Seeing the man struggle to get over to the hat to drop what little he had. He needed that money a whole lot more than I do. It moved me. Here I was only thinking about making music and money and this man was willing to give what looked like all he had. Tomorrow Nate and I are going to jam on the street again. I plan on bringing some food bags to help people out and my Bible to witness.

I didn't have the guts to bring a Bible, but the knot between serving those in need and music had been tied. That day on the street corner served as a kind of *Ite, missa est.* I was just beginning to see that you cannot keep what you don't give away.

* * * * *

"Good night, Kelly!" I said.
   "Good night, Tyler!"
   There was a pause.
   "Good night, Kelly!"
   "Good night, Tyler!"
   "Good night!"
   "Good night!"
I crept slowly back to the boys' side of church camp, dizzy with love.

The heart, also, was a sacrament, a voice at once immediate and infallible. The only problem was that, apart from girls, my heart was drawn to things I didn't quite believe in. Early in my adolescence, for example, I read a novel about a priest who ministered to his small-town flock, and I wanted somehow to *be* him. I read his story over and over again and lay awake dreaming about what it would be like to be a priest. It seemed almost too good to be true that a man could *do* the work of the Kingdom, that the day labor of salvation could be one's full-time job. But everything I knew about Jesus seemed to suggest that the apostolic priesthood (and all that it represented) was a corruption of the true, simple faith.

Looking back, I realize that my most fundamental beliefs about Christianity were in many ways inconsistent with my deepest longings. I believed that Jesus never asked anyone to form a "church", ordain priests, and develop elaborate rituals. He cut through all religious trappings to the heart. He reproofed those who claimed any dogma to be true or any tradition to be worthy, for his Kingdom was invisible and his ways were ultimately unknowable. Yet when my family hiked Gooseberry Falls in the winter of 1998 and the snow was falling on the cedars, I dreamed of building a monastery there. I imagined hearing bells. A few years later I pulled Richard Foster's *Celebration of Discipline* off my parents' bookshelf, and the opening lines resonated with me:

"Superficiality is the curse of our age.... The desperate need today is not for a greater number of intelligent people, or gifted people, but for deep people."² I wanted to be deep, and the spiritual practices of meditation, fasting, tithing, worshiping, Confession, and service seemed to offer a richer spiritual life. I wrote in my journal sometime around the turn of the millennium: "I have been discovering the delights of the Daily Office." Having read stories of Christian martyrs and sensing (but not recognizing) the value of *merit* in the economy of grace, I wrote: "I have been reading The Voice of the Martyrs' *Jesus Freaks* by D.C. Talk. It has opened my eyes to the power of God's love. He transforms. Consume me with your love, Lord."

Despite all this, even though I lionized both hard work and the heart, I somehow feared that my love for God would be jeopardized by outwardly serving him. In 1999, while touring Paris with my family, I wrote in my journal: "The heart cannot be caged by religion, rules, or an outer show. The heart is wild. I don't want this love to be ebbed away in the whirlwind of Christian service, activity, and religion. I don't want to move my spiritual life into the outer world of activity and internally drift. In the end, it does not matter how well we have performed or what we did. A life without the heart is not worth living. The heart is God's greatest gift."

I had accepted Jesus into my heart, and so I followed my heart. The summer before my senior year I solemnly wrote: "I refuse to make my faith suburban, because it's wild and unfettered. My life is hypocritical if I cannot live the way it moves me. I cannot be managed like a corporation. Don't place me in a box: that's not salvation. I am more than dutiful. I will never become another hollow man."

"We miss seeing you," a friend said, when I had skipped a few Sundays.

"I can love Jesus without going to church," I said.

Drawn to the priesthood and monasteries and the Daily Office yet simultaneously convinced that such things were a chimera, not knowing what else to do I grew dreadlocks and joined a spiritual community of Jesus followers called "The Porch". They held Sunday services above a café and sat on couches and lit candles. The Porch practiced open communion, inviting even the unbaptized to participate because it was believed that the Kingdom of God is like a wedding feast and everyone is invited to taste and see that the Lord is good. Full of tattooed yogis and granola moms, the Porch dabbled in "historic Christianity". It was there that I first recited the Nicene Creed, heard a modified version of Saint Patrick's breastplate, and participated in a Seder meal. I mostly just loved the candles and the aroma of coffee and that the Porch was so different from my suburban youth group scene. For the first time I was actively participating in a community of adults and carrying my own weight. They were welcoming and respectful, and seemed to appreciate me even more than I appreciated them, which was a great deal.

Throughout my time at the Porch, my battle cry became, "Live deep, not fast." I wrestled with the Janus-faced nature of the American Dream, at once obsessed with my "style" and yet longing to be free of pretense. In the autumn of my senior year I wrote:

> My wisdom teeth were pulled two days ago and my confinement to the house has given me time to realize that I have been living fast, not deep. I am worn out. I work hard, I get good grades, and I am involved in my youth group. I appear to be on top of things: I am preparing for the ACT, I own a mountain bike, I play guitar, I drive a car, I've got $1,000 in savings, $250 in my checkbook, a full tank of gas, $70 cash, nice clothes, a clean room, and well-groomed dreadlocks on my head. But it's all dust. I am nothing without God and must find my salvation in him. Thoreau said that when he had a table that needed dusting he threw it out the window shouting, "I do not have time for dusting, I am too busy living!" Thomas Young said, "A bold Christian is the highest style of a man." I need to find my style, my life, in God.

* * * * *

And then there was the sacrament of personal experience. I was seventeen and insecure, and Mason's advances made me uncomfortable. He sat next to me in math class, and I ignored him so that no one would associate me with him, even though at the arts high school being gay was common. Mason winked at me in the hallway, and I insulted him loudly. A week later, Mason hung himself.

I knew that Mason did not commit suicide because I insulted him in the hallway. His story was bigger than that. But when I heard of Mason's death, my heart suddenly circled the globe like a ship carrying New York's garbage. Hiding in a bathroom stall, I buried my face

in my hands and wept. I wished I could go back in time and say hello
to Mason, say something kind.

Around that time, I secretly began to worry that Christianity's
vision for sexuality was *bad news* for Mason. How could Christian
morality be good news for a lonely, gay, suicidal sixteen-year-old?
For the first time in my life, I had to ask myself: *Is Christianity good
news for* everyone?

Mason's death sent me on a journey. I wanted a Christianity of
compassion and grace that was rich with mystery. As I soaked my
dreadlocks in salt water and listened to Celtic music, I plunged almost
irreversibly into new and unplumbed mystic depths. I lived with the
dream of something worthy of complete surrender, something that
would demand my faith utterly and absolutely, but I could not get
around the fact that if Christianity were a *religion*, with all the moral
strictures and commanding dogmas of a religion, it would not allow
for Mason's happiness. And I believed very firmly that there is no
greater happiness on earth than romantic and sexual fulfilment. But
if Christianity were a *spirituality*, then Mason could fall in love with
another man and get married and be an upstanding citizen in the
Kingdom of God—regardless of his creed, sexual orientation, or
identity. After all, modern scholars were discovering that the Bible
isn't actually antigay, and I believed the primary way God reveals his
will to us is through the Bible (read with the help of scholars) and
personal experience.

Scholars and personal experience. The Catholics are content
with a single pope and that he is only infallible when he speaks ex
cathedra, but I gladly accepted popes by the dozen, and they were
infallible whether they stood in the pulpit or in their Birkenstock
sandals. When it came to sexual morality, I didn't have the guts to
say one way or the other, at least officially. I was grieving, and I
wanted neither to leave the shores of orthodoxy nor to break step
with Ani DiFranco or the Minneapolis music scene, and so I found
solace in my wager that ultimately faith is a very private affair. This
way Christianity could be good news for Mason because it allowed
him a personal relationship with Jesus while leaving the answer to
moral questions up to the discretion of the individual's personal
experience and private judgment. Jesus battled mightily against the
showy, legalistic Pharisees; he cared most for the heart, and who can

judge the heart but God? Suffice it to say, there were no conversions at the arts high school, though the fields were white for the harvest. In the name of compassion, but mostly out of cowardice, I kept the Gospel to myself.

I was thinking all this at the same time I was beginning to see that the more people freed themselves from religious doctrines, the easier it was for them to bind themselves to political dogmas. The people at the arts school were kind in their own way, but I shied from their arrogance, their boundless self-importance, and their belief in government programs. "Think for yourselves," my teachers said, but if I did and came to a conclusion other than the one prescribed, I was wrong. The teachers demanded an extensive and invasive compliance from their students unlike anything I had experienced at private school, and every one of us was encouraged to join the great mass of nonconformists. "Express yourself," they said. "Everybody's doing it."

Love and freedom were confused with free sex. "Truth" was an ideological ploy to cloak the dead white man's dagger. Thus we were taught that nothing ought to compel our devotion except global warming, the gay rights movement, and a woman's right to choose.

From the start, my opposition to feminism was based on a chivalrous and protective love for my mother. In almost all its forms, feminist theory somehow managed to insult my mother, holding her body and hard work in contempt. I was too young to name it, but when my civics teacher said that today's woman could be *so much more* than a mother, I felt at a gut level that *nothing* could be more precious than human life, and the woman's privilege of bearing new life rose above anything a man could ever do at the office. I might have been young and selfish, but I somehow recognized that without loving mothers, there could be no home, no civilization, only the noise of souls turning in on themselves.

With my views about motherhood I might as well have been a chauvinist, and with my belief in God I might as well have been a Bible thumper. I didn't consider myself to be religious, but compared to my friends at the arts high school, I was a hidebound archconservative.

"I'm not religious," Ashley said, who rejected heaven and hell but believed in an afterlife. "I don't need the past. I'm about living in the present. I'm about the future."

"I'm spiritual," Nick said. "There's really no religion that doesn't condemn other people and other values, and I believe in excluding no one." Nick didn't like names such as "Jesus", "Allah", and "Yahweh", but he believed very strongly that there was a nameless God.

"Jesus is my homeboy," Morgan said. Jesus was one of her many bodhisattvas, and she spoke of him as if he were a guru.

No one went to church except Mike, who attended a Unitarian church. "It's great," he said. "You can believe whatever you want."

Everyone listened to music. Little Buddhas decorated their dressers. If their parents could afford it, they went to the shiatsu massage clinic or an acupuncturist. Yet despite our disparate views, we all agreed on one thing: Mother Earth was in peril. The biology curriculum culminated in a project where we designed eco-friendly houses, and by the end of the first semester my concern for the fate of the planet was such that I called a family meeting.

"I'm not going to college," I said.

No answer.

"I am going to buy a hanging tent and live in the California Red Woods instead."

My parents would hear nothing of it, and it was decided before my senior year that we would tour several Christian colleges. I wrote in my journal that July: "I'm going to fast for seven days. We're going on a road trip to check out some colleges and it will be a chance to listen to God's calling. I have only one year of high school left and I want to know what God's plan for my life is. I seek purpose and mission, a cause I can dedicate my whole life to." The following day I wrote: "After talking with my dad, I've decided not to fast but to still search. He said that one should work up to a seven-day fast and that fasting on a road trip would not be wise. I want to live life fully and I do not want to miss out on any of it. I want to live for Christ."

Most of the colleges bragged about their football team or the size of their chapels, but I did not believe in large chapels or football teams. Bethel College was out of the question because it was "too suburban". Colorado Christian College offered downhill skiing and three-day weekends, but it didn't have anything to say for itself academically—but why did I care about academics? I had read a handful of Dallas Willard books and the usual C.S. Lewis and G.K. Chesterton, but I was not by any means scholarly. It is somewhat of a miracle that we drove to Michigan to visit Hillsdale College at all.

Yet my ears perked up at the casual dropping of phrases like "the Judeo-Christian, Greco-Roman Tradition", or "great books", or the "liberal arts".

"A good education won't teach you how to farm," a professor said, shaking my hand. "But it will teach you why you should." I liked the sound of that very much.

"Seek truth," another said, winking at me through a haze of pipe smoke, "and you will find the good and beautiful."

Even the students spoke of things enduring and of a longing for that which neither moth nor rust can corrupt. I had never heard anyone talk like that. They spoke as if they would never settle, never stop searching. They didn't mention their football team.

"Where's your chapel?" I asked.

Our tour guide gingerly led us to a closet. It looked like it could comfortably fit five people. I applied a week later. For me, it was a selling point that the college was planted in the middle of a nondescript town with nothing to boast of on its welcome sign except "It's the people." It reminded me of the book about the priest in a small town, and I imagined myself walking around like Robin Williams in the *Dead Poet's Society*, whistling and waving at professors with a worn book of verse in my hand.

Visiting Hillsdale's campus, the old brick and the cobbled walkways, the towering oaks and the small classrooms, hearing tales of a tradition and a heritage, shoved a poker into the hot coals of my heart. I didn't know much, but I knew that I didn't know much. I wanted to become a part of something bigger. I wanted to join the conversation.

* * * * *

Romance, wilderness, the Bible, work, rocking out, the heart, and personal experience—these are only seven of the rude and makeshift sacraments of my youth, but there were many more. Someone once said, I think it was Abraham Lincoln, that if people will not obey the Ten Commandments, they will obey the Ten Thousand Commandments. Without the sacraments, I turned nearly everything into a sacrament. Work and music, the Bible and personal experience, following my heart and, above all, romance and wilderness—I longed for outward signs of inward grace, for reconciliation, vocation, and

Eucharist. Looking back, I can now see that I wanted to be a saint, although I would never have put it that way.

So, I bought a yoga mat and drank inordinate amounts of carrot juice and discovered hesychastic prayer. I covered my bedroom with posters of Monet and Rembrandt, and printouts of my favorite quotes from Emily Dickinson: "If I read a book and it makes my whole body so cold no fire can warm me I know *that* is poetry. If I feel physically as if the top of my head were taken off, I know *that* is poetry";[3] and from Henry David Thoreau: "I sat at a table where were rich food and wine in abundance, and obsequious attendance, but sincerity and truth were not; and I went away hungry from the inhospitable board."[4] I pierced my cartilage and wore hemp necklaces and listened to Ben Harper, Mason Jennings, and Jack Johnson loudly. I preached sermons about how real Christianity is not suburban and how iceberg lettuce has no nutritional value, and my mother cried. But still I felt an almost audible gnawing. *Is this all there is? There is something more.* And I began to go mad with the threat of a God who was not impressed with my spirituality, even though my heart was in it.

In the hours when I worked in the coffee shop, in the battles and the poetry, in the dreaming and the rock music and the longing for a great love, I was doubled over by a hunger pang you could almost hear. Jesus was asking me the same questions he asks everyone: "What do you want?" "Do you love me?" "Will you follow me?" And I wonder if the call was not to act more spiritual, but to *become* someone. I longed to love God back—not with a love that boasts of having been saved, but with a love that *does* something and says, "This I do in the sacred name of the Most Adorable Trinity."

Good intentions are almost never good enough, but it is difficult to imagine where sainthood would begin if it didn't begin with the heart. Before anything else, it has to be about falling in love. And love is something that you need to *live*. Maybe this is why for the saints there is no spirituality apart from religion. Perhaps to say that you are "spiritual but not religious" is like saying that you love soccer but never play, or that you love music but never sing. It's great to be a fan or to have a nice record collection, but it's not enough. If you want to be a saint, you have to sing. You have to do the work.

I wanted to sing; I just didn't know it yet.

3

By Their Parties Ye Shall Know Them

Of Saturn we know more than enough,
but who does not need to be reminded of Jove?

—C. S. Lewis[1]

Feast after feast thus comes and passes by,
Yet, passing, points to the glad feast above,
Giving us foretaste of the festal joy,
The Lamb's great marriage feast of bliss and love.

—Horatius Bonar[2]

There was nothing special about Hillsdale College. It was an ordinary school in an ordinary town. With the usual beer and books and girls, no astonishing thing ever happened there. The students who went there were just regular students. And the professors were just plain old professors. Come to think of it, Hillsdale College couldn't have been more ordinary. But sometimes, when the world has reinvented every wheel and forsaken her patrimony, there's a chance that something as ordinary as a liberal arts education can become a little less ordinary. For me, it was a revolution.

"Greetings and salutations," said a student as I approached his table in the dining hall.

"Yikes," I said, and took a sharp left turn, dropping my tray on a table crowded with upper classmen.

"Sophistry!" said a senior. "Stop inventing these wild tales!"

"I'm not inventing," said another. "I'm just telling you the facts."

They all looked at me, eyes twinkling. "You're not a Donatist, are you?"

"No," I said, trying to look casual. "I'm still in Algebra 1."

35

I was clearly in over my head. It was only the first week, and I faced a long slog through the Code of Hammurabi, excerpts from Genesis, Exodus, and Deuteronomy, the entire *Iliad*, as well as writing a five-paragraph essay all while somehow learning how to conjugate Latin verbs. "The task will be challenging, but the rewards manifold," I read in the introduction of my Latin textbook, "so I bid you *bonam fortunam!*"

"Sheesh," I said, and turned up my Discman.

If I was going to learn "the best which has been thought and said", I would need to get it together. I threw my books into a leather satchel that I wore, because it made me feel like I was smart, and I wandered aimlessly around campus. Birds chirped. A breeze blew through the hair of freshman girls walking to the library. Eventually I collapsed beneath two towering oak trees where, after surveying the ground for ants, I endeavored to listen to music and to read a book at the same time. With Beck's *Odelay!* blasting in my headphones, I half-heartedly opened an essay by Russel Kirk and began to read: "Books give way to television and videos; universities, intellectually democratized, are sunk to the condition of job certification. An increasing proportion of the population, in America especially, is dehumanized by addiction to narcotics and insane sexuality ... as the phallic cult spreads, so does impotence."[3]

I took off my headphones and sat up. "We moderns lack moral imagination," Kirk continued. And then he said something I would never forget. He said there is no *culture* without a *cult*, and that a *cultus* is a joining together for worship:

> It is from the association in the cult, the body of worshippers, that human community grows....
>
> Once people are joined in a cult, cooperation in many other things becomes possible. Common defense, irrigation, systematic agriculture, architecture, the visual arts, music, the more intricate crafts, economic production, and distribution, courts and governments—all these aspects of a culture arise gradually from the cult, the religious tie....
>
> Our society's affliction is the decay of religious belief. If a culture is to survive and flourish, it must not be severed from the religious vision out of which it arose. The high necessity of reflective men and women, then, is to labor for the restoration of religious teachings as a credible body of doctrine.[4]

Percussive hisses shot out of my headphones, but I no longer heard them. Everything about Russel Kirk came across as dead and white and male, and yet, to my wonderment, I liked it. Could it be that there is no culture without "cult", no civilization without religion? Could it be that college could be more than job certification? Did I have what it takes to become a "reflective man"?

Even after four years of high school, diploma in hand, I found myself in a state of bewilderment. I sensed that somehow I had been cheated, that there must be something more to education than simply preparation for a career or the subversive "why not?" of so-called critical thinking. Then and there under the oak trees I resolved to cure my intellectual, moral, and spiritual disorientation, to uncover the story of what was indeed my heritage, and maybe the meaning of all my longing. But how?

My English professor had begun our first class by quoting Charles Péguy: "Homer is ever new; nothing is as old as the morning paper."[5] Having read nearly three whole pages of the *Iliad*, I knew that I did not like the blind bard; but I *wanted* to like him. I wanted to be that farmer they said a liberal arts education was all about. I imagined him to be something like Thomas Jefferson or the Marlboro Man in an old ball cap, at once rugged and cultured, as handy with Shakespeare as he is with a motor, looking up from a well-turned phrase in *Paradise Lost* to consider his freshly plowed fields. It was time to escape the provincialism of my own time and culture, a culture without a cult. It was time to climb Parnassus. It was time to play my part. It was time to smoke a cigarette.

* * * * *

"Jordan is passed out," said Stephen, sometime after our study group had fallen into disarray. "Throw water on him!"

"Throw beer!" said Matthew.

The boys cheered.

Davey ran for a glass of water. Jordan had a reputation for falling asleep while reading Virgil or Aeschylus with a bright lamp shining straight in his face.

Matthew knelt beside him. "Aristophanes was too much for him."

Davey returned with cold water and dashed it on Jordan.

"Throw some on me!" cried Stephen. "Aristophanes is too much for me, too."

Jordan, feeling the cold water, came to. He leaped from his chair, gripping his waterlogged book in both hands.

The boys cheered.

"He's up!"

Since I am a slow learner, I decided to use my moral imagination and to *pretend* to be a scholar. As often as I could I sat in the Heritage Room, a dark library with leather wing-backed chairs and a fireplace that made me feel almost erudite as I fumbled with Herodotus, Thucydides, Plato, Aristotle, Cicero, and Tacitus. I didn't understand anything I was reading, but I *wanted* to understand. There is an old piece of advice, "Fake it 'til you make it," and I found it to be helpful in my studies. Football practice, basic combat training, a dress rehearsal—we learn by imagination. To play is to learn, and the best way to learn is to play.

Friendship helps too. Philosophy, for Socrates, was ultimately about learning to die. Thus, it was something that could not be written down, but rather a way of life, a life of conversation. When Plato eventually put philosophy to paper, he wrote it in the form of dialogues. And so it was in friendship, and in the many late-night conversations that sought to know what *is*, that all my pretending to be a scholar became more of a reality.

Playing at scholar, I soon found myself surrounded by brilliant young minds, many of whom I was grateful to call friends. We bought tobacco pipes. We listened to Simon and Garfunkel and Rachmaninov. We played chess and cajoled the foreign exchange students into buying us beer. We applauded Socrates, the famous gadfly of Athens who was condemned to drink poisonous hemlock for his beliefs. We looked forward to translating Virgil's *Aeneid*, what T. S. Eliot named "the classic of all Europe",[6] and shouted in the halls at one another: "I sing of arms and a man!" We memorized poetry and talked about girls. Before long, the jest became fact: I was becoming a college student.

I was not a *good* student, to be sure, but I was willing to do the work of learning, at least most of the time. My grades were not very good, but I was slowly becoming more real, like in *The Velveteen Rabbit*. A good education takes a long time. It doesn't happen often to people who break easily, or have sharp edges, or who have to be carefully kept. And by the end most of your hair has been loved off, and your eyes drop out and you get loose in the joints and very shabby. But do any of these things really matter? Once you are a student you can't be ugly, except to people who don't understand.

Studying did not come easily for me, but it's just as well. Knowledge, too easily acquired, has never made a person more interesting. A quick answer, "googling" something, does not form a character. It does not develop what John Henry Newman called "a habit of mind" that "lasts through life, of which the attributes are freedom, equitableness, calmness, moderation, and wisdom",[7] all of which added up to what I wanted almost as badly as I wanted a girlfriend.

It was not effortless for me to learn Latin, but I threw myself into it with a will. The difficulty was not the Latin part, but the language part. I had no idea what people were talking about when they talked about prepositions, infinitives, conjunctions, substantives, or demonstratives. I bent over my textbook and blinked and blinked. I made color-coded flash cards and decorated them. I drank coffee until I shivered. At one point, I had a breakdown.

"I can't do this," I said into the phone. "I'm moving to California to live in the Red Woods."

"You have what it takes," said my father. "See the semester through."

I hung up. Desperate for some goal more accessible than a B+ and the heights of Parnassus, I resolved to get a tattoo. It would be in Latin, of course, and it would capture all that I had come to learn of the good, the true, and the beautiful. I read Augustine's *Confessions* and *The City of God*, Bede's *Ecclesiastical History of the English People*, the *Magna Carta*, Machiavelli's *The Prince*, Copernicus' *The Heavenly Spheres*, a little Thomas Aquinas and Martin Luther and John Calvin, a little Galileo and Harvey and Newton, a little Bodin and Hobbes and Locke, and always in the back of my mind I was planning my tattoo.

My first year of studies culminated in a road trip to Florida with friends and a trunk rattling with hundreds of beers, and eventually, on the sunny beaches of Fort Lauderdale, the acquisition of a tattoo, in Latin, across my shoulders, that read: "The Good, the True, the Beautiful". And so it came to pass that for me the "permanent things" got a little more permanent. Thenceforth, I would forever be more than just another white guy with a liberal arts degree; there would always be a "real me" that went deep, as deep as my skin.

* * * * *

"I shall begin by calling the roll. Michael?"

"Here!"

"Ben?"

"Hear! Hear!" said Ben, pulling a bottle out of his backpack. "Whiskey, anyone?"

No answer.

"We're not twenty-one," Michael finally stammered. Michael was the kind of guy who always wore a bow tie.

"So?" said Ben.

Just then Stephen staggered through the doorway shirtless, his body covered in blue paint. "I'm back!" he said in a triumphant voice. "What a night!"

Stephen collapsed in a chair and immediately grabbed the bottle from Ben and took an earnest swig.

"You ought to be ashamed of yourself," said Michael. "It would serve you right if you were hungover for a week."

What followed was an argument that would forever end "the Guild", a small association of freshmen who banded together to grow in fraternity and faith.

It had been a good run. We wore custom blue hoodies with our moniker printed on the front, and we had all signed a handwritten constitution that opened with notes most solemn: "We, the Guild, are a coterie of believers who gather together with the common pursuit of living out our salvation in Jesus Christ. Formed with the full understanding that the faith was never meant to be lived alone, we are committed and bound to each other in Christ." We met on Monday nights in my dorm to read excerpts from J. C. Ryle's *Holiness*, to light candles, and to confess the usual sins to one another. It was divined that the only Bible suitable for young scholars was the Cambridge King James Version, printed on India paper and bound in supple goatskin leather, and in the pursuit of holiness we wasted large sums of money going down this rabbit trail.

We considered ourselves to be an alternative to the Greek fraternity system. We had read Russel Kirk's essay about how there is no civilization without religion, and also the Mayflower Compact and the Salem Covenant of 1629, as well as John Winthrop, George Whitefield, and Jonathan Edwards, and all felt greatly awakened. In particular, we had been reading Alexis de Tocqueville, who admired the American penchant for making associations. Everyone had underlined selections from A. G. Sertillanges' *The Intellectual Life: Its Spirit, Conditions, Methods*, especially those lines that praised the workshops of old, where six or seven well-chosen associates, beside lectures and homework, would talk in the evening of all these noble things without pride or the spirit of rivalry, seeking only truth, their common soul revealing "a wealth of which no sufficient explanation would appear to be discoverable in a single part".[8]

"We gather within the circle of the Guild," said our constitution, "with the hope that our meetings and commitment to one another will be an inspiration for the cultivation of our souls and the encouragement to live a Godward life."

Our gatherings had been amiable until I suggested that we celebrate Holy Communion together.

"Without a priest?" said Michael from the lofted bed, his mouth full of potato chips.

"What's a priest?" I said in a snarky tone, looking up at him from my beanbag chair. Michael looked at me incredulously.

"Someone who has the authority to consecrate the bread and wine," said Michael. He leaped down from the lofted bed and offered me some of his potato chips.

"Oh, thank you," I said, and looked at Michael with round eyes. "But you don't need a priest to share the Lord's Supper," I explained. "Where two or three are gathered, Jesus always shows up. Everyone is welcome to the wedding feast!"

"Actually, no," interjected Nutkin, whose real name was Christopher. "You need a priest."

"Priests are for Jews!" shouted Ben.

A pained look shot across Nutkin's face. Michael fussed with his bow tie. Except for the blobs of wax ascending and descending in my lava lamp, the room grew very still.

"No," said Nutkin, finally, clearing his throat. "Priests are for Christians who want the Holy Mass."

"Jesus is enough for me," said Ben, standing up to leave. "You can keep your priests!"

We were divided on the matter of the Lord's Supper, and a house divided against itself cannot stand. We scraped together two more gatherings, but suddenly no one had any sins to confess. The conversations were pinched. And then, on that fateful night when Ben brought whiskey to the Guild gathering when Stephen also happened to show up drunk and half naked, it was as if someone had nailed ninety-five theses to my dorm-room door. Within hours, our small parachurch group fractured into a dozen different denominations, every man going his own way, Bible in hand, some to sit on coolers full of beer and others to sit in the library, some to churches with bimonthly memorial services of grape juice and others to churches with a eucharist of bread and wine consecrated by a priest.

"Phew," I said, when the last Guild meeting came to an end.

Leaning back in my beanbag chair, I watched the undulating wax inside my lava lamp. I had heard of schism before, but it had always been an abstract, historical footnote. Never before had I tried to gather believers together only to have our unity melt away in the heat of a disagreement. The reality of schism shook me to the core. It breathed and stared at me. It could be touched and felt like an animal. And it frightened me. If young Christian men from similar backgrounds—all virgins, all reading the same translation of the Bible, all wanting to pursue holiness in community—could not agree on underage drinking or the eucharist, what could we agree on? If the Bible wasn't enough to keep the Guild together, would it be enough to keep a church together?

That night I climbed up into my bed and wondered if divisions are inevitable, maybe even providential. Perhaps God is more glorified in dialogue than in dogma. It was then that I developed the theory that schism is the necessary evil of pneumatic unity, at least until the eschaton. I figured that, foreseeing that there would be disagreements, Jesus made provision for division and a plurality of beliefs by making the "real unity" of his Church *invisible*. This way, schism is only a surface-level illusion. In the end, it didn't matter if we splintered into ten denominations or ten thousand, because behind the division, running deeper than appearances, everyone who said the believer's prayer was already one in Christ. It was an improbable fiction, but it allowed for my Christian friends and I politely to go our separate ways. And my life was already a kind of living separation of church and state.

"Oh well," I said, and fluffed up my pillow. The Guild, like Christendom, had disbanded. Perhaps Lady Macbeth said it best: "What's done is done."[9]

How had I, born so late in history, come so quickly to a conclusion about which kind of Christianity was the truth? All I had learned about Christianity had come from an Evangelical Protestant perspective—my Baptist mother and father, my Calvinist elementary school teachers, the camp speaker in the Hawaiian T-Shirt, or the yogis at the emergent church above the coffee shop. When I had a question, I would check the commentary in the margins of my Teen New International Version of the Bible, and the answer was given through an Evangelical filter. When I was puzzled about theology, I would ask my Evangelical youth minister or friends, and they would answer according to their Evangelical beliefs. When the members of the Guild veered off in different directions, I took it as evidence of my preexisting position that sometimes the only thing a true believer can do is walk away. As a Protestant, I came from a long line of leavers.

* * * * *

But could it be that there is no civilization without religion, no culture without "cult"?

After the Guild disbanded, not knowing what else to do, I went out dancing on Friday nights and attended church on Sunday mornings, and quietly gave up on "Christian community". Christian faith and the stuff of civilization just didn't seem compatible, at least on this side of Christendom. At least the old Guild members could still party together. On the lawns of Sigma Chi's fraternity house we danced and sang as brothers, but on Sundays we parted company to worship in different churches.

Things were out of joint. We wanted to party like medieval peasants, but we did not have the key ingredient that made the old festivals possible. Our kegs of beer and crowded dance floors and bonfires and loud music exerted a more or less convincing spell, but they could not compensate for the lack of religious culture. A Friday night frat party is just "something different, for a change" or "having a good time", but a *festival* follows culture right up into its headwaters, and springs from the same "cult" as the culture itself.

Festivals are a thermometer of culture; they take the religious temperature of a community and hold it up for all to see. At first glance, the Guild's contretemps over drinking alcohol and the eucharist might seem unrelated, but I have come to see that they are in fact connected, and they come together in *festival*, in the old knot between sacrifice and thanksgiving that is *ritual worship*.

In voluntarily keeping feast days, people not only renounced that particular day's labor but also offered up the yield of their labors to God. And in return they received not only a sense of harmony with the world, but atonement, kinship with God and man, felicity. In this sense, *Easter* is the supreme festival, at once affirming creation and anticipating her future bliss, accepting suffering, embracing even death, and shot through with the hope of glory. On festival days the community affirms the goodness of existence as well as the glory of God by offering the response of joy. Such an affirmation shapes a calendar, marriages, births, funerals, heritage, and hope—the stuff of culture.

From the first ages of Christian history, the beating heart of the festival is the praise of God in public worship, the corporate *amen*, *alleluia*, and *eucharistia*. What the temple is to space, the festival is to time. The temple is the physical expression of the Sabbath, a sanctioned-off space, a day of rest. Like the temple, a traditional festival is removed from practical use, a grateful extravagance, "wasteful". And like the Sabbath, a festival is much more than simply a day free of work: it is an institution not altogether founded by men, "the Lord's day". Joseph Pieper has observed that when it comes to festival days, we can make the arrangements, but we cannot make the occasion; we can make the celebration, but we cannot make what is celebrated.[10] The *occasion* of a traditional festival is a divine gift. Here we receive something that it is not in human power to give: "For Christ, our Paschal Lamb, has been sacrificed. Let us, therefore, celebrate the festival" (1 Cor 5:7–8).

Because Easter absorbed the Sabbath into Sunday, Sunday is the day observed by Christians as a day of rest and religious worship.

Sunday is *the* festival day, of which Friday night is a pale, sublunary imitation. Yet Sunday was the one day of the week the old members of the Guild did not celebrate together. And by their parties ye shall know them.

As freshmen in college, and being for the first time in some sense "on our own", we felt the old impulse to party, but the religious element was missing. We were believers, but little about the practice of our beliefs was binding (*religare*, "to bind"). We attended church on Sunday, but Sunday was not a day of obligation (*religio*, "obligation, bond, reverence"). Raised by Baptists who did not drink or dance, and for whom communion was a time to recollect all that God had done for us over a thimble of pasteurized grape juice, most of us had never really considered Cana or the *koinonia* of the New Covenant. And so we were left to discover wine in the dark forests where not even Bacchus dares to tread, far removed from the Sacrifice of the Mass and its attendant fasts, penances, moral imperatives, and yes, *feast days*. The Guild's inability to agree on matters relating to alcohol and the eucharist simply exposed that we were, in fact, Christians without a culture.

* * * * *

It was the time of year that made me feel lonely for a girlfriend. By late November Hillsdale was stringing lights from one end of the campus to the other; freshly cut, beribboned greenery hung on lampposts, garlands of boxwood and holly politely draped the college monument, and students stuffed their dorm-room windows with everything from light-up Santa Clauses to Grinch posters. Everywhere I looked I saw couples holding hands or trees lashed to the tops of cars as families headed home to hang ornaments, or church steeples with winking lights reaching for the stars. It was also the time of year that made me feel like going to church. But every Sunday the Christians—including potential girlfriends—worshiped at different churches.

In the midst of self-contradictory simulacra of covenant, I continued my search for the real community of Christ, some remnant that bore semblance to the *kahal* of the Old Testament or the *ekklesia* of the New. By necessity, I imagined this community to be quite small.

And as I stood before the bewildering bazaar of denominations in search of those beliefs that would best corroborate my personal preferences, I saw very clearly that almost nothing was as beautiful as the Church of England and its liturgy, and when I first stumbled into an Anglican pew on Sunday morning, I saw clearly that no one was as beautiful as Emily.

"Hello," I said before the service began.

"Shhh," she said, and continued to pray in silence.

I looked around. The pews were dotted with only twelve or thirteen elderly congregants, all dressed in beige and bent over their prayer books. When the unmelodious organist began to pound the keys, Emily leaned over and explained that he was in fact deaf, which made me happy because I was tired of keeping up with worship trends, and also because it gave Emily an excuse to whisper in my ear. She wore a skirt with flower patterns on it and smelled of lavender as she showed me how to leaf through the 1928 Book of Common Prayer. She knelt often during the service and said all the prayers from memory. Her whole body was animated by a kind of reverence I had never seen before. I was spellbound.

The sermons were short and relevant, and I liked that. At one point, everyone said "peace" and I shook Emily's hand, and I liked that too. But more than the deaf organist and the short sermons, even more than Emily, I liked the poetry. My heart swam in phrases like, "We do not presume to come to this thy Table, O merciful Lord, trusting in our own righteousness, but in thy manifold and great mercies," and, "Almighty and everliving God, we most heartily thank thee, for that thou dost vouchsafe to feed us who have duly received these holy mysteries with the spiritual food of the most Precious Body and Blood of thy Son, our Savior Jesus Christ," though I hardly knew what I was saying.

I was getting pickled in the Anglican brine; or rather, praying with the Book of Common Prayer had put me in a pickle. In high school, Freud, Marx, and Nietzsche had seeped into my brain incognito—not because I had read them, of course, but because I had breathed the air around me. But now I was beginning to pray, "Assist us with thy grace, that we may continue in that holy fellowship, and do all such good works as thou hast prepared for us to walk in," even though I had always assumed that moral performance was how guilt-ridden Catholics cajoled God into saving them (Freud). Now I was praying that God would "dispose the hearts of all Christian rulers to the maintenance of thy true religion", even though I had always thought that religious organization was little more than a tool for the Magisterium to oppress the laity (Marx). Now I was reciting the Nicene Creed on a weekly basis, even though I had always suspected that truth claims were in fact power plays (Nietzsche). I thought all of this, in part, because as a child I had absorbed Luther's original idea that religion is just another form of works-righteousness.

These and other seemingly self-evident truths were reinforced by my theory of barnacles. The Old Covenant frightened me almost as much as the Catholic Church, and I believed that what Jesus did to Judaism the Reformers did to Christianity, as if Jesus came to abolish the law and not to fulfil it. I believed very strongly that the Jesus movement of the first century was a ship that had become over the years burdened with Catholic barnacles that dragged it down. Catholics had departed from the few really basic doctrines of historic Christianity and had added to the essential truths easily found in the pages of the Church's only authority, the inerrant Bible. Thankfully, the Reformation had not only scraped off the barnacles but had also restored what was believed by the primitive Church.

I believed in the Church as she was meant to be, before she became fat and short of breath from prosperity and cramped from administration. The Church of the Bible didn't make "acts of faith"; they believed. They didn't "do penance"; they trusted in God's mercy. They didn't "say their prayers"; they prayed. They were led by the Holy Spirit to bring people to God through Christ and were not held back by the rationalism of fundamentalism or distracted by the showy ornaments of the tradition-choked Catholic Church. There were no "Baptists" or "Lutherans" or "Methodists", only followers of Jesus, and I wanted to be a Jesus follower.

But I also wanted beauty and what I called "historic Christianity", and I had good taste, so I became Anglican. I knew almost nothing about the Church of England's hierarchies or theology, but I found the small church I attended to be rich and provocative and even comforting because it opened to me a tradition that I did not invent while also leaving papal dominion in the dust; and Jesus, I believed, would have strongly disapproved of the Catholic Church's varied institutional trappings. He critiqued the self-righteousness, exclusion, and power-mongering of organized religion and gave us something better—the Gospel. Religion was worse than immorality. In the parable of the two sons (Lk 15:11–32), the elder brother represented the religious leaders because he tried to control his father and exclude his irreligious brother. But in the end, he missed the feast. As far as I was concerned, the elder brother had done the unforgiveable—he had settled for religious observance. Sin, at least, was redeemable. "I'm just a sinner," I said, and meant it. The only time I was a saint was when I battled the Catholics, who talked about saints as if there were a catalogue of them, "Saint Anne" or "Saint Thomas More" and so on. Once, when a Catholic friend mentioned in passing *Saint* Thomas Aquinas, I retorted, "*I'm* a saint!" He tried his best to explain, but whenever a Catholic spoke all I heard was, "Barnacles, barnacles, barnacles!"

I admired Benjamin Franklin. When he heard a sermon that touched on points he would not have extrapolated from the biblical text himself, he was disgusted and "went no more to public assemblies".[11] Instead, he spent his Sunday mornings in his apartment drinking coffee and listening to podcasts of sermons that were relevant to his life of yoga classes and drinks with friends. "Had [the minister] been in my opinion a good preacher, perhaps I might have continued," Franklin confessed, "but his discourses were chiefly either polemic arguments, or explications of the peculiar doctrines of our sect, and were all to me very dry, uninteresting, and unedifying, since not a single moral principle was inculcated or enforced, their aim seeming to be rather to make us Presbyterians than good citizens."[12] You can almost hear in Franklin's voice a longing for Christendom, though it might only be my imagination: having already settled for democracy, the spiritualities of his day precluded the possibility of there being anything like a *Kingdom*, much less one on earth as it is in heaven.

"In America religion is a distinct sphere, in which the priest is sovereign, but out of which he takes care never to go," observed Alexis de Tocqueville. "All the American clergy know and respect the intellectual supremacy exercised by the majority; they never sustain any but necessary conflicts with it."[13]

I could sidestep this and other contradictions by keeping God's Kingdom an entirely abstract, "not yet" reality. When I recited the

Nicene Creed, I permitted myself to say the words "one" because I believed "one" originally meant *invisible* and "catholic" because I believed the original Greek *katholikos* meant "everyone". I deliberately referred to Catholics as "Roman Catholics" because it was oxymoronic—one word implied denominational limitations, while the other implied universality. And I believed no one church alone could be called "*the* Catholic Church". Catholics had their churches, and we had ours. But it didn't matter, because *Jesus* is the one foundation of Christians, and all who truly trust in him as Savior are by grace members of his global, invisibly united church. Maybe once or twice I prayed for the full visible unity of Christ's Church on earth *someday*, but not today, knowing it would never be completely realized until Jesus comes again. My spirituality was such that I pushed almost everything back up into heaven. Whether it was doctrinal agreement, moral perfection, or visible unity, I effectively delayed any realization until the final moment of Christ's return. I never thought about what it really meant to pray that God's Kingdom would come on *earth* as it is in heaven.

* * * * *

A cold winter passed, and then came spring. Every dorm-room window was flung open and graded papers took to the wind, sorority girls hosted car washes and picnics, and as the early bees were fumbling the flowers it became self-evident that I was not going to finish reading Montaigne, Cervantes, Chaucer, or even my Algebra homework. The Guild had disbanded, Emily had become Catholic, I had a lapidary tattoo on my back, and still all my Christian friends went to different churches on Sundays but partied together on Friday nights. We sang along to Weezer's *Blue Album* and danced to 50 Cent's *In Da Club*, and our coolers were well stocked. But we could not hear the music of the spheres, and our parties were more of a machine than a festival, saturnine and without apple-cheeked Jove, far removed from the eucharistic cup and the sword that pierces Mary's heart and Calvary's green hill.

What was the occasion? To what were we toasting all those nights we sang and danced and lifted our pint glasses to the sky? As college students clustered together from the farthest ends of the United States of America, hailing from different denominations, different liturgies, different doctrines, we should have had little in common. Yet we were uniform. With only a slipping grasp of localness and hardly a hint of regional dialect, we spoke the same radio and national television speech because we all consumed the same Hollywood and Billboard Hot 100. *Entertainment* was the lowest common denominator, the occasion, the place where Americans gathered together, and as such it was the only cathedral most of us had ever known. In the absence of real cult, a fake one is always propped up to take its place, such is the human need for ritual worship. Even if it's a poor substitute, baseball or vegetarianism, people will get religious about it. Even if they conflate temperance with abstinence and forsake the Mass for the traditions of men, there will be a jerry-rigged libation or toast. Every time you walk into a room *something* is being worshiped.

T. S. Eliot said that culture is deeply and irrevocably intertwined with religion. "No culture has appeared or developed except together with a religion: according to the point of view of the observer the culture will appear to be the product of the religion, or the religion the product of the culture."[14] And, of course, cultic worship expresses the virtues of agricultural life, for culture also draws its moral capital from the land. Hilaire Belloc put it another way:

> Wherever the Catholic sun doth shine
> There's always laughter and good red wine.
> At least I've always found it so,
> *Benedicamus Domino!*[15]

In other words, there can be no culture without the cultivation of the soil and winemaking; and depending on where you stand, a culture is the product of the cultivated grapevine or the vine the product of a culture. From the breaking up of the soil for sowing to the setting of the harvest table, people must acknowledge the goodness of God in the drinking of wine or ale, which is a kind of prayer and the stuff of culture. Agriculture is presupposed in the parables and metaphors of Jesus. He is the vine, the husbandman, the Lord of the Sabbath, the priest, the victim, the feast; he is turning water into wine at the outset of his public ministry and spilling his blood when it is finished.

Anthropologists debate which came first, bread or beer. East of Eden, the beginnings of civilization were spurred by the need for sacrifice, for Sundays, and for fermenting beverages. "No animal ever invented anything so bad as drunkenness—or so good as drink," said G. K. Chesterton. When a friend had a drinking problem, Hilaire Belloc advised him not to quit cold turkey but to distinguish between Bacchus and the devil:

> To wit: that he should never drink what has been made and sold since the Reformation—I mean especially spirits and champagne. Let him (said I) drink red wine and white, good beer and mead—if he could get it—liqueurs made by monks, and, in a word, all those feeding, fortifying, and confirming beverages that our fathers drank in old time; but not whisky, nor brandy, nor sparkling wines, not absinthe, nor the kind of drink called gin. This he promised to do, and all went well. He became a merry companion, and began to write odes.[16]

I do not remember anyone being a merry companion or writing odes. We had no taste for the fortifying beverages our fathers drank in old time; for we were all, to varying degrees, spiritualists. But spirituality alone cannot shorten the distance between the tabernacle and the tavern. Spirituality can only look at the freshness and purity of springtime, but it cannot make us fresh and pure. To mingle with the grandeur we see, we need something more. We need a culture that has preceded us and will endure long after we are gone; we need to be invited to participate. Like Jesus, the Church is a historical fact.

The Kingdom of God is heavy and inconvenient—like water, and children, and life. But for me, it was a physical impossibility. My spirituality had uprooted the Kingdom from the ground of objective reality and thrown her high into the ether of subjective experience. In Saint Paul's terms, I was satisfied forever to drink spiritual milk (1 Cor 3:2); I was content to hold little in common with other Christians except for what I called "the essentials", or "mere Christianity".

And there you have it. The Kingdom of God is like a wedding feast, but I had a short list of "essentials". Would not ecumenical dialogue be more rational than dancing? Much more rational, I dare say, but much less like a wedding feast.

4

The Beautiful Mess

Midway upon the journey of our life
I found myself within a forest dark,
For the straightforward pathway had been lost.

—Dante[1]

Lord, I have fallen again—a human clod!
Selfish I was, and heedless to offend;
Stood on my rights. Thy own child would not send
Away his shreds of nothing for the whole God!
Wretched, to thee who savest, low I bend:
Give me the power to let my rag-rights go
In the great wind that from thy gulf doth blow.

—George MacDonald[2]

Slouched in a stained bathtub, a cigarette dangling from my lips and
a photocopy of John Donne's *Holy Sonnets* steaming in my hands,
I did not move. The heat of an Indian summer pressed around me.
Hillsdale was usually chillier by now, with tidings of another Michigan winter beginning to blow under the doorways. As the water
soaked my skin, still dark from another summer of painting houses, I
plodded my way through a hangover.

Through the open bathroom door, I could see empty beer bot-
tles and stray clothing from last night's revelries. In the room across
the hall, a still-drunk Stephen was talking loudly into the phone. The
place reeked of stale yeast-fermented beverages and cigarette butts
from the parties we had thrown all junior year and every rowdy
weekend of the new year, our final year, our last hurrah.

I liked the tub. It made me feel removed from the storm, separate. In the tub I could feel morally superior to my brilliant, loyal, whiskey-swilling friends. In the tub with John Donne I could see that I was in a quandary. I could see that my spirituality was woefully inadequate for the realities of a world east of Eden. It warmed to literature and sunsets but was worthless in the face of cancer. It soared at the sight of a beautiful woman or a well-turned phrase in the Book of Common Prayer, but it froze at the sound of wails late at night. It was inadequate, but I didn't know what to do about it.

Returning my gaze to the dismal scene just outside the bathroom door, I realized how much had changed since I first cut off my dreadlocks and left for college—and how much had *not* changed. I was still hungry, still felt a summons that terrified me, and the gnawing feeling in the pit of my stomach had grown unbearable.

It was time for change, but what was the solution? Pancakes and coffee would provide an anodyne but not the antidote. Cleaning up would help, too, but I needed more than a clean, well-lighted space. I needed something more, something that could wring meaning from the mess. And then I remembered what had become my go-to solution for nearly every problem: poetry. I had run to poetry to understand some of the most defining features of the last few years—how my girlfriend broke up with me, my fear of Gnosticism, and my ironically Gnostic freedom in Christ debates about sola scriptura, transubstantiation, and Baptism, and why I had started my own painting business. Over the years I had developed a stratagem that seemed to resolve almost any contradiction within my self-styled spirituality and gave meaning to even my darkest hours, and I called it poetry.

Poetry wrung life out like a string mop, mud and all.

* * * * *

Where to begin? I needed poetry because I had been packing ice around my heart. The previous semester I had been studying at the Center for Medieval and Renaissance Studies in Oxford, England, that old city with spires where every pub played Coldplay's new album *Parachutes*. I was somewhere in between reading Saint Bernard and Saint Bonaventure when I got the call.

"It's over," Jess said.

I was not surprised, but still sad. I remember looking out the window as a bank of dark clouds moved in. It began to rain. I felt stiff and exhausted, like a cross-country trucker. Jess and I had been dating for almost two years, and our love was like a flower. Every stage of its growth had its own beauty, and the last phase was the most beautiful. Then very quickly it all went to seed. How had it come to this?

I met Jess the same week I read Dante's *Divine Comedy*, the story of how Beatrice leads Dante to God, and it had given me a sense of mission. I wanted our relationship to be like a steeple catching the brilliance of the sun. But the head can travel the globe while the heart sits in one spot. I had been reading a lot about "romantic theology", but my heart was still untrained. Beatrice (whose name means "the bringer of blessings") inspired Dante to holiness. When she would pass him on the street, her "Good morning!" (*salute*) was a proclamation of good news (*salvation*). So also romantic love summons all of us to holiness. At its best, marriage is a practice field for heaven. The image of God in you loves the image of God in her until, at last, the types and shadows give way to the heavenly reality—that's "romantic theology", but I was young and afraid to face whatever was beyond the curtain.

At first, Jess and I were on the same secret journey. And as we reached out for one another, we reached out for God. We played chess and listened to Radiohead and Damian Rice and the *Garden State* soundtrack. We went to the Anglican church together. We spoke of things we can now only know in part and not yet fully. But something began to snake its way into our love, winding like thin smoke through my heart, unnamed. And it wasn't until I was beneath Oxford's slate skies that I wondered if what had crept into my heart was *fear*.

Looking back, perhaps I had grown selfish with Jess. I liked the sound of her tennis shoes on the stairs, the look of amusement on her face when I tried to win an argument. I was attached to the bright questions in her eyes, and to the occasional breakthrough of a smile. I wished I could lock her love in a desk drawer of my heart and throw away the key. Even more than not wanting some other man to discover her, I wanted to protect her love for its rarity, for its—I couldn't find the word—fragility. I became jealous of Jess' other friendships. I wanted to be the center of her universe, to tie her to me somehow. Deep inside, I had pulled her so tightly to myself that the invisible cords of affection that bound us together snapped. It was nothing I *did*. On the surface, I was a fairly normal boyfriend. Rather, it was a secret posture deep within my heart. Perhaps she could sense that, and perhaps that was why it had to end.

Beneath a silver moon flanked by a fat springtime Venus, I read C. S. Lewis' *The Screwtape Letters*, in which the demons love someone by eating them. "Love", for the demons in *Screwtape*, absorbed the beloved's life into an extension of one's own. In heaven, love is self-gift; in hell, love is consumption. And I wondered, had I been so afraid of losing Jess' love that I had in fact stopped loving her, at least truly?

I stepped out into a city that seemed crowded with gargoyles and steeples and went down to a café on High Street to smoke Marlboros and look out the window. This was back when you could smoke inside cafés, and I remember they were playing Stan Getz and João Gilberto, and the barista came over to my table.

"I've never seen anyone smoke a cigarette like you," she said, replacing my ashtray.

I looked up. Clearly she had never seen anyone smoke a cigarette just after he discovered he had loved the way they do in hell.

The bell on the door jingled and I was grateful to be alone again. I sat and thought about how love is not neutral ground; here God and the devil are fighting, and the battlefield is the human heart. You can love bad things, and you can love good things badly. Even love can be disordered. Love can make a heaven of hell, a hell of heaven. It can lift you into the joy of the Trinity or thrust you to the utmost pole, far removed from God and the light of heaven. And all of it was but a shadow, an atrium, a "Farewell! thou art too dear for my possessing."[3]

My remaining months in Oxford were spent trying to make sense of it all. I was studying the theology of the Middle Ages and Eastern Orthodoxy; in the evenings I read everything by C. S. Lewis I could get my hands on, and it all swirled and eddied in my mind as I fell asleep to the sound of belfries at midnight: love as self-gift and love as consumption, cataphatic and apophatic theology, incarnation and divinization, marriage and celibacy, Beatrice and the beatific vision—and the more I read, the more I needed to write.

I wrote on a lumbering typewriter and drank tea and wore a "Narnian" bathrobe and leather slippers and pretended to *be* C. S. Lewis. It was around this time that I first discovered Pope Saint John Paul II's "theology of the body", and my heart instantly saluted him, even though he was a pope. I happened to be in Paris the day he died, and as I stumbled toward Notre Dame I was surprised to find myself weeping as seemingly thousands of pilgrims flocked the cathedral. Writing about a "theology of the body" or a "romantic theology" was my way of challenging myself, and also trying to put myself in a place to hear my vocation.

All of it—from the depravity of Dante's darkening pines to the glory of the beatific vision—I called "poetry". Poetry was a kind of salve. It seemed to express the romance of heaven and earth, the depths and heights, the beginning and the end of it all. Poetry seemed to be a fresh river of sun in what had been a long, dark iconoclasm.

* * * * *

A little poetry to stave off the hunger, that's what I needed—that and a strong dose of what I called "holistic Christianity". If I found ideas or situations that were opposed to one another, the explanation was poetry. If the second sentence appeared to be in flat contradiction of the first, the resolution was poetry. I turned to poetry the way a boy wipes back his hair in an unconscious gesture of annoyance. The sleight of hand was below the threshold of consciousness, an intuition, really, a kind of gut feeling. Poetry was a word the meaning of which I did not understand, though it filled my spirituality with a kind of meaning.

So when I came up against the dualism of Gnosticism, the remedy was poetry's alchemy. I had heard about Gnosticism before, but it wasn't until I was in Oxford that I began to wonder if my Christian life had embraced an unspoken dualism.

Gnosticism was a Christian heresy that arose in the early days of the Church that made a sharp distinction between the physical and the spiritual world, seeing the material world as evil. By the same principle, the history of Protestantism (of which I was heir) seemed to be a story of a scattered people who believed in a Creator yet became more and more suspicious of his creation. What started as iconoclasm became nondenominationalism, where churches are amphitheaters and preachers wear skinny jeans; and then, progressively, nondenominationalism became a strictly between-the-ears faith, where no one goes to church at all because they are "spiritual but not religious". By what principle did I believe God was in the sunsets, but not in the tabernacle? How had I concluded that Jesus could be the sacrificial victim, but not the sacrificial meal? And where did I get the idea that the eternal Son of God took on a body and became visible on earth, not as a phantom but as a reality, only to establish an invisible Church, a Mystical Body that had clearly been hanged, drawn, and quartered, with his remains displayed in prominent places across the world?

I had yet to see that if you destroy the altars, deny the sacraments, renounce the holy water, throw away the kneelers and pews, banish incense, candles, images, statues, bells, and chants, then by the same principle you destroy the very doctrine of the Incarnation. Fire the Magisterium and spiritualize the Kingdom, replace the bishops with a book and count yourself an able reader, and by the same principle you silence the living voice of Christ. Every appeal to Scripture is an appeal to an *interpretation* of Scripture; but did I have the audacity to stand up and say, "By God, I've got it!"? It's as if I believed God were hiding, not so much as a Creator but as a concept, a whim, perhaps even an image of myself.

Of course, I didn't see it at the time but my implicit iconoclasm was playing out morally. Nearly everything beyond a quick believer's prayer was optional for my spirituality. The Christian faith was quite simple and accommodating. If someone said that Jesus forbade divorce, I replied: "That's not the Jesus *I* know. *My* Jesus is all about grace." If someone challenged my newfangled theories about sexual purity, I replied: "The Jesus *I* know is not Victorian." When it came to morals I was terrified of becoming "Puritanical". I might not have had a problem with all the Reformers destroying the furniture of the medieval Mass, but I *did* have a problem with Gnosticism, at least in theory, because Gnosticism scorned the flesh and I like the flesh very much.

I think it was G.K. Chesterton who said that the heresies we most loudly denounce are the ones we are least likely to commit in the first place. As a young male eager to shake off the shackles of works-righteousness, I had every reason to scorn Gnosticism. It was almost as bad as Puritanism. And in the wake of my conclusions, I looked for poetry as one looks for a back door.

Not wanting to be Gnostic, but wanting to collect holy icons and to kiss girls, I decided to become what I called "incarnational". Having found within Eastern Orthodoxy's borders a wealth of interest and intrigue, I bought a few icons. I lit candles beneath the icons for mood lighting. I never venerated them, but I wanted an atmosphere of mystery and perhaps a touch of "historic Christianity" to complement my Sigur Rós posters. Terrified of Gnosticism and Puritanism, I threw away Joshua Harris' *I Kissed Dating Goodbye*[4] and tried my utmost to be "free in Christ", which mostly meant free to drink and dance. The heresies we most loudly denounce might be the ones we are the least likely to commit—but in flight from one expression of Gnosticism (the flight from flesh), I had unwittingly embraced another (the belief in gnosis). I had poetry, and poetry was all a Jesus follower needed—as long he had the correct interpretation of Scripture (*gnosis*) and the proper metaphysic (*gnosis*).

I had changed. But even after three years of encountering great minds and powerful ideas, it seems my fundamental beliefs about faith had not changed. As a Christian Studies major, my schooling appreciated the biblical and theological elements woven into the culture and imagination of Western civilization. Everything was connected, and nothing could be left out.

"Biology is not one thing and psychology another," one of my professors said. "English is not unrelated to civics. No, it is all of a piece. What the university says about God is inextricable from what it says about man. We worship one God, and he is the unity of the university. All the disciplines dovetail in theology, the Queen of Sciences."

I liked the sound of that. And as far as I was concerned, poetry was the mortar that held it all together, for God was a poet. I took as many classes on poetry as I could, and thankfully my favorite Christian Studies professor, Dr. Russell, taught classes that threw together poets like Chaucer, Shakespeare, Milton, Cervantes, and Philip Sidney with theologians like Saint Bonaventure, Saint Bernard, Saint Thomas Aquinas, Saint Thomas More, and Erasmus. It was a fireworks show. These bright minds shot up before me like grouse flushed from a distant wood, and I could only gape.

Yet all this gaping had not changed my faith, at least not yet. As I encountered new ideas, they simply went through the filter of what was essentially '90s Evangelicalism with an emergent church twist, which is to say that up until that point, like many spiritualists, I essentially thought that the Bible had been exclusively written for me and my life. However much I had outgrown WWJD bracelets and Christian T-shirts, I still believed that all I had to do was read the Bible and then figure out how it applied to my current situation. It was ultimately up to me to determine what the Christian faith was. But as my horizons grew, so did my thirst. And not having any authority outside of myself but the Bible, all of Church history was a grocery-store aisle with colorful options to choose from. Tradition was basically a dead thing, the Church a picturesque ruin. There was no *living voice* of authority that could proclaim the truth with certainty—but there was poetry. Disagreements over doctrine, division and schism, unclear or contradictory morals, incompatible interpretations of Scripture—all of this I called "the beautiful mess".

Looking back, I wonder if I was just beginning to feel the unbearable lightness of my spirituality's *being*. Like all spiritualists, I had a *right* to my own opinion. And if I had a right to my own opinion, why wouldn't I have a right to do with my body as I wished? And if I could do with my body as I wished, why on earth would church be necessary for entering heaven's gates? Thankfully, the via media of the Anglican church I attended could accommodate my personal opinions and lifestyle *and* my growing appreciation for candles and icons and old hymns. But when my priest converted to Catholicism, I was forced to show my hand. Disgusted, I quit going to church altogether and spent the morning at the kitchen table smoking unfiltered cigarettes and reading the New Testament.

For me, the *via affirmativa* was a custom lifestyle, a relationship with Jesus that demanded very little of me. Even as the riches of Scripture and Church history were opened to me, I still thought (without really thinking) that moral imperatives, social accountability, and even religious geography had gone the way of the Old Covenant. And not wanting to be Gnostic, I affirmed the flesh. I drank wine and kissed girls and collected devotionals and believed that, at least at its best, sexual love could be a carriage of grace, a finger pointing Godward. And not wanting to be Catholic, I affirmed the flesh in all matters *except* where it could pertain to salvation. There were no sacraments, to be sure, but the whole world was a kind of orbiting sacrament, a living poem. God was everywhere so long as he was nowhere. Jesus was not a Pharisee, but he *was* a lover and a poet. And when it came to love and poetry, E. E. Cummings put it best:

> Since feeling is first
> who pays any attention
> to the syntax of things
> will never wholly kiss you.[5]

Jesus loved the beautiful mess. He died for it. And all of this is to say that the God of the Old Testament scared the life out of me.

* * * * *

Now, I can remember three conversations in college that burrowed deep into my heart, though they wouldn't bear fruit for many years. It wasn't so much what was said, but what was whispered. And perhaps when it comes to those great clashes of the Reformation—*sola scriptura*, transubstantiation, believer's Baptism—a whisper is the only way to handle ties so fragile they would otherwise break. First, about *sola scriptura*.

"Tyler, what do you think?" Dr. Russell stood before the class, hirsute and browed like Einstein. The class sat upright in their chairs. "How can Christians know what is the truth?"

I breathed in the classroom's tentative air.

"The Bible," I said, wishing I could crawl under my desk and hide.

"How so?"

"The Bible is the infallible Word of God," I said; "the Bible is trustworthy."

"But all Protestant denominations claim to be biblical, and yet their different interpretations of the Bible have divided them into thousands of fighting groups."

"I don't know if anyone *fights* anymore," I said.

"So they're indifferent?"

"I mean—"

"Never mind. What good is a Bible if it only leads to different and even contradictory doctrines?"

"All Scripture is God breathed," I burbled out in summary.

"But what counts as Scripture? Do you know with confidence which books make up the Bible? The Catholic Church claims there are seven more books that are also inspired by God, not included in Protestant Bibles. Who's right?"

I clutched my pencil. "The Reformers, I suppose."

"How do you know? Why do you accept the Protestant canon of Scripture—or any canon, for that matter?"

My palms were sweaty. "Because the Reformers went back to the early Church, before all the medieval errors."

"Is it possible for smart and well-intentioned Christians to be wrong?"

"I don't think so," I said. *When was this going to end?*

"It is more than possible," Dr. Russell said. "If different Christians—all claiming to be 'led by the Holy Spirit' and all basing their beliefs on 'the Bible alone'—overlook common sense, disregard the apostolic traditions and the distilled wisdom of generations of Christians, and want to be fashionable, they may not only get *possibly* everything wrong," Dr. Russell leaned over the podium and glared. "They *will* get everything wrong."

"But the Holy Spirit is the Spirit of Truth," I said, my face growing warm. "God would never lead Christians to believe something untrue."

"Exactly," Dr. Russell said. "So would you agree that at least some of the Christians who think they are accurately interpreting the Scriptures are in reality not?"

I clutched my pencil so tightly it began to break. G. K. Chesterton's madman lost everything *but* his reason, and for one frightful moment I wondered if Protestantism had lost everything *but* its Bible.

"God either preserves his Church from errors, or he does not. But if he doesn't," Dr. Russell whispered, "we can only be *sorta* confident that *some* of our beliefs are *hopefully* true."

Hoping the former was true, I asked: "So which denomination has the truth?"

"Only Catholics, Orthodox, and Mormons claim to have the whole truth," Dr. Russell said, and then looked straight at me. "Perhaps you should become Catholic?"

I was skeptical.

Just then, he changed his tune. "Unless God is bigger than our ideas about him," Dr. Russell said, stepping out from behind the podium. He put his hands in his pockets and began to pace. "What if Jesus is comfortable with the mess? What if iron sharpens iron? What if it's supposed to be this way?"

"Phew." I breathed a sigh of relief. I felt at home in the beautiful mess. And there was the old poetry again. Dr. Russell's classes were rhapsodic, compelling, personal, and mettlesome. One minute you were scribbling his lecture furiously in your notebook, the next you were stammering as he launched questions at you like grenades. His use of the Socratic method kept you on your toes. Often the debates spilled over into the hallway, the cafeteria, the dorm rooms. Friends and I brought the conversation to the Finish Line, a greasy spoon where you could smoke indoors and get a "two of everything" (and they meant *everything*) breakfast for $5.99. For hours we hacked at an idea, searching for truth.

But someone once said that "no two persons ever read the same book", and I have found this to be especially true about the Bible. Like good books, every conversation seems to reach a point where you have to choose between turning the page and closing the book. In those days, the conversation about *sola scriptura* ended with a thud.

* * * * *

And this brings us to the second conversation, the conversation about transubstantiation. I'll never forget the dreary winter day Dr. Russell made a classmate, Susan, burst into tears. It was the same day I came to the conclusion that philosophy—Hellenistic philosophy—was bad news for Christianity. It had just snowed. Unlike most snows, this one did not bring the students out into the courtyard. This was a different snow, an ominous snow.

"Can you eat Jesus?" Dr. Russell asked Susan.

"No," Susan hesitated.

"What did Jesus mean by 'This is my body'?"

"Jesus was speaking symbolically."

"Luther didn't think so," said Dr. Russell. "Luther took Jesus at his word, but rejected the Aristotelean underpinnings of the Catholic dogma of transubstantiation. Luther favored a sacramental union where Jesus is present with and beside the bread and wine."

Dr. Russell began to draw on the board. "Zwingli, the Swiss Reformer, disagreed with Luther and the Catholic Church and believed that the eucharist *signifies* Christ's body. Calvin tried to find a middle way. Luther and Zwingli debated, but failed to agree. Susan, what do you think?"

The snow churned and swirled against the windows.

"Jesus couldn't really *mean* 'This is my body'," Susan said.

"If he were speaking symbolically, why does Jesus say in John 6, 'He who eats my flesh and drinks my blood has eternal life, and I will raise him up at the last day. For my flesh is food indeed, and my blood is drink indeed.'?"

"Jesus was just speaking symbolically," grinned Ben, who was doing his part to steam up the windows of the classroom.

"Was he?" Dr. Russell asked. "Open your Bibles to John 6. Up until verse 51, a purely figurative interpretation of the words of Jesus seems possible—maybe eating his flesh is just a strange way of saying that we need to believe in him. But from verse 53 to 54 onward, it only gets stranger. Jesus had been using a normal word for eating, *phago*, but when the Jews are confused, Jesus explains his meaning by getting even more graphic. He starts to use a different, more primal word for eating, *trogo*, which is animal-like gnawing. He basically says, 'He who *gnaws* on me abides in me, and I in him.' And look what happens. The crowds take him literally, and leave in disgust. Susan, what do you think?"

Susan looked pale.

"But the Twelve didn't leave," interjected Ben, who was reading ahead.

"That's right. The Twelve remained," said Dr. Russell. "If Jesus had been using a figure of speech, don't you think he would have told them so?"

The wind had cast torrents of snow against the old classroom windows, where it was freezing solid. We might have been swaddled in an igloo, filled with an eerie glow. In the darkness, the thought of eating Jesus made Susan cry.

After an awkward pause, Dr. Russell continued: "Zwingli's purely symbolic doctrine is not found in the writings of the Church Fathers and the other early Christians. Instead, we find only an affirmation of the Real Presence."

Barnacles! I thought.

Take Ignatius of Antioch, for example, who lived during apostolic times. He wrote against the Docetist heretics, who believed that Jesus only *appeared* to be a flesh-and-blood human being: "They abstain from the Eucharist and from prayer because they do not confess that the Eucharist is the flesh of our Savior Jesus Christ, flesh which suffered for our sins and which the Father, in his goodness, raised up again. They who deny the gift of God are perishing in their disputes."[6]

Dr. Russell went on to read quotes from Justin Martyr, Irenaeus, Clement of Alexandria, Tertullian, Hippolytus, Origen, all attesting the Real Presence of Christ in the Eucharist, but all I heard was, *Barnacles!*

"So what?" Dr. Russell leaned against the podium. "Either the Church was right for fifteen hundred years, or one of the Reformers was."

The class shivered in their chairs.

"Welcome to the Catholic Church," said Matthew, who was the only Catholic in the room.

"Are you sure?" Dr. Russell asked, returning to the chalkboard. He wrote "transubstantiation" in a loose script. "Or could it be that from early on Greek thought has infected the Church? Could it be that Christians were overeager to assimilate the Gospel to Hellenic philosophy, and in doing so, they forgot that Jesus was a Jew?"

I sat up in my chair and began to take notes again.

"All the Catholic Church's teaching about how the *substance* of the bread and wine offered in sacrifice at the Mass is changed into both the Body and Blood of Christ, all the talk about how the outward appearances, the *species* or *accidents*, remain unchanged—it's just Aristotelean metaphysics smuggled into the Church by Thomas Aquinas. Is any of it in the Bible?"

I scribbled notes furiously.

"Where in the Bible are we told to prostrate ourselves before a piece of bread? Where in the Bible do we find the word 'transubstantiation'?"

"The word 'Trinity' is not in the Bible either," said Catholic Matthew, and I dropped my pencil. I had never thought of *that* before.

"Yes," said Dr. Russell. "But unlike transubstantiation, the doctrine of the triune God is abundantly clear in Scripture."

"And, 'This is my body' isn't clear?" said Catholic Matthew.

"It's certainly not Aristotelean," said Dr. Russell, and the class laughed. "Look," Dr. Russell sighed and gave a warm smile. "In the end, all we can say is that the eucharist is a mystery."

My mind hummed with happiness. In addition to *barnacles* I could add another weapon to my arsenal: *Hellenism*. Catholic dogma was fastidious and "Greek", but Jesus was a salt-of-the-earth Jew. Christ's words in John 6 *seemed* to indicate that eating his flesh and drinking his blood are a matter concerning one's salvation—but because Jesus was a poet this was just another area where wide speculation was acceptable. Protestants might disagree about the *mystery* of the eucharist, but at least they didn't worship the Host, wrongly thinking Jesus was there, and use Hellenism to justify it. Like the Eastern Orthodox churches, I was happy to say it was all a mystery—isn't "sacrament" just another way of saying *mysterion*? As an Anglican, I said that the Lord's Supper was *more* than a memorial, but the "more" was the stuff of poetry.

Earnestly, hopefully, gaily, I raised the banner of poetry. I held poetry to a world of separation, disenchantment, and ten thousand contradictory biblical interpretations, like a candle to a black night. I waved it before Hellenism and barnacles like a knight's sword before a dragon. On a clear winter day in class I thought I saw the answer. Jesus was a troubadour, the primitive Church was like a young tree, and poetry was a fence to keep the deer from nibbling it, a fortified place with walls and watchtowers shining like the upper room at Pentecost. And this is, perhaps, why I thought Baptism was more a statement than a sacrament.

* * * * *

Before we enter the gilded world of Baptism, it remains to be said that I had not been baptized until I was sixteen years old. On a crisp June morning I gave my testimony before a crowd that had gathered to watch. The lake mirrored the blue sky, and the shadow of a plane passed overhead, and I was baptized in the name of the Father, and the Son, and the Holy Spirit. In the honest cold of a Minnesota morning, I was happy and grateful.

At the time, though, I thought Baptism was something *I* did for God. It was a stand I took, a message I sent to my church and the world. I had made the decision to give my life to Jesus, and I got baptized to show outwardly what Jesus had already done for me inwardly. I believed that God gave no grace through Baptism because I believed that I had already received the Holy Spirit when I asked Jesus into my heart and put my faith in him as my Lord and Savior. Everything necessary for salvation had already been completed, and getting baptized was just a public proclamation of my faith in him for all to see. So when I still attended church services, I was mildly irritated that we recited the following lines from the Nicene Creed: "We confess one Baptism for the forgiveness of sins."

What irritated me more was that Jesus seemed almost to *command* his disciples to baptize his followers (Mt 28:19) and that Saint Peter ordered people to be baptized and even linked it to receiving the Holy Spirit (Acts 2:38). Didn't they know that all the legalism of the Old Covenant was over? In my mind, the "necessity" of Baptism was superficial, and there was no causal relationship between getting dunked and salvation. To suggest anything more than poetry was "Greek", and Jesus was a Jew.

Perhaps a glaring problem of my theory that Greek philosophy was "bad" is that the New Testament is saturated with the stuff. Wasn't Saint Paul Hellenized, and didn't he put his philosophical tools to work in the task of articulating the New Covenant? But perhaps an even more glaring problem was that I was actually contradicting myself. I wanted Jesus to be a Jew, but I wanted the New Covenant to be nothing like the Jewish Old Covenant. When it came to salvation history, I believed in the *discontinuity* of covenants.

Regarding the discontinuity of covenants, shortly after I returned from Oxford my old crush Emily asked to meet me for lunch at a hole-in-the-wall sandwich shop downtown. I remembered that a few years earlier she had become Catholic, so there was no future for us. I was going to tell her I was busy but then she said she wanted to talk about the Bible, so I told her I would do it. A good Bible battle would surely turn the odds in my favor. And at least the food would be good.

As we sat down to our sandwiches and cracked open our Bibles, I was surprised when she proceeded to defend infant baptism on biblical grounds. She opened to Romans 4:11 to argue that just as circumcision was given as a sign to the "children of the covenant" in the Old Testament, so Baptism—the new sign of the covenant—should be given to the "children of the covenant" today. Emily opened up her Bible to Colossians 2:11–12: "In [Christ] also you were circumcised with a circumcision made without hands, by putting off the body of flesh in the circumcision of Christ; and you were buried with him in baptism."

"You see?" Emily said. "Baptism fulfils circumcision as the sign of the covenant. It should be applied to the children of the covenant members—Israelites then, Christians now. Don't you think that children of Christians today should then receive the sign and seal of the New Covenant just as the eight-day-old infants of Israelites did in the Old Covenant?"

"Um, no," I said, feeling a little uncomfortable talking about circumcision with Emily.

"Why not?"

"Because look at the context," I said, and turned back to Romans 4. "In verse 9, Paul says that 'faith was reckoned to Abraham as righteousness.' And verse 10 points out that this happened *before* Abraham was circumcised: 'How then was it reckoned to him? Was it before or after he had been circumcised? It was not after, but before he was circumcised.'"

"So?" said Emily.

"So Abraham's justification was not brought through circumcision, which came later, but through faith."

"I'm not sure I get what your point is."

"My point is that faith comes *before* circumcision. Babies can't have faith, so you shouldn't baptize them. My point is verse 11: 'He received circumcision as a sign or seal of the righteousness which he had by faith while he was still *un*circumcised.'"

"So why did the Israelites circumcise their baby boys?"

I stared at her.

"Circumcision was 'a sign and seal of the righteousness of faith,'" continued Emily, "and in obedience to God they circumcised their infants who didn't yet have faith for themselves."

I gave a laugh. "I think you're making a wrong assumption about the similarity between the Old Covenant and the New Covenant,"

I said. "The different signs of the covenants (circumcision and Baptism) cannot be administered in the same way, because the New Covenant is fundamentally different from the Old Covenant."

"Is it?" asked Emily.

"God covenanted himself to an ethnic people and their descendants, and gave them the sign of circumcision because the covenant was handed on within that ethnic group. But the New Covenant is not bound to an ethnic or national identity but is a Spirit-born reality open to all people."

"I'm with you."

"So while it worked to give the covenant sign of circumcision to infants in Israel, it just doesn't work to give the covenant sign of Baptism to infants in the Church. They don't play the same role."

"But why?"

"Because the New Covenant is the spiritual work of God," I said. "The Holy Spirit gives us saving faith and writes the law in our hearts. The New Covenant is a spiritual community, not an ethnic group. You can't be *born* into it. It's wrong to baptize children—they haven't shown evidence of being born again yet!" The Church isn't like Israel, where phonies were mixed with the true believers."

"I wonder what Jesus meant, then, about the wheat and the chaff? You don't think it's possible to be baptized into God's covenant and then to be unfaithful to it?"

"Look, Baptism is just an expression of the faith that we had *before* we were baptized."

Emily studied my face with a notch in her brow. "You don't sound like a very good Anglican. Besides, how can mentally disabled people enter the kingdom under your rubric?"

Emily took the Bible from my hands and opened to all the Scriptures that link being born again with *water* and *spirit*. She said she liked the part of Scripture that talks about Jesus wanting the little children to come to him, that the Kingdom was for them. She spoke of households being baptized into the household of God and outward signs of inward grace, and I vaguely remember a lot of familial language. But it was too late. Whenever a Catholic spoke, all I heard was, "Hellenism, Hellenism, Hellenism!"

And so I battled Catholic doctrines with a quip about how Jesus was a Jew, not a Greek philosopher. But when a Catholic made a

strong case that Jesus was a Jew and his New Covenant was a fulfilment of the Old, I argued that the New Covenant is *fundamentally*
different from the Old Covenant, that it was not so legalistic and
worldly but spiritual. The Kingdom of God was poetry, a beautiful
mess. And God answered the mess with one word: "grace".

At any rate, there was a second-century Christian who believed
that the wrathful God of the Old Covenant was fundamentally dif-
ferent than the God of the New Covenant, Jesus Christ. He believed
that the Old Covenant was lower, material, and evil, and that the
New Covenant was higher, spiritual, and good. The God of the Old
Testament seemed nothing like Jesus. Therefore, he concluded, the
New Covenant is *fundamentally* different than the Old Covenant.
Any expressions of the Gospel that were associated with the Old
Covenant *contradicted* the advance of the New Covenant and went
backward in redemptive history. But it would be some years before I
would read about Marcion and why he was denounced as a heretic.

* * * * *

The thing about trying to remember your life is you have to be kind.
You get the feeling you were dishonest, or foolish. You question
your motives. You're tempted to defend yourself. Sometimes you're
tempted to believe it's all futile. If I got so much wrong then, how
can I trust where I am now? The truth is, I am still growing. And in
any event, my poetry phase has a peculiar feel when I look back on it
that probably wasn't there when I was actually living it.

As I recall the conversations that eventually took my life in a new
direction, perhaps saying that I was "Gnostic" is too harsh an assess-
ment. But when I said that the Bible is just a "fallible collection of
infallible books", I can't help but wonder if a tiny part of me was trying to free myself from time, history, and politics. Or when I said that
I was saved "by faith alone", I wonder if I secretly wished salvation
were a form of escape rather than a lifelong pilgrimage. Or when I
said there were no sacraments, I wonder if I was in fact putting limits
on God's ability to act *in* and *through* matter, perhaps even alienating
myself from the goodness of creation. And when I said that the Bible
was authoritative, but that the list of books that make up the Bible was
fluid and nonauthoritative (e.g., I had no qualms about editing the

Old Testament Apocrypha), I wonder if I was in fact trying quietly to replace the authority of the covenanted community (which is the family of God) with a covenant only with myself and my private illumination. "Where do Bibles come from?" is a question not unlike "Where do babies come from?" and I seemed to think God's Word came via stork.

And yet, in spite of having best intentions, maybe I was coming at it the wrong way. What if what Gnosticism does to the body, *sola scriptura* does to Christ's Mystical Body? The doctrine seems almost to hate the universal Church. It seems to move faith *out* of the community of believers and in between the ears of the individual. Doesn't it seem to turn Christ's High Priestly Prayer into a whimper? Such a Gnosticism would reduce the Body of Christ to a buyer's market, placing churches in competition with one another as guests come and go following their own theological scruples and aesthetic preferences. At the time, from my vantage point, no one needed to wait for any clergy, pope, scholar, or ecumenical council to explain the *real* meaning of any passage of Scripture. There were no deficiencies in the Bible that needed to be filled with traditions, papal pronouncements, or developments of doctrine. I had the Holy Spirit, and the Bible was *clear* and *sufficient*. So all ecclesiastical authority was subject to the correction of my interpretation of Scripture. Doctrinally, what was I to do but to trust my own conclusions? Morally, where could I go but where my conscience led me? Socially, where was I to go on a Sunday morning but back to bed?

I was learning slowly, but life was moving so quickly. Looking back, I wonder how my mind was not a tangle of questions. Why did the God of the Old Covenant so little resemble my understanding of the God in the New Covenant? Where was the *continuity* between the covenants? Why did I recite the ancient prayers and creeds with so many qualifications? Where was the real presence of Christ with his people? Where was his *living voice* of authority and truth? Where was my cross? Where was the calendar? Where was the *leitourgia*? Where was the culture?

All of this raises the question, What did Jesus leave behind to finish his mission: a Church, or a Bible? Who did the Holy Spirit empower to speak in his name: a community, or a book? And does the Holy Spirit lead the Mystical Body of Christ into all truth, or into a beautiful mess? You could touch the body of Jesus, and you can touch the Church. You cannot touch poetry.

* * * * *

It would be remiss not to say that during my years at Hillsdale College I heard another kind of poetry, a toiling poetry. "He who hath a trade hath an estate," said Benjamin Franklin. If you have a skill, you have something of value, a source of income, and the means to acquire property. And in America, owning land was linked to freedom. "He shall sit under his vine and under his fig tree; and none shall make him afraid" (see Mic 4:4).

When I heard this in class as a freshman, I wished I had a trade. I wanted to work with my hands and do something *useful*, do some kind of work that had a tangible result. And then I remembered that I *had* a trade; I had learned the ins and outs of exterior house painting. That summer, I went back to work for the same house-painting company I had the previous year, except this time I paid attention. I learned to cut with both hands, how to save time with a better ladder and plank set-ups, how to caulk like an artist, and I became a little romantic about it all. I studied the time sheets, noted the equipment and the way the crew leader bossed us around; I listened as the company manager talked to the homeowners, and I even snuck a peek at the contracts. And when I saw the disparity between what the company was making and what I was making, I knew it was time to "ply my trade".

The following summer, I took out a business loan, registered with the state, got insured, purchased a truck and ladders and jacks and a power washer, branded the company "Rembrandt Home Painting Co.", and hired my brother to work for me. We listened to Bo Diddley and Flatt & Scruggs and Johnny Cash. It sometimes took new employees weeks to learn the vocabulary. Not only did they need to learn all the different meanings of the phrase "set up", which could mean almost anything, but also words like "jack", "set", "stinny", "cut", "flash", "feather", "tag team", "rock out", and "shit". Then there was the jargon unique to my crew. An area that could be painted within twenty minutes was called a "Lucé" after the Trampled by Turtles album *Live at Lucé*, which was a twenty-three-minute flurry of bluegrass. The pail that held the paint was called "a Hank", in honor of Hank Williams. The paint sprayer (which was seldom used on principle) was affectionately named "Nora" for Nora Jones. The six-foot stepladder was called "Kanga", and the two-foot platform ladder was called "Eeyore".

I hired friends and family, I was my own boss, and even more—I was a good painter. Except for when I was making bids or picking up supplies, I wanted to be the first on the ladder and the last one off. When we painted, my crew suffered long speeches about the "painter's life", the virtues of rising at 5 A.M. and not leaving the job site until 6 or 7 P.M., the latent beauty of certain techniques and equipment, the merits of staying hydrated, the poetry of hot coffee for hot weather, and the wisdom of Benjamin Franklin and all the Founding Fathers of our still United States.

It was a good balance of the body and mind, and it was around this time that I began to question the near-ubiquitous idea that college is inevitable, a hoop you need to jump through for the sake of making a living. What if learning a trade would make most of us not only happier, but freer? If you are naturally disposed to scholarship, if the reading of difficult books is an urgent need, and if you can *afford* to surrender four years of your young life to reading them, go to college. But if not, craftsmanship is as worthy a pursuit and equally ennobling as a college degree, even from a liberal arts college.

Compared to a real craftsman my skills were camp. But for me, house painting was anything but prosaic. My trade was poetry. A makeshift sacrament, work itself became a kind of poetry, at once exacting and liberating, demanding and satisfying. When I went to the grocery store after a long day of house painting, my white painter's shorts covered in latex paint and dried caulk, I was proud.

Today the university seems to celebrate potential rather than actual achievement; that is, students do not seem to learn any particular set of skills, at least ones that have a quantifiable result. What if in sending everybody to college, something is lost? "He that hath a trade hath an estate; and he that hath a calling hath a place of profit and honor. A ploughman on his legs is higher than a gentleman on his knees."[7]

* * * * *

And so I found myself in the stained bathtub in the heat of an Indian summer, still tanned from months of painting outdoors, brooding.

I had a successful house-painting company. My classes had opened new horizons. I had good friends. I was writing books and drinking tea. I was not a Gnostic or a Puritan. I was free in Christ. And now that my Anglican priest had become Catholic, I could sleep in on Sundays. I had a Bible and I followed my conscience. So why wasn't I happy?

I stood and put on my favorite "Narnian bathrobe". After studying in Oxford and painting all summer, it felt good to be back at "The Bench", the little yellow house some friends and I rented. I had missed the kegerator, the twinkle lights, the bar made out of an old bowling lane, the broken furniture, the familiar books, the antique stovetop. And as I made breakfast, I admitted my relative isolation. I was surrounded by friends, most of them Christians, and yet we were not *together*, not really. Even in my soul I felt a kind of loneliness. It was as if there was still a chasm between me and God, between me and others, and I didn't know what to do about it. I was so spiritual I was on the brink of evaporation.

The coffeemaker made hissing and crackling sounds. At least I had poetry. I had discovered that there is not only a real difference, a difference in *meaning*, between "old poets" and "poets old", but also that life—hungry, laughing, tear-stained life!—could be kind of *lived* poetry. More than verse, I believed poetry to be the answering voice, a kind of electric current that infused one's life with meaning. And this was a new year, our final year, our last hurrah. As I made breakfast in my Narnian bathrobe, I swore a new battle cry. It wasn't very new, but I couldn't think of a better alternative. Thenceforward, I would live a poetic prayer.

I used a fork to fidget with the bacon in the skillet. It was time for change. It was time to find others who also wanted to live a poetic prayer. It was time to muster the poets.

5

A Parliament of Owls

Yet Lord, instruct us to die,
That all these dyings may be life in death.

—George Herbert[1]

For it is in giving that we receive.
It is in pardoning that we are pardoned,
and it is in dying that we are born to Eternal Life.

—The Prayer of Saint Francis

Old hunting traditions were stocked with "nouns of assembly". For example, a *gaggle* was a term of venery for a flock of geese that is not in flight. Or when owls were seen together as a group they were called a *parliament* because they were considered to be of a wise disposition. And so in such a fashion, my friends and I gathered to form a kind of parachurch-cum-literary club. We had bonfires and sat on saggy furniture and read poetry out loud and threw crumpled balls of paper at each other in the heat of an argument. Having learned my lesson with the Guild, I did not suggest we celebrate communion without a minister. Dr. Breyers, a Congregationalist minister who liked the Book of Common Prayer, presided over the eucharist in our living room. Then we ordered pizza and threw a party. For these and any other sins I cannot now recall we were called "The Couch Society".

At first, we were little more than a gaggle. But Dr. Breyers kept admonishing us to repent of our sinful ways. And Stephen had a run-in with the police. And then Nutkin had an existential crisis, and there were a few bad breakups with girls. There was also a collective sense of reckoning that followed reading modern verse. Reading

A. E. Housman, it felt like *we* had been to Ludlow fair and left our neckties God knows where. Leafing through Seamus Heaney, the cold smell of potato mold brought with it the sad awareness that we had no spade to follow men like our fathers. It seemed that in our hearts we had killed some neighbor with whom, if we had met by some old inn, like Thomas Hardy, we would have wet many a nipperkin. By the time we finished Wilfred Owen, we felt bent double, like old beggars under sacks. A few of us started to confess our sins to one another, asking for accountability. We stopped messing around with girls. After several late nights of talking about James Fenton's "God, A Poem", Tom quit being an atheist. Slowly, almost accidentally, we began to pray for one another. We were no parliament of owls, but the Couch Society was smartening up. And people seemed to notice our affection for one another.

"What, are you gay?" a baseball player snickered in the lunchroom.

"Are you a business major?" Nutkin shot back.

"Poetry!" Stephen shouted after him in exhortation.

The accusation of homosexuality is worth pausing over. By then, the sexualization of everything was beginning to play out in my life in new and unfamiliar ways, especially in the depreciation of male companionship. For the first time, perhaps ever, boys and young men were reticent to go to the movies together, much less hug or sleep in the same bed—what if someone thinks they are gay? The reduction of almost every kind of affection to sexual attraction has been a strange and disappointing trend. It's difficult to believe on this side of Freud, but for most of human history sex was not considered to be the highest, most fulfilling experience possible. For the ancients, *eros* was not so much "erotic" but rather a kind of philosophical happiness, and *sexus* (a zoological term) was not a subject over which to spill ink. But friendship was everything. Friendship (*amicitia* or *philia*) was more highly prized even than romantic love (*amor*). "Your love to me was wonderful, passing the love of women," said David, when he learned of the death of his friend Jonathan (2 Sam 1:26). Shakespeare's sonnets express passionate love for a young man, a love that is not sexual (Sonnet 20). When Abraham Lincoln was a bachelor he shared a bed with his good friend Joshua Speed. Back then, men shared beds. Men loved each other. And they didn't need a "man hug" with a few pats on the back to make sure it wasn't sexual.

In any case, culture used to provide boys with clear and public ways to prove that they were on the way to becoming men—tests of endurance and courage, rites of passage, traditions. Today there are usually no such rituals and signs. Are we surprised boys invent their own?

The Couch Society brought about something that I have found not easily won, and that is male friendship. Testicular and chivalrous though they were, the friendships that formed within the Couch Society were a kind of forge. The arm wrestling, the memorizing of poetry, the intellectual breakthroughs, the taking of responsibility for our actions—it all added up to a kind of initiation. We didn't talk about it this way, but it happened. We challenged one another and had each other's backs, and the once-brief feints at adulthood became real blows. How rich and sweet and root-down-deep it was to have friends—not a clique, not a tribe, not a social crutch, but *friends*.

That being said, it must have looked like madness. One minute we were discussing Boethius and puffing our tobacco pipes and the next we were half naked and wrestling on the floor. Strong and earthy and sometimes almost erudite, our raillery and badinage was shot through with a deep respect for one another. We wanted to be better men. We were young and dipped in folly, but our camaraderie pointed us toward the virtues of fortitude and justice, prudence and chivalry, and maybe even a little temperance. We prayed together, studied together, slept together, made breakfast together, wrote poems for one another, and there was nothing sexual about it. In fact, there were times I felt that our gaggle was everything I wanted "church" to be. The only problem was I couldn't convince myself or anyone else that we really were a church.

And then there was Old Hickory, nicknamed because of his sheer height and lion's heart. A junior with biceps the size of cantaloupes, Old Hickory and I first met under a tree after class. He was playing guitar, and we agreed that trees have what the medieval man called "vegetable souls". We got to talking and he quoted Chaucer: "Whoso will pray, he must fast and be clean, And fat his soul, and make his body lean."[2] I did not recoil from such a religious sentiment, having been chastened by modern verse, and I loved him instantly.

When Old Hickory first sat on a green sofa with the other geese, he introduced us to Irish drinking songs. We danced to the Clancy Brothers, the Dubliners, and sang along to Luke Kelly. But Old Hickory brought more than his Irish heritage with him; he brought religion.

I realized I had no idea what to say to him. Every poem led him to the opposite conclusion; every song had a different meaning. He did not participate in our celebration of the. holy eucharist with Dr. Breyers. He cherished poetry but had no patience for poetry as a theological excuse. Never hurried, never resting, Old Hickory asked questions, but he didn't see the pleasure of unending dialogue. He wanted answers. I tried to introduce him to the concept of hanging out with coffee and the Bible on Sunday morning but he didn't get it, and I remember the Couch Society felt oppressively small with him moving about in it. He was blind to the hipness of my theological nuances; he was respectful and generous, but it bothered me that he was completely, totally unawed by my spirituality. What I learned from these experiences was that there were more cultural differences between Old Hickory and me than there were between me and anyone else I had ever met. He was the most unromantic man in the world, except he knew more poetry, sang better songs, and spoke more deeply than I had ever been able to speak in my long experiment with romance. And what he wordlessly held out to me— religion—felt so dear that it felt almost like home.

Meanwhile I was trying to stave off a restlessness that had developed. I noticed it first when I went to Mass, just to see what all the fuss was about. There was a crowd of ordinary people kneeling in pews, fingering rosaries, mothers bouncing children on their knees, and I was surprised to find the formality of the place was grounded in something almost wild. There was something about the people and the sanctuary, something primal, a kind of craving that was almost savage. The priest who greeted us in the narthex looked dangerous in his clericals. And Old Hickory was stooped over in the pew, rocking back and forth. He clutched his scapular in silence, and for a moment—it was very startling—I seemed almost to hear his prayers. I excused myself. Maybe going to Mass wasn't such a good idea after all. I hated walking through that gauntlet of praying people in the pews because none of them seemed to be sentimental or phony. I felt like a piece of driftwood.

Outside, the weight of my aloneness came down on me. I walked home and pushed open the door of my apartment, where the only movement in my absence had been the light moving across the desk with my Bible on it. I opened the leather binding, and the pages smelled like loneliness. The restlessness eased a little when I read the book of James, but only a little. And soon it spread, until the word "church" could make me cry.

I wanted one. With a priest. And a congregation and commandments and a calendar and children running between the pews. And the smell of incense and old missals, and the dark of the Confessional. And some kind of necessity or obligation to all of it. This honest wish seemed so impossible. Church was so different from the life I was living, and not even the friendships of the Couch Society seemed a satisfying substitute. There were no girls in the Couch Society, for one thing, no children and no old people; but most of all it lacked something I couldn't quite put my finger on.

That was my first hint that there's a kind of wisdom to religion, that if you clear away the white noise of spirituality and listen, faith and works might actually be allies. We are, after all, *creatures*, creatures made to crave what's good for us. It makes sense that a vestigial part of us should still be crouched over a votive candle somewhere or kneeling to receive the Host, chewing that which is not bread alone. Man cannot live on bread alone.

The longing for church might have come from the same primeval part of me that first told me to wear the brown scapular. Old Hickory gave me his after a long conversation about the saints by the fire, and I never took it off. The two pieces of cloth were threadbare, and it had a Marian symbol on it that I didn't understand, but it seemed somehow to mean something just to have it fall square on my chest, a band on each shoulder, and drop down my back. And after I graduated Hillsdale College and returned to Minneapolis, the first thing I did was look for a church.

* * * * *

"It's good to be home," I lied.

"Well, you can't stay here," my parents said.

I called an old college friend, Nutkin, and we rented a small apartment in Uptown. Clueless and walking around with eyes as big as saucers, we were fortunate enough to make a living wage our first year out of school. Nutkin taught history at a private school, and I painted houses. Inspired, perhaps strangely, by Mark Rothko and Jackson Pollock, I painted acrylic paintings on large canvases and sold them to rich bankers. When I could, I worked on my book about "romantic theology". I missed Dr. Russell's classes and my friends in the Couch Society. That winter I tried to buoy my sinking heart with the vision that had rushed me out into the world again—the poetry, the cigarettes, my invisible church theory, the beautiful mess—and spent long hours pounding on my typewriter, listening to the silent sound of snow falling and the hissing radiators.

Minneapolis was so cold the snow was squeaky. It was so cold I didn't get a haircut for six years. It was so cold I wished I had a wife, and I imagined her to be a librarian with tortoiseshell glasses. It was so cold, and this imaginary woman seemed beyond my reach, that instead of trying to find her I decided to take what I called "a vow of celibacy"; for one year, I wouldn't date any girls. I wanted to wear my brown scapular at all times and to rid myself of my sinful ways and figure out if I should become a monk. Because I had seen *The Boondock Saints*, I hung a rosary on my wall. But first, I had to break up with my girlfriend.

"It's not you, it's me," I said.

"What do you mean?" Allison asked.

"I'm becoming a monk."

"You are?"

"Well, just for a year."

"You're a real jerk," she said, and hung up.

I hung up, too, and breathed the rarified air of celibacy.

That night, Nutkin and I went out for burritos and watched *The Office* in our apartment while it snowed outside. The next morning, being "celibate" (by which I meant something like *chaste*), I threw the covers off my bed and drove to a small Anglican church nestled in the suburbs. The music was unadorned but elegant, and the sermons seemed biblical enough. There were no eligible girls in the pews, but it didn't matter because I was a monk. The parish seemed always to be flooded with sunlight. Folks soon knew me by my name, and a few even became close friends. I memorized the Creed and the prayers. I still felt like a piece of driftwood, but one that had found safe anchorage.

Soon thereafter a gaggle of old friends from college moved to the Twin Cities and rented apartments nearby. Some painted houses with me, and others worked at coffee shops. We grilled beer can chicken and sang along to Old Crow Medicine Show. We crammed an upright bass and a banjo and several guitars into my apartment and stomped our feet and ate frozen pizzas. We argued about Modernism (that "synthesis of all heresies", as Saint Pope Pius X called it[3]) and stomped around Minneapolis like we owned the place. More than anything—more than making money or settling down or anything else associated with "growing up"—I wanted to keep the poetry alive. I didn't want to be alone in the world.

I purchased a set of harmonicas and began to write songs on my guitar with a will. Believing art could do what God's breath did to the dead bones in the prophet Ezekiel's dream—"Son of man, can these bones live?" (Ezek 37:3)—I established a record label called Ezekiel Records & Creative Group and dumped thousands of dollars and the long winter hours of 2008 into recording the music album *Out from the Darkness*. These were the songs I wrote and sang with the Couch Society, and playing them in bars and music clubs made Minneapolis feel a little less lonely.

All the while I was endeavoring to land a book contract. Every month I sent a manuscript and proposal to various publishing houses, and every month I received rejection letters. One publisher expressed great interest in my "romantic theology" (at the time I think the book was unfortunately called *Sex & First Snowflakes*) only to drop it. When I got the news I cried for twenty minutes, then ripped the rejection letter into a confetti and threw the pieces into the air. Then I took a long nap. Then I splashed cold water on my face, shouted something like a war cry, and immediately began writing a new book called *Mud & Poetry: Love, Sex, and the Sacred*. In writing it, I seemed to see the world so clearly—the holiness of Matrimony, the perils of what I called "savvy bachelor sex", the depths and heights of love. But by the time the book was finally published in 2010, the revelation of romantic love as a carriage of grace, even a means of sanctification, had lost its freshness. Instead, I felt tired and maybe a little tricked. When at last I was sure that I wasn't called to be a monk, I started dating a girl named Lauren. But after what proved to be an operatic year of romance, I began to despair of ever finding a Great Love.

"It's not you, it's me," Lauren said.

"What do you mean?" I said, looking at the engagement ring I had just bought.

"I don't like poetry."

"You don't?"

"I mean, I'm not a deep person," Lauren said. "I know it sounds shallow, but I just want to have fun."

Two days later, Lauren became a lesbian, which only made me feel worse—what kind of guy makes a girl want to give up on guys altogether? I sat around in my underwear until noon and then made breakfast, looked at my newly published book about "romantic theology", and wondered if my life would ever amount to much more than a romantic fiction. But deep down, at least when I was honest with myself, I knew that I didn't miss Lauren as much as I missed the chance to get married. I felt a little better when I realized I had loved the idea of marriage more than I had loved Lauren, but I also felt like I couldn't look at myself in the mirror.

Being angry felt better than being sad, so I decided to be angry. There was no one to blame for my loneliness, so I blamed God for everything, especially my virginity. About this business of being a virgin, after breaking up with Lauren it seemed that I had paid so heavily for a lifetime of abstinence that I felt entitled, now and then, to get some sort of return. The reward for chastity, I thought, was a happy marriage, and God wasn't keeping up his end of the bargain. I doubted his love for me, and what's worse, I seemed almost to revel in my heart's defiance. All the while I was absorbing the values of Minneapolis and its half-baked, prairie home companion ways. Like the other hipsters, I feasted on saturnine gruel and drank the cup of disillusionment. Slowly, almost imperceptibly, I turned in on myself like a clenched fist in a sock puppet.

They were dark and starless years, years of waiting. Waiting to become the man I thought I was always on the verge of becoming. Waiting for the woman I thought I deserved. For two years I waited for my life to really begin. But even in the darkness, there was a flicker of light. For example, I remember reading a poem about this guy who would lend one of his books to a girl on the first date. This way, she would get to know him, and she would have to see him again in order to return the book. But what really happened was, she didn't have the time to read his books, and she was afraid that if she saw him again, he would expect her to talk about it, and maybe even lend her another one, so she cancelled the date. He ended up losing a lot

of books. So one day his therapist told him something brilliant: he
should borrow hers. When I first read this poem I chuckled nervously
because I was that guy. I lent girls *my* books. But I was beginning to
learn that sometimes—not all the time, but sometimes—"giving" can
be self-interest in disguise.

Not long after my relationship with Lauren ended, I figured out
that love works the same way. Nothing is wrong with wanting to be
known and understood, but you have to *start* with wanting to understand and to know. A man in love asks questions. So when I started
dating Natalia I borrowed her books, tried to enter her world. I still
had a long way to go, but I was learning how to love.

We listened to Björk and M83 and quarreled incessantly. I think
we mostly just liked the idea of each other. Natalia clawed at life the
way an animal might rip open an orange and eat it, rind and juice
and all. She was from Lithuania and told stories of the Baltic Sea and
mountains of tangled crucifixes left behind by Christians on pilgrimage. She wanted to talk about God, which bothered me because I
was packing ice around my heart. In fact, she seemed only to want
to talk about God. Despite my spiritual sloth and perennial concupiscence, God would not be thwarted. Before it was over, Natalia was
baptized. For God, that which is not flint is tinder.

In those days I still attended the Anglican church in the suburbs,
but it no longer felt like safe anchorage. For me, "church" was still
essentially Lockean social contract theory dressed up in spiritual
skinny jeans, a shriveled and subjective thing. Even as an Anglican,
I harbored the opinion that the Lord's Supper was essentially a time
to think about Jesus on the Cross while I waited in line to receive
the wine and the bread. The eucharist was not sharing in the Body
and Blood of Jesus, at least not really, for I didn't acknowledge that
my Baptism had united me to the Body of Christ. "Church" felt
unrelated to the real me, and to the extent that I lived as though the
"real world" were not related to the worship of God, it wasn't. It
was inevitable that for me the Kingdom of God would be bereft of
scruples and civic duties and customs. My faith was inherently private, otherworldly, nonpolitical, and this great theoretical separation
of church and state helped me enormously in separating faith and
works. I bought a bicycle and stayed out late with the other hipsters.
I prayed when I felt like it, which wasn't very often, and tithed even

less. As for Corporal Works of Mercy, there weren't any. One night my friend Petrie and I were sitting outside a café when a homeless man asked if we had cigarettes.

"Call me Ishmael," said the man, inhaling. "I won't answer to it, because it's not my name."

"So why do you want us to call you Ishmael?" Petrie asked.

"Because it's a lot better than most of the things I've been called."

"It was nice to meet you, Ishmael," I said, hoping he would leave.

"Here," said the man, handing Petrie a half-empty bottle of mouthwash.

"What is it?"

"You'll never taste better. Go on, take a nip, I won't tell anyone."

Petrie unscrewed the cap, turned the bottle up, and took a snort. He passed it to me, nearly unable to speak.

"No thanks," I said.

And for one miserable hour I sat as Petrie and Ishmael polished off the remaining contents of the mouthwash, and it was cold so Petrie gave him his coat and let him keep it. I was annoyed, but I was also a little inspired.

When the thought first came to me, I should have dismissed it as mere whimsy. But like most of my harebrained ideas, it wouldn't go away. Within days of watching Petrie drink mouthwash, I resolved to launch a music record project that would raise awareness about homelessness. I asked local musicians to add accompaniment to my songs, or to contribute their own songs, and poured all my savings into the album's production. Years later, in debt but happy with the outcome, *Think Out Loud: Music Serving the Homeless in the Twin Cities* was finally released. It was the greatest nonevent in the history of Minnesota music, raising no more than a whimper of awareness about the problem of homelessness in Minneapolis and St. Paul.

Even if it had been a smashing success, it wouldn't have changed the fact that in the name of fighting homelessness I had avoided homeless people. For all my shiny efforts, for all my collaboration with local stars and rocking out in cool recording studios, I never once volunteered at a homeless shelter or sat on the curb to drink mouthwash with someone who was so poor they couldn't afford bottom-shelf vodka. I never once gave away my winter coat. But they were dark years, and whether it was fighting homelessness or living my Christian faith, I didn't really want to *do* anything. I was not the authentic man I thought myself to be.

Early on in the *Think Out Loud* project, I met with Mary Jo Copeland, the founder of the Sharing and Caring Hands shelter, to receive something like her blessing. She listened, and then handed me—of all things!—a rosary.

"Will you pray with me?"

"Um," I said, conflicted.

"In the name of the Father, and the Son, and the Holy Spirit," Mary Jo crossed herself.

As she began to say her say Hail Marys, I listened with a self-righteous, almost self-loathing anger, barely sensing the awkwardness of my life's situation. There I was—praying with Mary Jo but not really praying, wearing a brown scapular and fingering a rosary but not believing in the Blessed Virgin, serving the homeless with my right hand and not serving them with my left, going to church on Sunday but resenting God in my heart, wishing I were married but not doing anything that would suggest to anyone I was ready for marriage, pouring everything I had into producing yet another music record with hardly a passing thought to my own future—and the situation seems to be a kind of snapshot of how things were then.

* * * * *

"I don't know what I'm doing with my life," I told my friend Paul after church one day.

"What should you be doing?" he asked.

"Discovering myself, I guess."

"Says who?"

"I don't know. Everybody. Books."

Paul raised his eyebrows.

"This is my chance to have fun," I sighed. "You know, before real life sets in."

Paul was quiet. "So why are you so miserable?"

That night, I thought about why I was so miserable. Why did I stay out late with people I did not admire or respect? Why didn't I just break up with Natalia when it was obvious we were not right for each other? Why did I stream videos rather than go to sleep? The answer, I think, is simply that I was afraid of being alone. I wanted to belong, to feel at home in the world, and yet I had never felt so forlorn.

As a child, making friends had been so easy. You waited at the same bus stop, partnered with someone for Bio Lab, moved into a dorm, started a Couch Society—and *wham*, you had friends. But Minneapolis was different. At times, it felt like I was a figurine trapped inside a snow globe. As the years rolled on, the small gaggle of friendships that had formed in my neighborhood proved not to be very meaningful or enduring. There was no accountability, no exhorting in righteousness, and in matters of faith and morals every man was left to himself. We had always been busy, but we didn't share the same experiences anymore: we no longer went to the same classes, ate the same lunches, or hung out until midnight over books. We had left college for a world of divorce, cohabitation, careerism, private spiritualities, and casual sex, scrambling to find a foothold. My early twenties were more hectic than I anticipated—and lonelier.

Where were the old people? Where were the children? And where did we find the time? When we talk about the emergence of "young adults" and "thirty-is-the-new-twenty" we often leave out what could be the most influential change in the history of growing up: the doubling of the human life span from around forty years to eighty years. Until the end of the nineteenth century, death and children colored every moment of a person's life. Not so long ago, a woman choosing to delay childbirth until her late thirties was as unimaginable as claiming to live long past the age of sixty-five. To grow old was exceptional—almost as exceptional as living a whole decade disconnected from children, or caring for the elderly, or family.

Extended life expectancy has made extended adolescence possible. Industrialization, urbanization, agribusiness, technology, and shrinking population are all factors circumstantial and otherwise correlated with "young adults"; yet, even taking them all into account, the picture remains incomplete without the lengthening of life span. Death has been moved to the periphery of our social imagination and exercises less influence over young people's minds and hearts today than it did in the past. In combination with technology and post-agrarian economies, lengthened life span has, understandably, reshaped how we think about every aspect of life. Work is no longer directly linked to staying alive. Advances in sanitation and water distribution and the specialization of work, so removed from the soil, veil the very human link between labor and survival. Young people entering the workforce have time to brood. More than putting food on the table, "work" is viewed through the lens of personal fulfilment, lifestyle, and vocation (a term originally used for religious life). As a young twentysomething I was aware that people die, that some- day I would die, but death was not an ever-present reality. I went to no funerals. Father Time with his scythe and hourglass, grim Chronos, the old hymns, the eschaton, judgment, and hope—no influence could be received, such was the nature of our world.

It often happens that what we take most for granted has the most impact on our lives, and taking for granted that you will live until you're eighty is undoubtedly a game changer. As I reflect on the emergence of "young adults" and on my own years as an "emerg- ing adult", it seems indubitable that the marginalization of death has made the marginalization of moral norms possible, especially those regarding sex. The urgency to reproduce is less urgent. Mar- riage's mortal origins are obfuscated. The once-familiar purposes of marriage—to care for children and the elderly in covenant—are recast to account for the doubling of life span. The feelings and "experi- ences" of young people may well be considered as surrogate children. Community becomes something of a commodity.

Life as a hipster was life in limbo. The once brief and intermedi- ate stage between childhood and adulthood had become a decade of indecision and irresolution so idealized no one dared admit just how miserable they were. But we lived in a generational ghetto. Our grand- parents had been shoved into dark corners with the other grandparents. Time with parents was segregated to isolated situations far removed from our social circles and "real life". We had no children. Most of us twentysomethings lived with other twentysomethings, ate with other twentysomethings, talked with other twentysomethings, went to churches (if we went at all) with other twentysomethings, often worked with other twentysomethings, and beneath our smug and uncritical satisfaction with ourselves lay a constant suspicion that we were missing something. The PBR tallboys, the crowds, the pairing off, the social media, the tattoos—behind the noise, we stood before life's deepest questions in paralyzed silence.

The hipsters around me—was there anyone else?—wanted to "change the world". To that end, it was thought enough to ride a bicycle, eat expensive organic food, and go out for drinks with like-minded friends. Everything else was a policy problem. For us, the generation of children of divorced parents, it was simply assumed that the family was a broken institution; it certainly had no vital role to play, at least not really. The government seemed a more trustworthy caretaker of children and the elderly, and anyone else who happened to be in the way.

"I'd rather die than sit in a nursing home, wasting tax dollars," someone said.

"A burden to society," someone chimed in.

What was this thing we called society? And how light and insubstantial did someone need to be in order not to be a burden? Free from the responsibility of children and cut off from the wisdom of the elderly, segregated into our own self-contained circles and applauded by our own urban tribe, who were we to decide what made life worth living? The salmon did protest—"We will not swim upstream to spawn and die!"—and I mimicked them because I didn't know what else to do. It's not like I was about to move into my parents' neighborhood. I enjoyed playing cribbage with my grandparents, but it was obvious that I didn't fit in at the nursing home. The families at the Anglican church in the suburbs were welcoming, but their world had nothing to do with mine. The world which lay beneath the shadow of my grudge against God was not the world I knew as a boy. I could not call it home any more than I could call my urban tribe a community. In college, generational homogeneity was excusable and checked by the authority and presence of professors. But for "young adults" is there any excuse?

We did not remain unmarried on purpose, but by reflex. In flight from death, we relinquished the family, for the family reminds us of our own mortality, of God. Saint John Paul the Great once said that "God in his deepest mystery [the Holy Trinity] is . . . a family".[4] Made in God's image, we are families. The family is the created image of the uncreated Trinity. And with neither children nor parents nor grandparents in our "real lives", we had no real community—no *family*—with which to see God.

Perhaps community, like cake or family or anything else worth making, cannot be made of only one ingredient. I am speaking of generations: babies, fathers, grandmothers, siblings, the conjugal bond, stirring, mixing, baking, cooling, cleaning, till death do us part—all of this takes tenderness and careful attention and time, but we didn't have time. Life's duration had doubled, and we didn't have time for what makes real community possible. It's not that we wanted to have our cake and eat it too; it's that we thought we could buy it at the store. But real community is always homemade.

Death keeps us moral. The fact that we die strongly suggests that our choices have consequences, that there is judgment. And it seems that if we pretend that death is not a part of life, we will never be ready to understand that dying is actually living, much less that death is not the end. For we are born toward death, and in living our dying is already underway. Remembering death helps us to find our place in the passing of generations. Caring for the dying and burying the dead, especially when linked with conceiving new life and caring for children, can only teach us how to live. The denial of death and children has never made a community healthy.

In my hipster days, religion, like community, was an optional association that could be discarded voluntarily depending on personal preference. Death didn't matter, and religion was relevant insofar as it promised happiness in *this* life, and only those who accumulated "experiences" really lived. G. K. Chesterton turned this idea upside down. "Death is not dead for any of us," he said. "The hour comes when death will be very much alive: the awful hour when death will be more alive than we. Are we then to deduce that we cannot experience perfect joy till after that has happened?"[5]

I return to these memories, these sad subjects, as to unfinished business, for they are my life's work. When Israel fell into disbelief, divorce, and avoidance of children, Malachi called them back to God and moral order: "Has not the one God made and sustained for us the spirit of life? And what does he desire? Godly offspring" (Mal 2:15). What community is depends on what the human person is, and the fact remains that every single one of us was born of a woman, begotten of a man. Made in the image of the Trinity, we are made in the likeness of a family. The natural family is the human icon through which we see the Trinity. And the doubling of life span—to say nothing of artificial birth control—has helped to fabricate a decade wherein young people are cut off from this icon. Is it any wonder we did not see God? We hardly saw each other.

* * * * *

After I returned the engagement ring, I justified my mortal and venial sins with a complex web of biblical interpretations and theological nuances. Blaming God for my loneliness and doubting his goodness, I was not as interested in God's rights as I was with *my* rights. But perhaps the fault was not in my stars, but in myself. Always I was waiting. More than anything, I think I was waiting for clarity. I galloped like a mad horse at it. As my relationship with God became dry, fissured, cracked, I was desperate for clarity: Why did I exist? Where was life going? What was my vocation? But the more I sought clarity, the more unhappy I became. I began to feel that maybe God could have given me clearer instructions or more obvious signs. What was he keeping secret?

One of the saddest things about this season in my life is that I was not grateful for half of what I could have been. I was not even grateful for half of half of it. Not even a tiny fraction, to be honest. And one of the reasons I found it so hard to say thank you was because deep down I didn't trust God. I was afraid that God might be hiding something from me, that what I had would be all I was going to get.

And then one day—I was probably twenty-six and Minneapolis was seething with millennials costumed for the annual Zombie Pub Crawl—I remembered a story about a man who worked for three months at "the house of the dying" in Calcutta. He was seeking a clear answer about what God wanted him to do with his life. He asked Saint Teresa of Calcutta (Mother Teresa) to pray for him.

"What do you want me to pray for?" she asked.

"Pray that I would have clarity," he said.

"No, I will not do that," she said.

When he asked her why, she explained: "Clarity is the last thing you are clinging to and must let go of."

When he mentioned that *she* always seemed to have clarity, Mother Teresa just laughed: "I've never had clarity; all I've ever had is trust. So I will pray that you will trust in God."

I knew then that if I was going to stop blaming God and doubting his good intentions for me, my hipster lifestyle would be turned upside down. I knew I would have to stop seeking clarity and risk trusting God. Both prospects looked reckless, and I didn't want to do either. And the stakes were high. I was going to have to learn to trust God or spend the rest of my life in an endless quest for clarity. The suspicion that God might be holding something back, that maybe he didn't want the best for me, made me try to pave my own way, come up with my own plan. Fear of the unknown made me want to read another book, pose another question, demand another sign. But Jesus never said, "Follow me and everything will become crystal clear." He said, "Let not your hearts be troubled; believe in God, believe also in me" (Jn 14:1). I glimpsed an idea, a way forward. I pulled at it and, wrenching it free, saw that I needed to step out in trust.

As a crowd of twentysomethings dressed as zombies and feigning apocalyptic terror scuttled outside my apartment window, I realized that this seemingly simple act of faith, stepping out in trust, is a religious gesture. For the first time in my life I truly doubted my spirituality. In the popular phrase "I'm spiritual but not religious", the word "spiritual" was not true spirituality. My spirituality was an easy assurance. It assumed all the light of the beatific vision without admitting the darkness of concupiscence. It bid me to lie down in green pastures without walking through the valley of the shadow of death (Ps 23:2, 4). But what is homecoming without the difficult journey? And what is sainthood without some kind of sacrifice?

I sat on the windowsill and lit a cigarette, and tried to imagine what a life of trust would look like. I looked back over the years and considered the frightening implications. Spiritual but not religious, I had moved from one thing to the next, one moment gushing over a "new insight" only to be bored the next. And I had to admit that such a spirituality had afforded a kind of instant gratification, which, due to being instant, had proved to be not so gratifying after all. And so the "new insights" got more and more exotic, and less and less orthodox, and I could see that the quest would never stop. Scratch a Christian who has bold new ideas and you find a slave to fashion.

I was beginning to feel claustrophobic. I decided to go for a walk. Outside, they staggered past me—half-drunk young adults dressed as zombies and fouled with a strange sexuality, their faces bleached with death, their laughter dinning fiercely. I felt like I too had been living like the walking dead. My "spiritual life" was not life, not really. And against my flimsy, cardboard version of Christianity stood religion, ominous with its warnings and demands and first principles. With religion there was no shortcut to the heavenly holy of holies. Here the pain of Good Friday and the sorrow of Holy Saturday went before the bliss of Easter. Repentance and penance, sacrifice and submission, obedience and oblation, and, yes, eucharist—I saw that all of it was part of God's gift for the salvation of mortal flesh. And I strongly suspected that once I dined on fare as rich as this, I would never again settle for the thin gruel of spirituality. The only problem was, I didn't know what to do about it. But maybe that was the point—I didn't need to know; I needed to trust.

What does it look like to love God? Maybe it looks like trust. Perhaps trust is human love by another name. In this fallen world, maybe it's the only way we're able to love God back. A heart that recklessly trusts in God looks up into the sky and says, "Thank you." And I wondered if maybe I didn't need to wait until things become clear to start living. Maybe no one can honestly say in his heart, "I believe in God," until he has said, "Jesus, I trust in you." When all else is unclear, only *trust* can lead you to the same place it took Job: "Though he slay me, yet will I trust in him" (Job 13:15 KJV).

All of this is to say that I was impatient under the ordeal of young adulthood. There had been a lavish expenditure of music and cocktails and organic eggs and coffee, and I basked in the free feeling of it all. But it was not quite what I had expected, and like so many I bore it with an air of irritation. I would turn thirty feeling vague relief.

Still, when I recall those years, I now see a mother kneeling, her tear-stained face upraised, her brow veiled in lace. For I was wearing the brown scapular, and the Immaculata was on the move. And for a moment, it seemed an angel, ruffled and fierce, flew over me. And sometime after the Zombie Pub Crawl, I was brought gradually back to the old idea of the priesthood. Being a priest seemed to put first things first. "Seek ye first the kingdom of God, ... and all these things shall be added unto you" (Mt 6:33 KJV). Or, as G. K. Chesterton put it, "The first things must be the very fountains of life, love and birth and babyhood ... flowing in the quiet courts of home."[6] The Holy

Trinity, covenant, the family icon, the priesthood of Christ—to me the priesthood cracked open the heavy-set doors of young adulthood to something antecedent and primary. I didn't know where to go or what to do, so I started writing again. Natalia and I broke up; I stopped going to the clubs and bars and became somewhat of a recluse. I was not better than my peers (I was, in fact, a big mess), but I needed to distance myself from them. Somehow, I needed to start putting first things first.

If first things are put first, second things will follow. As a twentysomething, I put second things first only to find that in doing so I lost not only the first things, but also second things. The Guild, the Couch Society, the bewhiskered millennial hordes, my footloose ecclesiology and uncertain church attendance, my clenched heart— none of it would do. The only thing that could make sense of life, the only thing that could allow for the possibility of truth—not just private, sort-of-true-for-me truth, but real, public truth for everyone, truth for adults—was eternal life. I am speaking of generations, of a past and a future that mean something. Procopius, a sixth-century historian, marveled at the Christians he encountered, "whose life is a kind of careful rehearsal of death".[7]

6

The Spell to Break the Spell

These are indeed the barn; withindoors house
The shocks. This piece-bright paling shuts the spouse
Christ home, Christ and his mother and all his hallows.

—Gerard Manley Hopkins[1]

O Blood and Water, which gushed forth from the Heart of Jesus
as a fountain of Mercy for us, I trust in You!

—The Divine Mercy Chaplet

The first time Brittany happened upon me I was performing with my guitar and harmonicas in "The Whole", the University of Minnesota's student union. By then, my hair fell well below my shoulders and was so wild I looked like a toilet brush. The second time she saw me was at the First Avenue Music Club, and I was dancing to dubstep in skinny jeans. She didn't see me the third time, but later heard that we were at the same concert and that, much to her disapproval, I thought Andrew Bird's repertoire was disappointing. Then we were at a Halloween party and I was half naked in a bearskin, and I thought her name was Bethany. Six months later, when my sister gave me her number, Brittany did not call me back.

"I want to go on dates," I had told my sister.

"You want a girlfriend?" she asked.

"No," I said, "I mean, I want a girlfriend, but I want to meet different people, go on dates."

"You want to be a player?"

"I want to *date*. Do you know anyone?"

My sister thought for a moment. "Do you remember Brittany?"

93

"Bethany?"

"Brittany," she laughed. "A few years ago we stopped by Mom and Dad's before going out and played dominos. Mom said that you would be perfect for each other."

"And she didn't tell me?"

"Would you have listened?"

"What's her number?"

My sister watched as I called Brittany. I left a voicemail, but didn't know what to say. *Hi, I'm your friend's brother. I was wondering if you wanted to grab a cup of coffee or something?* My sister rolled her eyes.

Brittany did not call back, and the days plodded by slowly. I went on dates and enjoyed getting to know other girls, but I was distracted by my mother's praise for Brittany. I tried to remember the few times I had seen her. How had I not noticed her before? Unlike the other girls, loud and showy and easily dodged, Brittany was quiet. I remembered that she blushed, and the color seemed to rise from a hidden strength, a kind of unstoppable dignity that demanded you look her in the eye. I wasn't used to that. Perhaps out of discomfort, almost like selective hearing, I had not seen her because she made me feel like a fake plastic tree in the sunlight. As the weeks turned into months, my mind kept coming back to these salutary memories. I left another nonsensical voicemail, worried that I had missed my chance. But late that spring, after Brittany had been assured that I had no abnormalities and was quite safe, she called back.

* * * * *

When I opened the door it was as if time stood still. Brittany and I regarded each other and for a fleeting moment something passed between us, a faint sense of some common doom. When I tell the story—Brittany remembers it quite differently—this is the moment that counts as the beginning. I felt it physically, before I could turn it into words. The sun shone on her freckled shoulders, and I saw a twelve-year-old Brittany with whom I might have climbed a tree and a grandmother Brittany sitting next to me in a rocker. Standing there I heard a voice in my heart, a quiet voice. *You're going to marry this woman.*

I had made a chicken soup. We laughed and she leaned against the windowsill, cheerful and almost festive, yet temperate and magnanimous. We walked to the lake and read poetry and watched the sunset. Under stars only half muted by the streetlights, I walked Brittany back to her car. Going for a walk at night is profoundly different from going on a walk at night with a beautiful woman. Brittany talked about her childhood and all the books she wanted to read. She loved walking around campus with a thermos of hot coffee and taking notes by hand. As she spoke, the air around us felt charged with expectation and hope. The saturnine shadow cast over Minneapolis seemed to lift and the dead hopes were brought back to life, decayed longings were reawoken, and I sensed very strongly that I was walking next to a woman made by God himself, a woman deserving nothing less than to be wooed with sobriety and cheerfulness and wed under sacerdotal authority.

Immediately after Brittany left, I called my mother.

"I'm going to marry this woman."

"Wow." I could almost hear her smiling. "So what are you going to do?"

"Nothing," I said. "I mean, this time I'm not going to *do* anything. This is in God's hands."

Immediately after she left, Brittany called her friend.

"He was so easy to talk to," she said. "I must be getting better at conversations with strangers."

Her friend laughed. "So when are you going to see Tyler again?"

They were tranquil, halcyon days, days of heartsease and gladness. I lived on 28th Street in an attic above a recording studio with good light. I painted houses in the summers and then hung up my brush to write books and make music albums in the winter, changing the oil in my power sprayer one season and dog-earing pages of Thomas Aquinas the next. I liked to sit in front of the windows and drink coffee and look down on the people walking by as I wrote. Brittany came over often, and always we made food. I cooked for her as seduction, as courtship, so that she would know I was serious. And while we cooked we never stopped talking, except to listen. We talked about what matters in life, how to order our astonishments, how to love. Brittany's will stunned me with its presence, its pregnant reality—a reality that did not negate my will but put it in its place. She pushed against me and held me at the same time. Brittany was very liberal, at the time, and we argued about politics a lot. She scoffed at my lack of knowledge about current bills being put before

Congress, and I smiled at just how unprincipled her arguments were. We brought our frustrations with one another to the chess board, looking to checkmate.

Brittany had an aurifying influence on me. Her very existence summoned me to gentleness and strength, to a fuller-bodied manhood. As the mists of my early twentysomethingness cleared, she turned my gaze to the utter east, to God, and to what needed to be done.

"What are you going to do with your life? I mean, to provide for a family?" she asked me as we prepared dinner.

"Maybe my music will take off?" I said. "Or a book will sell?"

She wrinkled her nose, saying, "I wouldn't count on it ..."

Speechless, I watched Brittany slice the carrots thin, dust the slices with a little brown sugar and salt, and lay them in a skillet of sizzling butter.

"But what are you going to do?" she said.

I knew the answer, but it felt weird and almost embarrassing to say it. "I've always wanted to be a priest," I said.

After a pause, Brittany chopped the vegetables into a rough chiffonade. "You wouldn't be able to marry, then?"

"Anglican priests can get married."

Brittany removed the carrots, and I lay the chicken in the skillet. To the pan, she added a splash of the white wine she had brought. She turned and wrapped her arms around me.

"You should become a priest."

This little nudge was all I needed to take action. That night I prayed and then called my parish priest. Within weeks, a process of prayer began, and a discernment team was assembled at my Anglican church in the suburbs. I began to read up on parish ministry and tried to imagine what life would be like as a priest. How would God use me? What kind of qualities did a good priest have? It was not so much soul-searching as it was God-searching. I was coming to God with honest questions. In the process, little by little, I began to open my heart, to trust.

I saw then that I was wounded, and that the cause of my hipsterness, all my years of darkness and waiting, had begun after I listened to a liar—"the father of lies" (Jn 8:44). What did he tell me? Of course, he told me the old lie: *Did God really say that? Surely you will not die!*

God had told Adam and Eve that if they ate from the forbidden tree, they would die (Gen 3:3), and yet I ate. I ate because the serpent made God look like a liar. I ate because he made God look jealous, selfish, and scheming. *For God knows that when you eat of it your eyes will be opened, and you will be like God* (Gen 3:5). I ate, and all my subsequent sadness sprung from this singular lack of trust in God's goodness. In a sense, I didn't want to know God's plans for me: I didn't want to be exposed in my nakedness. Seeing Eve eat the fruit, and not wanting to be separated from her, Adam followed (Gen 3:6). Brittany was doing the opposite. She was stepping out in faith before God, and I was compelled to follow. I loved her, and I knew then that the triune God was my first love.

While Brittany was writing her senior thesis on George Eliot, I made early preparations for becoming an Anglican priest. I also endeavored to read "all of Shakespeare" (I only read about three plays) and write my new book. We listened to Fernando Ortega and Cantus on repeat. We went to Bordertown to drink mochas that were thick with dark chocolate and prodigal with whipped cream. As I applied to seminaries, Brittany helped me study for the GRE (Graduate Record Exam). She even took the test with me for moral support, because she's a genius, and when we went out for a celebratory breakfast at Al's Diner afterward, she revealed that she pretty much aced it.

Love seems to be expressed best not in proclamations but in presence. Brittany allowed me to live at once more patiently and more expectantly. Quiet and respect were the beginnings of our affection. Fresh air and the sun's warmth, the smell of fresh snow and the cedar trees, homemade bread and strong coffee, reading in the late afternoon—these were its ingredients. Brittany loved the Fleet Foxes, pumpkin pancakes, and peeking under the lid of the pot. Together, we fell in love with playing Scrabble and drinking Lapsang Souchong tea, going for winter walks while wearing Santa hats, sighting old-soul trees, and eventually sitting next to each other at church.

Around that time, I had reconnected with my old friend Nate from the high school for artists, and he came over often to make music as the Minnesota sun warmed the attic floor. Nate and I played guitar and sang, and Brittany sang along. We called ourselves "The New American Folk". I had been writing new songs, richer songs, and we played shows around the city and recorded an acoustic album that was never released.

One night in the attic after hours of playing, we put down our guitars and had a poor man's wine tasting with Charles Shaw "Two Buck Chuck". We held our glasses to a hanging light bulb like professional sommeliers and listened to James Taylor and Louis Armstrong on the turntable.

"What do you think of the cab?" asked Brittany, looking very much like a wine steward.

Nate examined his glass, inhaled deeply, and sloshed the red stuff around in his mouth. "It's like shoving your face in a bouquet of flowers," he said, wiping his moustache.

And I remember thinking that life with Brittany was much the same. Falling in love seems to be "given" to a person. A man or woman may be "in love" whether he or she truly loves or not. But real love can only be seen in action, an interplay of devotion and struggle, seeing and savoring, self-gift and even self-denial. Love works more like squiggles than straight lines. For us it was a fluid, lively interplay of ideas and dreams and confessions. We pushed into love, nestled into the insides and edges of the thing, always climbing higher up and further in. Under the rubric of love, our bodies, our books, our pastimes, the little minutes of the day became happier, almost regal.

Brittany was hungry for depth, for religious moorings. She was in her senior year at the University of Minnesota with a triple major in French, global studies, and comparative literature. A member of the atheist club and an activist for LGBT rights, she believed secular public policy was the vehicle for change and that religion was, as Peter Berger once put it, basically something "that was done in private between consenting adults".[2] But while dating a dark and mysterious atheist in Paris, she saw that nihilism was quite dark in an unromantic kind of way and not so mysterious after all. In college, she had befriended two Christian men from the Minnesota north woods and was surprised to discover that they were neither ignorant nor moralizing nor aggressive when voicing their opinions. On the contrary, they were among the most generous, thoughtful people she had ever met. Brittany was intrigued by the story of Jesus, and was surprised by the intense hunger she felt for him. So when she visited the very small Bible church they attended, she nearly cried with disappointment. The narrowness of that church's vision and the almost smug simplicity of its we-are-the-remnant message sent her reeling.

"Want to check out my Anglican church?" I asked. "Anglicanism is the one, holy, catholic, and apostolic church. We have sacraments and priests and a beautiful liturgy, a sense of reverence, real tradition." I didn't mention that my Anglican church was not in communion with the other Episcopal and Anglican churches in the metro area, but was at the time a part of a self-governing church that started under the oversight of bishops in Rwanda—not because I was disingenuous, but because I didn't know and didn't care. It was a good church with good people.

Brittany instantly warmed to the intellectual culture of the Anglican church in the suburbs, and they embraced her with open arms. Together, we explored the story of Jesus in history—his birth, life, death, and Resurrection. It came to light that the Holy Spirit was just stirring up an old baptismal promise, that Brittany had already been baptized as an infant, and that it was time for her to live into that Baptism. After her father died—Brittany was only six months old—she had been raised in a decidedly secular home by her loving mother and stepfather. But the keep-your-chin-up, you-can-do-it optimism of the American Dream was beginning to pale before the strong and jocund hope of Christianity. Brittany believed in Jesus, in the work Christ had begun in her at her Baptism; that Easter our Anglican church invited her to share her testimony and reaffirm her baptismal vows.

To believe is not to have all the answers. To discern the truth as honestly as you can does not mean you will foresee where it will lead. Brittany understood that we see through a glass darkly, and she affirmed her Baptism with humility. She did not apologize for "becoming a Christian", but she invited those around her to approach everything new and other with a sense of curiosity and wonder. She was still herself. But she spoke as one with questions, real questions that had real answers, and I think everyone could tell that she had in some fundamental way changed.

Her parents were not indifferent. How had their political activist, pro-choice, atheist, American Dream girl suddenly become a spiritual, contemplative, Bible-thumping Christian? Not having followed her along her long journey back to the Christian faith, they thought the only explanation for her precipitous change was her new boyfriend, the one with the long hair and guitar who lived in an attic filled with books and "made art" for a living. Graciously, her family attended the service and listened to Brittany's testimony, but for Brittany the joy of that Easter season was also tinseled with sadness. Understandably, her family felt like they were becoming estranged from their daughter.

It wasn't just Christianity. While I applied to seminaries and began the discernment process for the Anglican priesthood, Brittany had resolved to apply for Teach for America, an organization that recruits top college graduates from top universities to serve as teachers in low-performing schools. She wanted to teach students from disadvantaged backgrounds and try to give them some of the same opportunities she had treasured. This career choice was far from the high-profile, profit-making dreams Brittany had as a teen, dreams of being a lawyer or a banker or business executive, and her family struggled to understand. What was perhaps even more frightening for them was that she was hinting of marriage at the ripe age of twenty-one!

And here, perhaps, Christian morality had opened a door that had thitherto been left unopened to her. Until Brittany reaffirmed her baptismal vows, her desire for chastity had felt unnatural, almost embarrassing. Growing up, Brittany had been barraged with politically correct narratives of men and women hooking up indiscriminately and yet had intuited over time that such behavior was anything but empowering. The culture at large simply didn't value her virginity, her body, her heart's deepest desires. Suspicious of authority and not wanting to be too strict, the baby boomers had surrendered parenting to professionals, even when it came to sexuality. But Brittany found the endless moralizing about condoms and risks to be self-evidently empty slogans. Yet so many of her friends clung to these slogans as deep truths while their parents nodded in approval. If parents said anything at all, they often told their daughters not to get married just because they want to have sex (as if any woman marries for this reason) and instead, just to have sex. But when it comes to love, hooking up is a dead-end street.

Sooner or later, women do not want cafeteria-style sex. They want marriage. And from the start, what I offered Brittany was my hand in marriage.

* * * * *

The previous year, my roommate's Croatian grandmother had traveled all the way across the Atlantic to see her children and grandchildren probably for the last time. We were drinking wine on a saggy couch, and it must have looked like I needed some marriage advice.

"The secret to a successful marriage," she said in a thick accent, "is complicity."

Her eyes were bright. She lifted a crooked finger. "Complicity," she said.

A few years later, when Brittany and I started dating, I remembered the old woman's crooked finger and told Brittany about *complicity*. We noticed that the couples we most admired were complicit. What they had was bright and inviting, a long, slow burn. Complicit couples made for the best company. They were not worried about what you thought of them, so they were able to be genuinely interested in you. They built each other up—and they built you up in the process. We loved just being around them. We could never catch them winking at each other, but we saw the twinkle in their eyes. And it felt good. Most of all, we noticed that the couples who were complicit were intentional. They were on the same page, a unified front. They had a punch line, and everything they did led up to it. Only the two of them were in on the joke, but we loved being around them because they were laughing. We decided that complicit marriages are the happy ones, even in the face of sorrow and hardships. They are the marriages that last.

We had just left a dinner with couple of friends who were getting married. It was dark and snowing thick, and it would have been romantic except that we were freezing. As we footslogged through the snow, the conversation drifted toward marriage. And yet, even as we shivered and struggled somehow not to breathe in the biting air, the subject didn't feel awkward or impulsive. It felt welcoming.

We began to see our love as a kind of conspiracy, especially in our shared faith. In her pursuit of heaven, I was Brittany's accomplice.

We were in on a secret, partners in crime, co-conspirators in love. We wanted to plot something beautiful—a parable of heaven.

"Complicity is *not* being the same," Brittany said. "In marriage, you should not want to be the same. You are a man; I'm a woman. I'm a linear thinker; you're, well, nonlinear."

"Yes, different," I said. "I'm an old mop and you're, well, a goddess."

"So the opposite of complicity is *not* being different," Brittany said. "The opposite of complicity is 'a relationship', a marriage that's nothing more than a kind of domestic political system where the couple is constantly talking about their rights."

"What do you mean?" I asked.

"In that Wendell Berry book I'm reading, he says that you don't want a marriage where rights and interests must be constantly asserted and defended," she said. "Berry describes it as a marriage that takes the form of divorce: a prolonged and impassioned negotiation as to how things shall be divided. During their understandably temporary association, the 'married' couple will typically consume large quantities of merchandise and a large portion of each other."

"The opposite of complicity is competition," I said.

"Marriage as consumerism."

We decided that the secret to a joyful, God-filled marriage is complicity. Would the mission of our marriage be the Great Commission? Would our in-laws accuse us of being outlaws? We hoped so. A lot of marriages are successful in terms of 401(k)s, two-car garages, and manicured lawns. Still more have succeeded in great sex, great conversation, and great emotional intimacy. But what makes a marriage truly successful? What if our marriage could be about more than living a Christ-glittered version of the American Dream? What if there could be something more?

We were idealistic and infatuated with one another and lacking experience but could at least see that earthly marriage was of eternal significance. And the idea of *complicity* helped us ignore the warnings and discouragement popular culture threw at us. If baby boomers wrote a book of marriage advice, it would be entitled *Marriage: It Only Gets Worse*. But we didn't want what we called a "baby boomer marriage". We wanted something more.

But how to get there? I was in debt from producing the *Think Out Loud* music album. I knew that I didn't want to be a house painter forever, but seminary was expensive and it would be years before I would have anything remotely resembling a salary and benefits. I needed more than just a livelihood, though, something that went deeper, something almost religious. And that's why I wanted to go to seminary. What was I missing?

My twenties had started out like a wilderness adventure. But now the sun was going down, the temperature was dropping, and I was getting hungry. To survive, I needed light, I needed warmth, and I needed a way to cook dinner. I needed *fire*. Or maybe I hadn't really started yet. Maybe I was still saving up for gear, looking at the maps, and trying to plan my adventure. I needed something like an "Ultimate Camping Guide" for life. Whether I was preparing for marriage or feeling "lost in the woods" when it came to faith, I wanted seminary to help me save myself, to protect my soul from the despair that surrounded me, and help make my potential marriage to Brittany a happy, lasting marriage. Even more, I was looking to start a life of trusting God again.

As I discerned the priesthood with parishioners and men I respected, my prayer was that the vocation would breathe fire into my heart, that together Brittany and I would live our marriage for the glory of God. When it came to religion, there seemed to be no quick fix. But Anglicanism seemed to offer a tool box, or a first-aid kit, or a backpack. There was appropriate gear, and inappropriate gear. And I wanted to travel light. Pound for pound, my prayer was that becoming an Anglican would be worth its weight on the trail. To leave Minneapolis, to start over, to learn Greek and Hebrew and patristics, to pray—as far as I was concerned, there was no goal to reach in 7 days or 30 days or 365 days. The goal here was *forever*.

Brittany was blithe and sharp, youthful in joy and savvy in making plans. Her questions about Christianity forced me to discern the tenets of my beliefs, to know their texture, to revisit and cleave to the first principles. As much as one could say that our Lord used me to draw Brittany closer to his Sacred Heart, so much more could be said, I feel, in how God used her to change the trajectory of my days and hours.

Wanting to grow in trust, I likened my priestly "call" to Abraham's. My wound, my lack of trust, seemed to find its antidote in this father of trust. God called Abraham (who was then named Abram) from his home to an unknown land that God would show him, and Abram believed and left everything behind. One night, God directed Abram's gaze to the multitude of stars in the sky and promised him, "So shall your descendants be" (Gen 15:5). Abram believed, and even though he and his wife were beyond childbearing years, they conceived a son. God promised Abram, who was now Abraham, that through that son, Isaac, he would establish an everlasting covenant with him and his descendants. And then, of course, God commanded Abraham to slaughter Isaac, the only son through whom God would establish an everlasting covenant (Gen 22:1–19). What an impossible test! Yet Abraham did as he was told. And just as he was about to thrust the knife into his son, God stepped in. Unlike Eve, Abraham believed that God was not a liar, that God was good. He trusted that God would keep his promise. For me, this example of unbelievable *trust* helped me overcome the effects of my sin and doubt. Like Abraham, I wanted to trust in God's promises, to leave Minneapolis for seminary not knowing whither.

* * * * *

I slid out of bed and scampered barefoot across the cold wooden floor. I got my clothes off a chair. The early morning was mine. As the coffeemaker coughed out the last few drops of freshly brewed coffee, I flipped through a spiral-bound notebook. Every winter I hung up my paintbrush so I could rise early to write. I would write until about noon, and then eat breakfast for lunch. I would read and nap. Before dinner, I would exercise and then connect with Brittany or friends. And then I would climb back up the three flights of stairs to my attic apartment to drink tea and write until midnight. This particular morning, I remember standing by the coffeemaker as I tried to make sense of just how much I had changed. Brittany's love, her deepening conversion to Christ, had not only brought a certain healing into my life; it had focused my attention. I was praying again and in bits and pieces learning to trust God. The old longings had awoken.

They say that when a man is in love the whole world is lovable. I had fallen in love with Brittany and, unexpectedly, I had fallen in love with Jesus all over again. No longer was I kicking against the goads. The triune God had my attention, and it felt like putting on a pair of perfectly calibrated prescription glasses after a long period of squinting through life. I was so childlike in those winter months, so ready to love and to believe. I did not deserve this unexpected gift, but to me that was the whole point. All is gift. After years of pride and anger, I was hymning praises in my heart. And to make sense of it all, I returned to writing, the old habit.

I was hungry for what I called "fairy tale", which was an expression I picked up from Dr. Breyers during one of the Couch Society's many meetings. He had brought a bag of licorice and photocopies of C. S. Lewis' essay "Myth Became Fact" and handed them out.

"Do you like fairy tales?" he asked.

"We like them," said Davey. "Myths are almost better than poetry, and we like poetry very much."

"What's your favorite myth?" I asked, looking at Dr. Breyers.

"The story of the Redemption," he replied, simply.

Shocked, the gaggle of geese didn't know quite what to say. How could a Christian minister believe the Gospel was a fairy tale? How could he dare to celebrate the Eucharist and think it was just a myth? Dr. Breyers bade us to light our pipes and listen to his reading of Lewis' "Myth":

God is more than a god, not less; Christ is more than Balder, not less. We must not be ashamed of the mythical radiance resting on our theology. We must not be nervous about "parallels" and "pagan Christs:" they ought to be there—it would be a stumbling block if they weren't. We must not, in false spirituality, withhold our imaginative welcome. If God chooses to be mythopoeic—and is not the sky itself a myth—shall we refuse to be mythopathic? For this is the marriage of heaven and earth: perfect myth and perfect fact: claiming not only our love and our obedience, but also our wonder and delight, addressed to the savage, the child, and the poet in each one of us no less than to the moralist, the scholar, and the philosopher.[3]

"You see," said Dr. Breyers when he finished reading, "myths are stories full of gods and adventures that never really happened; yet they ring true because they are echoes of the *fact* of Jesus. Fairy tales are *like* the Redemption because the Redemption is the *real* fairy tale."

Now, for some time I had a growing suspicion that the doctrines of the Enlightenment were, to make a sweeping generalization, what was wrong with the world. Modernism was the death of fairy tales, and as I saw it, the opposite of poetry and a simulacrum of reason. Where did all the know-it-alls come from? It was as if "science" had cast a kind of spell. The spooky incantation was first whispered in the twelfth century when Averroës insisted that reason was somehow *opposed* to revelation, and was eventually shouted from the rooftops in the seventeenth century when philosophers like Descartes, Locke, Newton, and Bacon shook their wicked wands and said, in so many words, "The world is now a machine." As my heart relearned enchantment and as my brain became more rational, as I began to gawk at the splendors of God on display in the Scriptures and the world around me, a deep conviction began to settle. God is *wonderful*. The whole world is on fire, a burning bush alive with his presence. Worship is like children playing or peasants feasting or a skilled carpenter wholly engaged in his labor, and we were made for worship. But Modernism, I believed, had emptied the world of its sacraments and reduced the brain to a machine and even life itself to bytes and bytes of digital information. Modernists did not see God in the stars or water or bread or a baby laughing because the whole world had already been reduced to a windup toy.

That winter, I began to practice worship the way someone might practice the piano. To my surprise, my modest efforts seemed to draw me not only into a closer relationship with God but also into a relationship of felicity with the world. I saw a world crowded with angels and demons, curses and blessings, cloistered incantations of the psalms and the prayers of the faithful, and the constellations in their seasons. My situatedness, my embodiment, the fact that I lived in a particular historical moment—I began to feel how it all cohered in Christ.

I remember one morning realizing that I didn't actually agree with my own theological claims. When it came to theology, at least, my head made my heart sad. As a child my heart just knew that there really were burning bushes, talking serpents, crowing roosters, and magic apples that, if bitten, would steal your immortality. My heart knew that faith without works is dead, that something terrible happened at my Baptism, that the eucharist was more than eating bread and drinking wine while "thinking about Jesus". So why had my head said otherwise? How could I have claimed that the eternal Son of God became a visible man, died and rose from the dead, flooded believers with the Holy Spirit, and sent them into the world to baptize in the holy name of the Holy Trinity—and yet also have claimed that Baptism was just a symbol, that Communion was just a memorial, or that the Church was essentially invisible? I sounded like a modernist!

No sooner had I thought this than I wondered, did the Reformation presage the Enlightenment? Of course the Enlightenment's emphasizing reason and individualism rather than tradition was a problem—but were Descartes, Locke, Kant, and all the rest riffing on an intellectual movement that preceded the Enlightenment? After all, iconoclasm was the central sacrament of the Reformation, expressed not only in the denial of apostolic succession and priestly authority, but in stripping the altars and the wholesale removal of holy images, vestments, sacred vessels—everything except for the Sacred Scriptures. The entire movement was arguably based on the denial of the Mass. As Luther put it: "It is indeed upon the Mass as on a rock that the whole papal system is built, with its monasteries, its bishoprics, its collegiate churches, its altars, its ministries, its doctrine, i.e., with all its guts. All these cannot fail to crumble once their sacrilegious and abominable Mass falls."[4] The Reformers replaced the Mass with a communion service, a mere meal in which the risen Christ was present only in the minds of the individuals. As in the sanctuary, so in the street. Reduce the holy words of Jesus at the Last Supper, "Hoc est corpus meum" ("This is my body" [Mt 26:26; Mk 14:22; Lk 22:19]), to mere "hocus-pocus", and eventually religion itself will be considered hocus-pocus. Were the Modernists just breathing the air of Reformed Europe?

From my attic window, I remember looking out to the snow-covered rooftops and feeling caught off-balance. The possibility that all my Muggle doctrines were only superficially the result of the modern era's rationalism and individualism, and were rather the fruit of an older problem, frightened me. As I mulled over it, I felt just how ineffectual was my theory of the "beautiful mess", how my idea of "poetry" was a poor substitute for a world of deep magic, a world where something like a priest or a sacrament was a real possibility—a *world* of worship.

Researching the sacraments felt like stumbling through a wardrobe into Narnia. I learned that the sacraments are the means through which God unites his creation to himself and shares the fruit of the Incarnation with mankind. They are not only signs, but signs which effect what they signify and signify what they effect. Though confected by human hands, the efficacy of the sacraments does not depend upon the personal worthiness of their ministers or the imperfect understanding of their recipients. The primary agent is God, and the triune God truly offers grace in the sacraments, even though sometimes the offer is refused. My theory of "poetry" was gassy and conveniently vague. But the sacraments implied a Kingdom that was not only magical but real.

All of this was beginning to sound Catholic, but the thought of Catholicism was so crazy-sounding I safely dismissed it as absurd. As an Anglican, thankfully, it seemed I could sweep *sola scriptura* and memorialism and all other forms of iconoclasm into the dustbin of the modern era without becoming a Catholic. With the Church of England, I could keep the good parts of the Reformation—and all the magic too. The phrase "Anglo-Catholic" began to evoke for me a world of holy wonder and enchantment, a world with dew still on it.

And so the days turned into weeks, the weeks into months, and I returned to the scribbles in my spiral notebook and brewed many pots of coffee. My book about rediscovering the mystery and wonder of Christianity was coming along. Before winter was over I signed with a publisher, and the royalty advance paid off my debt and helped me to save for seminary. Brittany wrote papers and studied for exams, and I was on something of a quest, a holy pilgrimage.

I was hungry for God, but I lived in the world. Shouldn't the world be crowded with him? Was God knowable only in books and ideas, or was he knowable in other ways, physical and even carnal ways? Did we live in a world where something like a sacrament was even possible? As Minneapolis slept beneath a blanket of white snow, I began to live into these questions. I read a lot of Czesław Miłosz and Gerard Manley Hopkins and was fascinated by "inscape" and "instress". I dusted off what C. S. Lewis called "the discarded image" and Owen Barfield called "that discarded garment", and began to feel very strongly that what popular Evangelicalism needed was a holy renaissance, a recovery of the Middle Ages, a recovery of the one true *fairy tale*. Above all, I hungered for Christ in the most holy sacrament of the altar. If the Enlightenment (or was it the Reformation?) had cast a spell of disenchantment, what was the spell to break the spell?

This much seemed clear: when Christ ascended into heaven, he did not leave behind a Bible. He left behind the Church, and the Church wrote the Bible. It also seemed clear that I was born late in Church history. To be obedient to the succession of apostles was to be obedient to Christ. Yet, despite its thousand different claims, the Reformation was predicated on what might be called religious autonomy. The opposite of autonomy is, of course, heteronomy: being ruled by something alien to oneself. One's personal relationship with Jesus is considered primary, even antithetical, to one's relationship with the universal Church. In a faith predicated on autonomy—whether among ten sects or ten thousand denominations—it is difficult to think clearly about *obedience* (the faculty that joins us to the Church) because everything outside your own head is a potential source of heteronomy, and therefore a threat to your personal relationship with Jesus.

This might sound like an overstatement, yet it seems implicit in the view of Christianity we have received from the early modern thinkers who forged a new and radical notion of "Church". I wondered if obedience to Scripture might not be a viable alternative to apostolic succession, for the Bible is not a *living voice* of authority and we read the text with assumptions that might blind us to the text. For example, if we assume that we live in a world where the incarnate Son of God could never become transubstantial bread, then we simply will not *hear* Jesus when he says: "This is my body." To admit a real apostolic authority, let alone to admit that "unless you eat the flesh of the Son of man and drink his blood, you have no life in you" (Jn 6:53), put me at odds with deeply embedded Evangelical reflexes. But thankfully, Anglicanism looked like the best of both worlds, a via media that removed all that was wrong with Modernism and kept all that was right about Christendom.

The deeper I journeyed into the darkening pines of Church history, the less infallible my interpretations of Scripture seemed. My hodgepodge collection of catholica and accumulated beliefs began to look more like loose threads, and less like the original tapestry. I began to think less highly of myself. The path through Christendom was old and dangerous, and I quickly learned that careful reconnoitering was necessary. I felt more than ever how important it was for me to go to seminary.

* * * * *

And so as the late winter snows began to melt, Brittany and I drove out to tour a seminary rumored to be Anglo-Catholic and called, strangely, "Nashotah House", with bells and liturgy and cassocked priests looming out of a fog of incense thicker than wood smoke. When we arrived, it felt like someone had dropped a tiny piece of Oxford in the woods of Wisconsin. And everyone seemed to like the Middle Ages. We walked through the school's fields and wooded trails, entranced.

"So what do you think?" I asked.

Brittany took a few paces before answering. The sun shone through the bare branches above us. "I think this is the right place for you," she said, cautiously.

"For me?" I asked.

"I know it's the right place for you—I'm just not sure it's the right place for me."

Her intelligent eyes were bright with humor, but she was earnest. We talked about how much we wanted to marry and yet how we both felt so unprepared to marry, about how Brittany wanted to go forward with her application to Teach for America, and how it was obvious that I would love Nashotah House. Marriage looked like it was just above us, a high summit, but we couldn't climb the cliff face. In order to get there, we had to take the long way around the mountain. And Brittany had reservations about the timing. What about her career in teaching? What about saving money and traveling Europe? Maybe there was wisdom in waiting a few years, or even longer?

We left the Anglican seminary in Wisconsin and drove to Michigan. I wanted to show Brittany Hillsdale College and also to introduce her to dear old friends. Much to my consternation, many had become Catholic. I warned Brittany to be on her guard. That night, while having dinner with a newly Catholic Davey and his wife, I remember arguing very foolishly that the scapular I wore had "nothing to do with Mary". The next day, when staying at Old

Hickory's crucifix-laden home, his wife looked up from spoon-feeding their toddler.

"Does it bother you that the Church of England is the phallic extension of Henry VIII's lust?" she asked.

"Anglicanism didn't start with Henry VIII," I shot back, offended.

"Oh?" she asked.

"It was already there," I continued. "All the Reformers did was send the pope back where he came from."

"Ah," she said, looking unfazed.

On the way back to Minnesota, I was so upset about the hubris of Catholicism I got a speeding ticket. Flushed, Brittany happened to thank the police officer, which only made me more upset. But when we returned, the snows in Minneapolis had all melted and springtime had come, and I forgot all about the hubris of the pope.

Brittany was accepted to Teach for America and was assigned to teach math at a high school in rural Mississippi. I had been accepted to Nashotah House and was trying to read up on Anglicanism. We savored our last sun-filled days together. It felt like we were pressing our hearts into whatever is good, fat, and happy, reaching out into life's unmapped geography and then making a run for it. The day we said our goodbyes, we went to church and then walked to a park nearby. We sat on a bench and promised to write letters by hand. Brittany cried, and my jaw kept twitching. Her bags packed, Brittany left for Mississippi. I sold most of my possessions, moved back in with my parents, and painted houses that summer. But the work had lost its romance, and every night I rushed home to call Brittany or went out to play a show with Nate.

Grilling burgers with my father, taking the family dog on walks with my mother, enjoying a fridge stocked with fresh vegetables and sparkling water—leaving Minneapolis and settling into my child-hood bedroom felt almost liberating. I didn't miss the Zombie Pub Crawl, and I didn't miss the used bookstores or the cafés. I didn't miss my attic apartment above the recording studio, even though it had good light.

"It's good to be home," I said.

"Well, you can't stay here," said my father.

7

A Vision Glorious

Give us grace that our way of life may be pleasing to you,
that we may have the patience to wait for you
and the perseverance to look for you.

—Prayer of Saint Benedict

℟. Behold the handmaid of the LORD.
℣. Be it done unto me according to thy word.

—The Angelus

In the beginning God created the Church of England. And England was overcast and an old ruin with moss on it, so God said, "Let there be light." And the sun shone through a stained-glass window depicting Saint Augustine of Canterbury, thank God.

And God said, "Let there be bangers and mash and toad in the hole." And it was so. And God said, "Let there be parchment so as to write the Book of Common Prayer." And it was so. And God said, "Let there be more clouds and rain, and also a spring to bubble at Saint Alban's feet." And it was so. And God saw that the Roman and the Eastern churches had valid orders, even though they were not English, so he said, "Let there also be the branch theory." And it was so.

Now there was darkness upon the altars in the Church of England because there was no one to light the candles. So God created the people of England; male and female, he created them. A liturgical people he made them. And he made them just right; men to be priests, and women to be priests too. And God blessed the Church of England and said unto them, "Be fruitful and multiply, for the branch theory is sure."

And the people of the Church of England made every church according to its kind. And behold! High church and low church and broad church! And God was happy, and said, "Catholic faith, Anglican tradition." And behold! TEC and ACNA, ACiA and AMiA, and of course GAFCON![1] And God saw that it was as he wished—one tree, many branches. (But God liked the Tractarians best, for they were less branchy than the rest.)

Knowing this old lore, I was eager to begin my studies at Nashotah House Theological Seminary, that outpost of Anglo-Catholicism sticking out into the wilderness of Wisconsin. Because the priests in the pictures I had seen had shaved heads, I buzzed off my Rapunzel-length hair while Skyping with Brittany in my parents' kitchen. The summer spent preparing for seminary involved other negations as well. I took psychological exams, interviewed with priests, attended Safeguarding God's Children classes, memorized the Greek alphabet, and began an ongoing fundraising campaign with my parish to support me while I prepared for the priesthood. I found asking parishioners to support the financial burden of grad school to be humiliating, but it forced me to hone my long-term vision, which was to return to the Twin Cities to "plant" an Anglican church rooted in Word and sacrament. I also had to get a letter from my bishop.

"Who's our bishop, Father?" I asked my parish priest.

"Call no man on earth *Father*, for you have one Father in heaven," said my priest, quoting Matthew 23:9.

"I'll tell my dad you say hi," I said, teasing.

"Our bishop is visiting next week," said my priest. You should meet with him. I think he's staying with Dr. Olson."

"*Doctor* Olson?" I said, and quoted Matthew 23:10: "Call no man *Teacher*, for you have one Teacher, the Messiah."

The following Sunday, I wore a suit and tie because I was very nervous to meet my bishop and to persuade him that I was called to be a priest. I waited in the narthex with sweaty palms. I did not know to call him "your grace" or to kiss his episcopal ring. At this point, I had not yet put a scissors to my locks of hair, and as I introduced myself and explained that God was calling me to become a priest, the good bishop kept staring at my hair.

"I love your hair," he said, finally.

"Thanks," I said.

He wrote the letter, and I passed my psychological exams, submitted my GRE scores, and interviewed well enough. In the heat of August, at the age of twenty-seven, I loaded up my red Ford Ranger and left Minneapolis for the small seminary nestled on the shores of a beautiful lake and surrounded by the forests and cornfields of Wisconsin and just beyond, a sprawl of suburbia.

Apart from the stone buildings and wooded acreage, the most striking thing about Nashotah House is that the students never take off their black cassocks. At a priest's garage sale, I acquired a very old and threadbare cassock that made me feel like I was a young Saint Francis or Gerard Manley Hopkins, and I wore it at all times—during the daily morning prayers and Mass in the Chapel of Saint Mary the Virgin, in all my biblical and Church history classes in Kemper Hall, while dining at the communal breakfasts and lunches in the refectory, and when I studied beneath the oaks or in the old library among what was affectionately called "The Migne", an enormous collection of the writings of the Church Fathers that was enshrined behind bars on the top floor. Every afternoon at Evensong, I threw a white surplice over it with all the rest to intone the ancient prayers. In the evening, I read and prayed among the dead priests who had gone before me. Nashotah House, which was affectionately called "The House", has a very old graveyard where many country parsons and bishops are buried. Upon matriculation, when you become a "son of the House", you may be buried in that cemetery. Parsing Greek among the tombstones in the half light of autumn made quite an impression on me, and I remember calling Brittany to talk about death and the urgency of ministry. I tried to share all that I was learning in my theology classes, especially about the implications of the Incarnation.

"The eternal Son of God became incarnate of the Virgin Mary," I said, as if I had made an original discovery.

"I know," Brittany laughed.

"But this *means* something," I said. "It means that when Jesus established a Church to finish his mission, he established something *visible*. As his Mystical Body, one could almost say that the Church is the social continuation of the hypostatic union."

"The what?"

"The combination of divine and human natures in the single Person of Christ," I said.

"Okay," Brittany said. "But what does this have to do with death?"

"Christ is death's antidote," I said. "But he ascended into heaven and left behind the Church to be a hospital for sinners."

"What do you mean by *the* Church?" Brittany asked.

"The apostolic Church," I said.

"Including Anglicans, I hope?" Brittany asked.

"Yes," I said. "How are classes going? How's Mississippi?"

"It's hard," Brittany sighed. "But I love it. I'm just grading papers right now. I'm so grateful for my housemates. Tonight we're going out for catfish and hushpuppies. I'm obsessed with Southern food!"

"I miss you," I said, sitting among the headstones.

"I miss you too," she said, and paused. "This is good for us, though."

"What?"

"This. You at seminary, me teaching. We're changing."

The thought of change made me shiver. But maybe Brittany was right. Maybe change was good for us. What I was learning about the Bible and theology was changing me—Brittany could hardly recognize the way I talked about Christianity on the phone—but there was a change deeper still. For me, the priesthood was a matter firstly of love—better to receive God's love and better to love him back. But what does it look like to *love* God? "If you love me, keep my commands" (Jn 14:15). When someone loves God, he obeys him. And his service is perfect freedom. So for me, the question of whether or not to be an Anglican priest was firstly a matter of *obedience*. I was beginning to believe in the Church, yes, but I was also eager to obey the Church as one would obey Christ himself. I was just beginning to learn how Jesus is the Head of his Body, the Church. And if for the Head, so for the Body: to be obedient to bishops, the successors of the apostles, is to be obedient to Christ, the one true apostle whom the Father *sent*. But which bishops? And what did obedience entail? And would my studies and desire to obey Christ's Church change anything for Brittany and me, for better or for worse?

* * * * *

Once dressed in a black cassock and cincture band, the first thing students at Nashotah House did was read Bonhoeffer's *Life Together* and Saint Benedict's *Rule*. The idea was that seminary should not be a time of information but of spiritual formation. I liked the sound of that, and I often spoke of things like a *rule of life* and *sacred time*, *vespers* and *lectio divina* and *conversatio morum* (fidelity to monastic life), in hushed and reverent tones. Just reading about liturgy made me feel like a deep person, a little more pious. But it was immediately clear that I liked the idea of the Benedictine Rule much more than the reality. By then, of course, I no longer scorned religion, and one could say I even wanted to *be* religious. Yet to my dismay, I found the actual experience of spiritual obligations and definable expectations unbearably stifling.

After only a few weeks, I was stir-crazy. In Minneapolis, I had lifted weights four times a week, ran every other day, and painted houses. I rode a bike and skateboarded and went for long walks with Brittany. I was my own boss and did what I wanted to do when I wanted to do it. But seminary was different. Because it was loosely modeled after the Benedictine idea of *ora et labora*, we were required to complete ninety-six credit hours in three years, which was typically three to four classes a semester; attend two hours of "chapel" daily, which consisted of Morning Prayer, Mass, and Evensong; eat both breakfast and lunch with the community; participate in "work crew", which involved shoveling snow, washing dishes, vacuuming floors, and taking out the campus' garbage; as well as do an internship at a local parish, complete CPE training, prepare for canonicals, and attend numerous formation events and lectures. What all of this mostly amounted to was hours and hours of sitting. I sat to pray, to learn, to eat, and to think, and to my great dismay, I had to sit next to the same people without respite. Like popcorn on the stove top, I felt like I could burst. One could say I "grew up" at seminary, and I am grateful for the forbearance of my professors and classmates as I experienced something not unlike growing pains.

And still I reveled in seminary life. I breathed in the aroma of the incense at the High Masses and felt like I could almost see the Shekinah glory of the Lord on the altar. I marveled at the beautiful vestments, the many priests who taught and counseled us, and was swept up in the hymnody. Singing as many as four hymns a day, every day, only repeating hymns during Lent, I was practically percolating in the poetry of our fathers. Every night I would stay up late talking to

Brittany on the phone or studying with friends. And every morning, much to my delight, the Javatokos (so named after the Mother of God, the Theotokos) would bring carafes of hot coffee to the classrooms. Students would guzzle the stuff while studying Aquinas or Augustine, reading Raymond Brown or N. T. Wright, skimming Jaroslav Pelikan or Gregory Dix, highlighting lines in Francis Hall and Jeremy Taylor and Thomas Cranmer, and generally discovering that in the beginning, God created the Church of England.

The telling of Church history at Nashotah House read like a taut novel. When Jesus ascended into heaven, he did not leave behind a Bible, but his apostles. He promised that he would send the Holy Spirit and that through the Holy Spirit he would always be present with them. The Church was new, but she was also old. She was a fulfilment of the Church of the Old Covenant, and as the Old Covenant had rulers, so also Jesus appointed the twelve apostles to be the rulers of the New Covenant, with Saint Matthias in the place of Judas' office (and an office has successors). When the apostles died, bishops succeeded them—not as eyewitnesses to the Resurrection, but as rulers of the Church and custodians of "the faith once delivered for all". "Christ's Holy Catholic Church," wrote John Keble, "is a real outward visible body, having supernatural grace continually communicated through it by succession from the apostles, in whose place bishops are."[2]

To read of the fledgling Church was to fall under a holy spell. And the Church Fathers took us deeper into a world, a God-lit world, a world where the Holy Spirit did still brood over his Church with warm breast and bright wings. For several centuries bishops gathered in ecumenical councils to condemn heresies and to define true doctrines, issuing decrees that were binding upon all the baptized faithful. But at a certain point in history, for reasons unknown, these councils ceased to carry that universal teaching authority of Christ. What mattered now was who could make the most convincing appeal to antiquity and the Scriptures.

What happened next was always told with a self-deprecating chuckle. After an age of darkness, King Henry VIII saw that the bishop of Rome had grown fat. He saw that Cranmer was a talented liturgist. The best monasteries were no monasteries. The Romish doctrines of purgatory, pardons, adoration of the Eucharist and of images and relics, and the invocation of saints was a fond thing vainly invented and repugnant to the Word of God. There were only two sacraments ordained by Christ, Baptism and the Lord's Supper. The king of England was the supreme head of the Church of England. In America, this recovery of the early Church chose the name "Episcopal", because it meant "with bishops" and not just "English". But still: Catholic Church, Anglican patrimony. The stories would sweep me away, as good English writing is wont to—or rather, they drew me in. I felt like I was a part of a tradition much bigger than myself.

Reading the Church Fathers, and reading them in translation with the original Greek and Latin texts at hand, reading them with the Scriptures open and the sound of birdsong outside my window, wrought in my mind a profound and notable transformation. Even more, the liturgy at Nashotah House began to work on me. The Daily Office, the thrice-daily Angelus and the ringing of the bells, the lectionary, the liturgical year—all of it anchored the domestic realities of the seminary, supplying color and refreshment to a life that was mostly drab, sometimes absurdly comical, on occasion tragic, but just as often happy. The Mass, which held together both our past and future, was how we endured the present. On a much lower plane, bacon helped. And late-night conversations down by the lake.

I was hardly an aspirant for Holy Orders and already I was anxious about preaching. After washing dishes for work crew one day, I invited two students, Guy and Alex, to join me in a preaching exercise. The sun was hot and the corn was still, and we walked along the fields in our black cassocks as I preached loudly to the corn. In an act of near sacrilege, I ripped a cob from a stalk and baptized it in the name of the Father, the Son, and the Holy Spirit, and then hurtled it back into the fields, which looked white for the harvest. Alex and Guy watched, frowning, not understanding why I had dragged them along to sweat in the middle of a cornfield, then asked if we could return to campus. Mildly embarrassed, but feeling like perhaps there was an old-time preacher somewhere inside of me, I consented.

Some of the students were men and others were women. Some were older, some younger; a few of us were under thirty. Almost everyone believed they were called to the priesthood of Christ. Early on I befriended two particularly tall, muscular students. While Guy was half British and spoke with an English accent and drank English tea, Sven was an enormous Swede. Quick and intelligent, they were much more capable students than I; but like me, they were young and their sense of calling to the priesthood was grave and beautiful. After translating passages of the New Testament together, we drank beer and talked about girls, sacraments, angels, rock music, liturgical minutia. Our conversations were not idle chitchat, but aimed to get to the bottom of things. They helped to clarify our experience of Nashotah's liturgical life. In their company, I thought critically about my own thinking. The three of us would triangulate our theological discoveries in a way that put our initial interpretations at risk. In this way, our arguments—waged with the weapons of criticism and charity—were almost a moral accomplishment. We wanted to love the truth more than we loved our own current understanding.

Liturgy was trending, and for good reason. Nashotah House had a way of shoving you, almost against your will, into the waters of the Daily Office and the Church calendar without so much as a "Don't worry, the water's warm!" Once I got over the initial shock, I didn't want to get out of the pool. Liturgy made daily life feel like a nonstop prayer. It felt like we had somehow entered God's time zone. I began to feel the passage of time as something sacred, an arrow pointing to God. The Daily Office was a way to live in thrall to our God and King, to participate in his Kingdom. Liturgy ($\lambda\epsilon\iota\tau o\upsilon\rho\gamma o\varsigma$) is public work, worship of the gods, and translates into Latin as *officium*. When we went to chapel, we went to pray "the Office", to do the work for which we were made. In hymning praises to our Lord we were joining the song of the spheres, the ceaseless worship of Christ that holds the universe together. And liturgy created the context for us to do good work, starting in Nashotah's Chapel of Saint Mary the Virgin and hopefully spreading out into the whole world.

"What's the difference between a liturgist and a terrorist?" asked my professor.

There was no answer.

"You can negotiate with a terrorist."

Liturgy was law. In order to understand this point, it might be helpful to pause a moment to ponder what happened after God parted the Red Sea so that England might escape Roman Catholic captivity. During their desert sojourn, God said to the British people,

"I will rain down collects from heaven for you and you are to gather enough to put in the Prayer Book." And Thomas Cranmer went out to gather them. But with so many changes to the worship service, the British people began to grumble. So God said, "Here are the rubrics, so that future generations can hear the collects I gave you to pray in the wilderness when I brought you out of papal dominion." And were it not for the Tractarians this ancient lore would have been lost: "Thou shalt not genuflect with thy left knee," and "Remember Elizabethan English and keep it holy," and "Thou shalt not wear the cassock-alb," and thus and such. If you transgressed these ancient laws, upperclassmen were ready to pounce, the instructor of church music or the chapel director made an example of you, a professor pulled you aside. For in the beginning God created the Church of England, and a liturgical people he made them.

I was in love. I loved the lakes and forests and cornfields of eastern Wisconsin. I loved learning Greek and discovering that the Bible is the Church's book. I loved Christ, and I was struck that Christ loved his Church so much that he promised to lead her into *all* truth, not just some truth (Jn 16:13). I loved that his apostles and their successors, the bishops, could speak with the authority of Christ, and I was comforted to belong to a tradition that traced back to the original twelve apostles. I loved how every heresy leads to a clarification of the truth, and how it never stops. Doctrine develops because the Church must speak with the universal authority of Christ yesterday and today, so she must be speaking with a *living* voice. Empowered by the Holy Spirit as she is, how can she not? I loved the old hymns. I loved kneeling, bowing, kissing, and everything else that went into the work of worship. I loved Keble and Newman and Andrewes and Webb and Pusey and Ramsey. I loved my professors and my classmates and the serious mood on campus that history was going somewhere, and it rhymes. I was in love, and I was also in way over my head.

I flew to Mississippi to see Brittany. She rented an old house on a swamp chock-full of cypress trees. I arrived to find a rat in the cupboard, roaches in the bathroom, fleas in the laundry room, something scurrying up above in the rafters, and the bumping sounds of wild dogs beneath the floor. The swamp was beautiful, but buggy. It was all very otherworldly. Brittany and her roommates, also with the Teach for America corps, were exhausted from long hours of corybantic and mostly untaught students. Everyone had flea bites and bloodshot eyes. Yet, for all this, Brittany was happy.

She was hardier, more resilient. She leaned into teaching as into the wind, and her faith in Christ was more established. Up to that point, to some degree her faith had been experienced in the shadow of others. We had gone to church together, prayed together, talked together. But now she was on her own, and her relationship with Jesus had become much more personal. She and her roommates had been exploring the local churches. The town of Indianola seemed stuck in a long-ago era; it felt almost frightening to visit a town where black people literally lived on one side of the tracks and white people on the other. The pews of the Episcopal Church were dotted only with rich, white folks, and the sermons were so vaguely Christian the only one who liked them was Brittany's Unitarian roommate. The Methodists were a negligible improvement. The sundry Baptist churches were also racially segregated, but the sermons were Gospel-centered and inspiring. The Catholic Church was the only black and white mixed congregation in town, but they were Catholic. Thus, while their Unitarian roommate was at home with the Episcopalians, Brittany and the others attended a Baptist church, and I had to admit: the preaching *was* good.

We drove through the cotton fields of the Delta countryside until we arrived at a small shack called Po' Monkeys, one of the few juke joints to survive into the twenty-first century. We were the only white people, and it was hot and smelled of barbecue so I ordered Budweisers and wanted to sit discreetly in a corner. But Brittany wanted to dance, and so with beer in hand we danced to the blues and rubbed elbows with the locals. The next day we toured the B.B. King blues museum and learned about how almost all American music has roots in the Mississippi Delta soil. We went out for craw-dads boiled with potatoes and corn covered in Cajun seasoning and it all tasted awful. Yet after only a few days I began to feel at home in the Deep South. The people were warmer and less hurried, and the world seemed almost quieter.

Brittany and I talked about marriage and considered whether I should move to live with her while she finished her two-year commitment with Teach for America. Brittany sought advice from her spiritual director, an Episcopal female priest from the neighboring town, but when she found out I went to Nashotah House the only advice she had was for me to pull up stakes and transfer to Sewanee, a much more open-minded seminary. Still, I began to make phone calls and we dreamed about renting a house in Greenwood, Mississippi, praying I could find some work in ministry, Anglican or not. But everything was tentative, and Brittany wondered about the timing. It felt impossible; perhaps we should wait at least a few more years to get married after all?

* * * * *

Inevitably, a story about Anglo-Catholicism is a chronicle of longing, of unrequited desire. So what happens when some of your most intense memories of grace involve sacraments you hadn't actually tasted? Memories of imaginings, of received histories, a collective yearning produced by nearly five hundred years of separation, enveloped me. And the melancholy ruins that fueled Anglo-Catholicism's nostalgia for an idealized Catholicism were freighted with meaning: the ravaged monasteries of England, the broken rood screens, the toppled headless statues of saints, and even after British colonial expansion the general sense that the island that is England remained, even when holding a Lambeth council, an ecclesial island. I'll never forget when a Russian Orthodox archbishop visited Nashotah House with an entourage of priests with beards as long as Gandalf's. That night, during his speech, he publically rebuked not just the Episcopal Church but global Anglicanism for its schisms, attempts to ordain women, doctrinal confusion, and immorality. I was offended and also disturbed.

Like most Anglo-Catholics, I looked to the churches of the East with awe. The beards and the mysticism and the beautiful iconostases, all of it shrouded in mystery and tradition—here were ancient churches with a noble heritage! Now, the bishops of Rome had long held that Anglican churches do not have valid orders, that our rite of ordination did not make a real Catholic priest. Yet Rome acknowledged Eastern Orthodox orders to be valid, thus proving that one can be Catholic without being a papal Catholic. As Anglicans, we already believed that the authority of bishops was not derived from the papacy, but from Christ himself. The apostolic succession continued without a break; bishops were consecrated by bishops of the old apostolic line during and after the Reformation. The sacraments continued. The English church did not need the Roman See to be Catholic. And if the Orthodox were legit, it was widely thought on campus, so were we. Together, Anglicanism and Eastern Orthodoxy and the Roman Church comprised the one, holy, catholic, and apostolic Church.

Yet it was clear that the Russian Orthodox archbishop was not on the same page. He spoke as if every Anglican decided for himself, or chose clergymen who decided for him, what is Catholic. As he spoke, I blushed with shame for the chaos of the so-called Anglican "communion". It was obvious that in his eyes we were a fractious and obstinate people, breaking camp with Rome only to break camp with one another. The archbishop's speech struck close to home because there was no visible entity to which I could point and say, "That is the Catholic Church to which I belong." And his priests had longer beards than ours. And vodka seemed a purer drink than gin. And I very much wanted Eastern Orthodoxy's approval. And so it was with mixed feelings that I purchased one of his many books and asked him to sign it.

Now, the claim to *catholicity* stands or falls on the apostolic succession, for apart from succession there is no reliable ministry of Word and sacrament. As an Anglo-Catholic, I believed fervently that possession of apostolic ministry in direct line with the apostles made the difference between the Catholic Church and a sect. For me, apostolic succession mattered because Jesus is *King,* and I wanted to live a life of total obedience to my King. With this goal in mind, I returned to the Scriptures to find that the apostolicity of the Church goes deep, as deep as the Old Covenant.

It felt like I was reading something out of Tolkien's Middle-earth. God planned to bless the world through the twelve tribes of Israel, but they had scattered. Jesus grieved to see his people "harassed and helpless, like sheep without a shepherd" (Mt 9:36), so he turned to his disciples and singled out *twelve* men to be the special leaders of his new Kingdom (Mt 9:37–10:1). Jesus was the "anointed one", a title given to a Davidic king anointed at his coronation. By choosing *twelve* men to be his apostles, Jesus, the son of David, was gathering the twelve tribes of Israel. He chose twelve apostles because there were twelve princes of the tribes of Israel in the wilderness (Num 1:4–16). He was saying, "Look, I'm restoring the kingdom of David!"

"The New Testament lies hidden in the Old," wrote Saint Augustine, "and the Old is unveiled in the New."[3] Could it also be said that the Church lies hidden in Israel and Israel is unveiled in the Church? I found it fascinating that David and his lineage, the anointed kings of Judah, did *not* govern alone. As King Solomon appointed twelve officers to rule his kingdom (1 Kings 4:7), so also Jesus appoints twelve apostles to rule his Kingdom after his Ascension (Mt 19:28). The Twelve were his royal cabinet, the body of men authorized to do the King's will, entrusted with viceroyal authority to represent him in his New Israel, the Church: "He who hears *you* hears me, and he who rejects *you* rejects me" (Lk 10:16).[4] As God planned to bless the world through Israel, he now plans to bless the world through these twelve apostles, "through *their* word" (Jn 17:20). If you want to listen to King Jesus, just listen to his apostles.

The Twelve knew that Christ had appointed them to an office, and that *an office left vacant must be filled.* After the death of Judas, Peter said to the others: "His *office* let another take" (Acts 1:20). There was no debate. And Matthias was chosen to be numbered among them. To be an apostle was to hold an office, and an office has successors. The Holy Spirit transmitted the authority from the apostles to their successors, the bishops, through the laying on of hands, and then in turn to their successors (cf. 1 Tim 4:14). Through apostolic succession, bishops remain "the foundation" of the apostolic Church (Eph 2:19–20).

This research was a turn in the road. I could no longer say that the Bible was the pillar and bulwark of the truth because, according to the Bible, "the Church of the living God [is] the pillar and bulwark of the truth" (1 Tim 3:15). The apostles and their successors—the bishops—are empowered by the Holy Spirit "to feed the Church of the Lord" (Acts 20:28). To submit to their authority is to submit to Christ: "He who receives any one whom I send receives me" (Jn 13:20). The Kingdom of God is not yet consummated—but it's here. It's now. And the apostolic fathers agreed: where the bishop is there is the Catholic Church.

What did my parish priest back in Minnesota think of all this, and did my bishop believe it too? Surely he did. Why else would he carry his crozier or wear his episcopal ring? If Anglicanism was truly apostolic, it followed that parishioners could not hold their own interpretation against Anglicanism's interpretation of the Scriptures, since the Anglican bishops have true authority in the Church. The Bible was not intended to be studied apart from the apostolic tradition and the teaching authority of Christ's Church, and since Anglicans know who has rightful authority (based on the orderly succession of bishops, from the early Church down through today) they ought to submit to the teachings of Anglican bishops, teachings that must be proclaimed with the clear and universal authority of Christ the King.

All of this is to say that before my final exams, I detected that *sola scriptura* does not get us creedal Christianity. Without a *regula fidei*, the Bible was a vast and uncharted canvas, me a flea scurrying across. I could either give up the *normativity* of the creeds (made by the successors of the apostles, the bishops) or give up *sola scriptura* for good. I could still *think*, still ask questions, but ultimately my private interpretations of Scripture were no substitute for the apostles' teaching. Besides, if the Church is truly apostolic, her official dogmas will never contradict Scripture. Ever. As there is no error in Jesus' teaching, there is no error in his Church's teaching. The Holy Spirit descended on the Church. She is the mouthpiece of Christ on earth, his vehicle for salvation. In short, I was beginning to detect that the Bible is the *Church's* book.

I also detected that the sooner Brittany and I could marry, the better. Being apart felt like trying to break the law of gravity. Every morning I woke up feeling like I had bruised ribs. Brittany was content, but her heart felt sore. We did not know what the future held, but on this we agreed: we needed to marry.

* * * * *

One of the most challenging things about Nashotah House was the Society of Mary. Not only was our chapel named "Saint Mary the Virgin" *as if* Mary were still a virgin, not only were the statues and icons of Mary everywhere, not only did we stand to say the Angelus (the old devotion commemorating the Incarnation) three times a day as the bell ringer tugged on a two-ton bell named Saint Michael, but the students in the Society of Mary said the Rosary every Tuesday morning. I recoiled at the phrase "the most holy Rosary" and "the most holy Mother of God", and every Tuesday morning I turned the pages of my Bible loudly while they repeated their Hail Marys. Now, some Anglicans believe the saints can hear our prayers and intercede on our behalf, and others believe such petitions are on the knife's edge of idolatry. So the Angelus was said silently. The Saint Michael bell rang out the Angelus, the students would stand, but everyone was silent. Silence was the via media applied to Mary. Silence allowed for truth and lies to mix without discord. This way, no one was offended—except me. I heard the fellow next to me muttering his vain and repetitious prayers. I coughed and sanctimoniously prayed extremely spontaneous prayers to Jesus instead. In the hallway one day—and I am ashamed to admit this—I verbally assaulted a fellow seminarian caught wearing the Society of Mary's medal.

"Mary was just a sinner," I said.

He winced.

"Mary is dead. She can't hear you."

There was no response.

"You have mom issues," I said, and walked away.

Growing pains. I was trudging through a muck of contradictions. For years I had worn the brown scapular yet didn't believe in its Marian origins. I had hung a rosary on my wall and had started a small collection of "Anglican Prayer Beads", yet felt foolish kneeling to rote and repetitious prayers. I believed in sacraments and the communion of saints, but it was a communion of sleeping saints. I was convinced that without bodies, the souls of the faithful departed were sleeping. They would not wake up until the final resurrection of the dead. Even if they weren't sleeping, even if they were alive in Christ, they certainly would not pay any attention to the Church. They would be too busy worshiping God! It simply had never occurred to me that the baptized faithful who have passed through death would continue to participate in the Kingdom, would continue to do what Jesus does. I simply could not imagine that the faithful departed would join Christ in his twofold mission to bring glory to the Father *and* to bring salvation to the world. In heaven, I thought, the second commandment is no longer like unto the first. In heaven, thou shalt not love your neighbor as yourself.

But as we lived the liturgical year, hearing salvation history afresh and singing the Magnificat every day, I began to marvel at Mary's *trust.* Even though she was a virgin, she believed the angel's words spoken at the Annunciation, that by the power of the Holy Spirit she would become the Mother of God's Son (Lk 1:26–35). "Filled with the Holy Spirit" and "with a loud cry" (Lk 1:41–42) her cousin Elizabeth proclaims: "Blessed is she who believed that there would be a fulfilment of what was spoken to her from the Lord" (Lk 1:45). Mary's faith reminded me of Abraham's—except even greater. Her faith cooperated with the Holy Spirit to conceive the Son of God in her own womb!

Mary trusted God throughout the hidden life of the Holy Family—when her Creator became a creature of her own flesh, when King Jesus was wrapped in swaddling clothes and resting in a dirty manger (Lk 2:7), when the eternal Son of God was nursing at her own breast, during the slaughter of the innocents and exile in Egypt (Mt 2:13–18). Mary trusted when the rulers sought to stone her Son, the Messiah (Jn 8:59; 10:31), when they contradicted him and plotted his death (Jn 11:45–57). She remained steadfast and held on to the words spoken to her by the Lord and pondered them in her heart (Lk 2:19), and just as Abraham's trust met its ultimate test when he was called to sacrifice Isaac, so Mary's trust met a similar test. But *unlike* Abraham, who did not have to go through with the sacrifice, Mary had to watch as her Son was sacrificed on the Cross. The angel had told her that "of his kingdom there will be no end" (Lk 1:33), and as Mary remained present at the slaughtering of her own Son, she believed the impossible, "that God was able to raise men even from the dead" (Heb 11:19). In trust, Mary suffered with her Son, just as Simeon said she would: "And a sword will pierce through your own soul also" (Lk 2:35). On Calvary she stood in darkness, her heart bleeding and broken, and still her cousin's words rang true: "Blessed is she who believed that there would be a fulfilment of what was spoken to her from the Lord."

What did trust look like for Mary? From the start it looked like sheer joy: "My soul magnifies the Lord, and my spirit rejoices in God my Savior, for he has regarded the low estate of his handmaiden." (Lk 1:46–48). For Mary, trust takes the form of joyful praise! And as far as I could tell the whole world seemed to be made for this one purpose—to savor and adore God. I did not believe in praying to Mary, but I *did* want to join the anthem, I wanted my priestly vocation to be an act of joyful praise.

When I left Minneapolis as one not knowing whither, I had looked to Abraham as my father in trust. But in the growing pains of my first year at seminary, I began to look to Mary as my mother in trust. The Annunciation seemed to reveal the meaning of the Christian vocation. By saying Yes to the God who created the world, Mary made it possible for God re-create that same world through his Son. I felt summoned to say and believe, "I am the handmaid of the Lord; be it done to me according to thy word." And yet, I was scared—for following Mary's example of trust seemed impossible without also following her example of suffering and sacrifice.

Every day as we sang the Magnificat I joined in. I worshiped the Lord as best I could, and prayed that God would help me to sing a better, more trust-filled song of praise and thanksgiving. Mary's witness inspired me, and I wanted my whole life to be like her fiat, to have my whole life—the joys and sufferings, sickness and health, richer times and poorer times—all of it, body and soul, my whole being, be a heartfelt Yes to God. I longed for God to "take flesh" in my life, as it were, as the Lord took flesh through Mary's fiat of surrendering love. And when I stepped out just a little further in Mary's way of trust, even though very little in life felt certain and almost nothing was clear, I knew it was time to stop talking about marriage. It was time to act.

I flew back to Mississippi that Christmas break. We visited Oxford, Mississippi, and drank coffee on a balcony of a used bookstore, and I got down on my knee and asked Brittany to marry me. She said yes and—I did not plan it this way—the town hall bells began to toll high noon. We went out for croissants and walked the town square. Even now the memory of it is a blur of color and joy.

* * * * *

Being in a theological seminary that had a society of Mary and now being engaged to Brittany, who was of course a woman, I began to think about the part women played in salvation history, especially Mary's part. The Incarnation was a divine achievement, but it involved taking a real human nature from a real human woman. The conception of Jesus was a work of grace, but grace does not abolish the freedom of Mary's will. Thus, the Incarnation *waited* on Mary's consent, on the freely given cooperation of a human mother. While Eve failed to trust, Mary succeeded. While Israel failed to obey, Mary obeyed. As Saint Irenaeus of Lyons put it around the year 200, "The knot of Eve's disobedience was loosed by the obedience of Mary."[5] In Mary, I saw the culmination of God's relationship with Israel, the total self-gift of God and man. How could the daughter of Zion not rejoice? Mary prophesied, "Henceforth all generations will call me blessed" (Lk 1:48), and I felt that the obligation was mine to esteem her so. If Elizabeth could shout, "Blessed are you among women" (Lk 1:42), when Christ was in Mary's womb, surely I could say the same now that Christ was in heaven. She was to be honored and esteemed, but only the Lord was to be worshiped and adored. As far as I was concerned, she was still just another sinner. She was dead and therefore sleeping until the final resurrection of the dead. She was just a normal human being.

And so while I began to think of Mary as my "mother in trust", I most certainly did not think she was the Mother of the Church. While I saw clearly that Mary gave a human nature to the eternal Son of God, I rejected the idea that she herself was without sin, let alone immaculately conceived, as Pope Pius IX unilaterally announced in 1854. I agreed that Mary was not merely an appliance in the Incarnation, as the Gnostic Valentinus wrongly maintained, and was happy to call her Theotokos, the Mother of God, but I could not agree that she is, as the Eastern hymn put it, "higher than the Cherubim, more glorious than the Seraphim". She was obviously the Spouse of the Holy Spirit, but I could not accept that she was the Mediatrix of All Graces. I certainly did not believe that she was assumed into heaven. In short, I admired Mary for her life of trust and joyful praise, but there was no way I would ever say the Rosary.

But I *did* honor her, and for me this was a big leap. I honored her because I saw that Jesus wanted me to become like her. Her role in Cana, her intercession, was to be my role in the Kingdom. Jesus even held up Mary's fiat, her hearing the Word of God and keeping it, as a model for every Christian: when a woman of the crowd cried out like cousin Elizabeth, "Blessed is the womb that bore you," Jesus replied, "Blessed rather are those that hear the word of God and keep it!" (Lk 11:27–28; cf. Lk 1:42). Of course, I couldn't physically give birth to Jesus, but in Mary's way of trust I could become a God-bearer. Wasn't this the evangelical mission of the Church, to receive the implanted Word and then show it to the world?

Again, I might not have prayed to Mary, but I wanted to *be* like Mary. I wanted to be rich soil for the seed of God to grow. I wanted to be blessed. Even more, I wanted my priestly ministry to be blessed, to be a blessing. And I wanted my marriage to Brittany to be blessed. And so it was around that time that I began to pray that God would make our love look like Mary's, a life of trust and joyful praise, a living liturgy. And often I wept in the Chapel of Saint Mary the Virgin when we sang the Te Deum, incense overspreading the high altar and votive candles flickering against the dark. Where was I when God laid the foundations of the earth, or when the morning stars sang together and all the angels sang for joy? It seemed to me that I was born to sing this hymn, that all creation had been singing from the start, and that I had arrived late. I had catching up to do. Because I am a slow learner, this did not come to me as a surprise.

I'm sorry to say I became somewhat distracted in my studies. As a child I was often accused of being absentminded, but that winter my inattentive disposition seemed only to get worse. "I am not absentminded," G. K. Chesterton once said in his defense. "It is the presence of mind that makes me unaware of everything else." I was no G. K. Chesterton, but in those days it *did* feel like I was becoming aware of everything else—Abraham and Mary, Brittany and Mississippi, that I had no choice but to trust God with my future. I couldn't help but to peer eagerly through the gloom.

8

Don't Waste Your Suffering

Do this in remembrance of me.

—Jesus (Lk 22:19; 1 Cor 11:24)

We are afflicted in every way ... always carrying
in the body the death of Jesus,
so that the life of Jesus may also be manifested in our bodies.

—Saint Paul (2 Cor 4:8, 10)

Being apart made our love feel interrupted, almost abstract, and I'm afraid to say we became sentimental. I purchased four white coffee cups with matching saucers and sent two of them to Brittany in a care package along with freshly ground coffee so that we could drink the same coffee from the same mugs at the same time, 5:30 A.M., every morning while we Skyped. I sent her mix CDs and cards and books. Brittany sent me letters and tea bags with a different love note attached to each string. We played online chess when we weren't talking, the games lasting sometimes several weeks. The care packages made our conversations by webcam over the Internet less exotic and more familiar, almost cozy. But the fact of the matter was that we were apart. And I was beginning to feel like I wasn't only in a long-distance relationship with my fiancée, but also with my future.

My whole life felt suspended in midair—my finances, my job, my marriage, my beliefs, the way I lived my faith, everything—and I wanted to take action, to *do* something. Unfortunately, as I've said before, seminary involved an enormous amount of sitting. In Minneapolis, I did not hesitate to take a seat—it meant I wasn't painting houses or at the gym. But at seminary, I couldn't seem to get off my buttocks. I worried my spine was becoming permanently bent into the shape of a question mark. Trapped in the sedentary confinement of choir stalls and classroom chairs, I seemed to experience something like visions. They were almost mystical, and at times alarming.

For example, sometime during the February of my first year—I do not remember if I was sitting in the chapel or in class or in the library—I saw Robin Hood roasting a rack of red deer ribs in the Year of Our Lord 1183. And it got me thinking. If there were a way to compare the total caloric value of what he and his band of merry men ate with the total caloric output that went into hunting it, it would likely explain why those guys fit into tights. They fought for every ounce of meat by running upstream, climbing jagged rocks, stomping through thick forests, trudging through knee-deep mud, usually with fifty-pound sacks on their backs, and usually with the Nottingham sheriff hot on their trail. Meanwhile I was cramming for the upcoming exam in biblical Greek. I bought my meat wrapped in plastic.

Unbidden, Robin Hood's tights flashed before my eyes when I was studying eucharistic theology. It was not so much a thought as it was a feeling, a listlessness, an unsettling suspicion that something was not right. A thought rose just above the surface. *Real men do not get their meat with the swipe of a credit card. They bloody their own hands butchering every single cooling carcass. Their freezers are stocked with black bear, squirrel, whitetail deer, feral hog, and who knows what else. Real men hunt.*

Startled, I shook my head and went grocery shopping. I filled my shopping cart with eggs, orange juice, salads, frozen pizzas, and beer. That night I read about the Old Testament's sacrificial cult while eating frozen pizza. I ate a lot of frozen pizza at school because all I had to do was unwrap it and stick it in the oven and—voila!—a hot delicious pizza.

As I ate and read, another vision flashed before my eyes. I saw the slaughtering of bullocks in the hot sun, and the immolated victims burning on the altar at the Jerusalem temple. The priests didn't just unwrap a sacrifice and stick it in the oven. The temple was a sacred butcher shop. It was said you could smell the blood from miles away. I wasn't used to this.

The ordered bloodletting of cultic *sacrifice* was the lifeblood of the Old Covenant, and yet I had always been safely insulated from such holy violence. There was no room in my Christian spirituality for cultic sacrifice, for the strangling and butchering and burning and sprinkling of blood. I saw Christ's death on the Cross as a sacrifice, but in my mind it had no connection to the Lord's Supper. The Protestant Reformers made the sacrificial element of the eucharist appear less important than it really is and emphasized instead the eucharist as a communal meal. And there was, of course, the small matter of where I was standing, which was downwind from the Reformation. Growing up, I had firsthand experience of meals but absolutely no contact with crucifixes, much less the smell and heat of a half-butchered bullock. I did not know what to make of the phrase "the Sacrifice of the Mass", and not knowing what else to think, I simply assumed Catholics believed that Jesus was being resacrificed every Sunday morning.

I chuckled at how silly I could be. But it was there: the Jerusalem temple and Robin Hood's tights. And I was struck by how in the past both *eating* and *sacrifice* were involved, participatory, laborious. For a moment I saw them, and for a moment I saw just how otherworldly the eucharist and the Christian life as a whole had been for me. Up until then, my custom spirituality came to me like my meat, precut and wrapped in plastic. It was easy, but also abstract. Christian religion did not work the same way. It was not waiting in the freezer, just waiting to thaw. If I wanted union with God, I would have to work for it. Jesus said, "The way is hard" (Mt 7:14).

The only appropriate response to Christ's sacrifice is with sacrifices of our own. Saint Paul relied entirely on the righteousness of Christ imparted to him at his Baptism, but he knew that in his flesh he had to "complete what is lacking in Christ's afflictions for the sake of his body, that is, the Church" (Col 1:24). And Paul fought for every ounce of this redemption by denying the flesh, traveling on long journeys to preach the Gospel, climbing spiritual mountains, getting whipped and imprisoned and beaten with rods and even stoned, shipwrecking three times—all this usually with the daily burden of his concern for all the churches, and usually with Satan hot on his trail. Saint Augustine put it this way: "The God who created you without yourself will not save you without yourself."[1]

I needed to stop sitting. The Christian life is not an armchair adventure. Jesus said that whoever wanted to be his disciple must "deny himself and take up his cross and follow [him]" (Mt 16:24; cf. Mt 10:38; Lk 14:27). I wanted to *do* something, and a tiny part of me wanted to join my life to the sacrifice of Christ on the Cross. But I had never put it this way before, and I wasn't sure what exactly to do.

In fact, in the past I had pointed to the good thief on the cross (to whom tradition assigns the name Saint Dismas) as the supreme example of doing nothing to be saved (Mt 27:38; Mk 15:27; Lk 23:32). But when I revisited Luke 23:32–43 I began to wonder, did Dismas really do *nothing*? First, he was being crucified for his crimes. Second, he was contrite. Third, he publicly rebuked a sinner. Fourth, he believed in Jesus. And finally, he publicly petitioned the Lord to remember him in his kingdom. Far from nothing, the good thief seemed to have done much more than I had ever done!

But what, exactly, was to be done? For one thing, Baptism. As an Anglo-Catholic, I had come to believe that this sacrament of birth into the new life of Christ was necessary for salvation. Saint Dismas was not baptized and yet Jesus assured him that he was saved and even promised that he would go to heaven that very day, but clearly he was an exception to a rule: "Repent, and be baptized every one of you" (Acts 2:38).

I began to feel the weight of my Baptism. No longer could I dismiss Saint Peter's words, "Baptism saves you" (1 Pet 3:21). Jesus told Nicodemus that no one can enter into the Kingdom of God unless he "is born of water and the Spirit" (Jn 3:5). Saint Paul said that Baptism is the means of union with the death of Christ (Rom 6:3–11; Col 2:13). Titus 3:5 mentioned "the washing of regeneration and renewal in the Holy Spirit". In Ephesians 5:26, Baptism is the means by which the Church is cleansed. Here was the remission of sins and justification, adoption as children of God and heirs of the kingdom of heaven! So it was that for the fledgling Church, Baptism was death unto sin (cf. Rom 6:3), the door to heaven (cf. John 3:5), the garment of immortality (cf. 1 Cor 15:53), the clothing of Christ (cf. Gal 3:27), the laver of regeneration (cf. Titus 3:5). Here was something real that didn't come wrapped in plastic, something one had to do—or rather, something done to you.

But what else must I do to be saved? As I pored through the Scriptures in search of an identifiable (hopefully short) list, it soon became clear that there wasn't one. In fact, everywhere I turned I saw not a list but an entire life. What must I do to be saved? There was only one answer: everything. In order to be saved you must give

God *everything.* "Whoever does not *bear his own cross* and come after me, cannot be my disciple" (Lk 14:27; cf. 9:23; 16:24; Mk 8:34). "Christ also suffered for you, *leaving you an example, that you should follow in his steps*" (1 Pet 2:21). We are to "put on Christ" (Gal 3:27), to imitate him, so that we might "become partakers of the divine nature" (2 Pet 1:4). In order to redeem us, the Son took on flesh and gave everything to the Father. Likewise, in order to be Christlike, we must take up our crosses and offer God everything. As a royal priesthood, our being (nonministerial) priests means that we make *sacrifices.* And I shuddered to learn that all the sacrifice and self-denial, all the suffering—none of it stops. We are called to be witnesses, to be martyrs. "Our crosses," wrote John Henry Newman, "are the lengthened shadow of the Cross on Calvary."[2]

But everything is a lot. It's vague. It wasn't long before I wanted something a little more specific to do. And I noticed that many Anglo-Catholics, like Roman Catholics, referred to the Eucharist as the Sacrifice of the Mass. It was believed that just as the ministerial priests in the Old Covenant offered sacrifices for the sins of the people, the ordained priest, as a representative of Christ, offers sacrifices at the altar for those who would share in Calvary. But how could the Eucharist be a *sacrifice?* Perish the thought!

That winter I began to wonder if the reason I was not more like Robin Hood was because there were layers and layers of economic and social impediments between me and the hot smell of a butchered carcass. I was not a full participant in the preparation of my own meals. Food was abstract. I did not work for it, at least directly. And I began to wonder if something similar had happened with my faith. Were there layers and layers of theological and ecclesial impediments between me and the Sacrifice of the Mass? Was I not a full participant in filling up what is lacking in Christ's afflictions? Was my faith abstract, something for which I did not work? Was I doomed forever to sit, or was there something specific I could do?

* * * * *

Brittany flew in from Mississippi to visit for several days. We were so excited to see one another, so lovesick, that when I finally picked her up from the Milwaukee airport she began to cry. I had to pull over and throw up. We dreamed about our wedding. We wanted a morning ceremony followed by a lunch buffet with mimosas, homemade invitations, an emphasis on the liturgy, and time to connect with friends and family. As we talked, it felt like we were just getting started with life, and yet it also felt like we had always known each other.

Where do you pick up the story of an engagement? With the late-night conversations? They went on for hours. With the evening flirting in the library while I crammed for an exam? It was romantic. Getting caught by a seminarian roommate making out? That was embarrassing. At the time, I was strangely not only *for* priests being married, but strongly *against* priestly celibacy. Of course, even today clerical celibacy is not an unchangeable dogma but a disciplinary rule—a biblical, pastorally fitting *norm*. Saint Paul saw it: to take vows is to "choose well" (cf. 1 Cor 7:38). But it was self-evident that (in Pauline terms, at least) I burned with passion; it was better that I prepare for marriage.

Brittany, perforce, returned to Mississippi to teach while I remained at seminary to learn. Wisconsin was gray and buried in snow. The naked branches looked wind-tossed and frazzled. The sun rarely shone, and all the grayness weighed me down. I seemed always to feel hungry and maybe a little beat up. But my mood was occasioned by more than the weather: the reality of the Eucharist was beginning to sink in.

I had been attending daily Mass, and the way I described the Eucharist back then was like a hammer. The Eucharist was like a medieval bludgeon to my heart. Kneeling there before the high altar I knew that Christ meant what he said in John 6 that his "flesh *is* food indeed" (v. 55), and if I did not eat him, I had no life in me (v. 57). He was the victim and the priest, and I trembled to draw near and take the Body of the Lord and drink the holy Blood so outpoured. I began to see just how childish I had been in writing off transubstantiation with a single categorical sweep, as mere "Greek philosophy". The very use of reason (*logos*) in the prologue of Saint John's Gospel was clearly an incorporation of Greek philosophical thought with Revelation. I did not flinch at the "philosophy" behind other doctrines. I already believed, for example, in the doctrine of *concomitance*, in *recapitulation* and *theosis*, that the Son was *consubstantial* with the Father and that Christ's two natures came together in the *hypostatic union*—why was transubstantiation a dirty word? Only when it came to the Eucharist did I prefer vague phrases like "real presence" or "mystery" to theological precision. But I was growing up. Dogmatic precision is in fact the stuff of sonnets, the fence around the playground, the bulwark against the desecration of the holy mysteries. Dogma keeps the fairy tale *real*.

"You are what you eat," wrote Saint Augustine.[3] He believed that celebrating the Eucharist brings us into intimacy with Jesus—both with the baptized faithful who are his Mystical Body and with his transubstantial Body, which is the consecrated bread and wine. At the altar, we are united not only with the Head of the Body but also with every member of the Body of Christ. This is why we call it "Communion". We who have been baptized into Christ must be fed on Christ. Saint Augustine invited parishioners to the Eucharist, saying, "Be what you see, and receive what you are."[4] I felt it in the silence of my bones, in fear and trembling of my mortaling flesh, that the King of kings in human vesture—very God, born of Mary—gives as heavenly food his own self to all the faithful in the Body and the Blood.

"The cup of blessing which we bless, is it not a participation in the blood of Christ?" asked Saint Paul in his first letter to the Corinthians. And "the bread which we break, is it not a participation in the body of Christ?" (10:16). The word Saint Paul used for "participation" (*koinonia*) is where we get our English word "communion". Participating in the communion of the Blessed Trinity, in the communion of the "communion of the saints". This *koinonia*, this communion by participation, challenged me; and in those days I began to pray the words of an old hymn: "Here let me feast, and feasting, still prolong the brief, bright hour of fellowship with thee."[5]

As always, Brittany had to endure my enthusiastic soliloquys as I attempted to convey the awfulness of what was being given to me. I resisted being in the presence of the all-holy God; I wanted to flee. As Joseph Cardinal Ratzinger put it, "We do not want God as near as that; we do not want him so small, humbling himself; we want him to be great and far away."[6] But I went forward to receive the Eucharist. Every morning at Mass I tried to lay my heart down on the anvil. The Eucharist was the hammer.

Many of these light-bulb moments and sea changes would make their way into my book about rediscovering the mystery and wonder of Christianity, and I'm afraid to say that my publisher initially signed a much less Catholic-sounding book than the one I eventually submitted. It was published with the title *When Donkeys Talk: A Quest to Rediscover the Mystery and Wonder of Christianity* and argued that the Kingdom of God is not a machine. To enter it one must become like a little child. To work out one's salvation with fear and trembling takes more than a moment, but a life. It takes humor, angst, and a dash of imagination. It takes grace.

This was a time of conversion for me, a deep transformation in my religious life. Reminiscing about those distant days, I used to say that my theological studies were an outward sign of an interior change taking place.

Having finally admitted the Eucharist to be the risen Christ—Body and Blood, Soul and Divinity—and having finally confessed the covenant reality of *koinonia*, perhaps my faith was becoming a little less childish and a little more childlike. I was certainly thinking less highly of myself. And I set my gaze to the holy altar upon which the priest confected the Eucharist, asking, *Is this a sacrifice?* as I had once run down to the lake as a child to look up at all the stars flickering in the blackness, asking, *Lord, how can I love you more?*

* * * * *

This bit about sacrifice is so important that it is worth lingering over. Growing up, I had argued that the Last Supper was only a Passover meal, nothing more. But what happened on the night of Passover, and how were the people of Israel to keep the feast? Looking for answers, I turned back to Exodus 12. Every spring the Passover was celebrated as a "memorial day", the festival of the Lord to last "for ever" (v. 14). This was the Paschal liturgy Jesus "did" at the Last Supper, and clearly it was meant to go on for all time.

First, the father of each household chose an unblemished male lamb to be offered as sacrifice on behalf of his family. In the springtime, he slaughtered the lamb, being careful not to break a single bone. Having slit the throat of the lamb and let the blood pour into a sacred vessel of some sort, he then spread the blood on the doorpost of his home so that the angel of death could see who had offered the sacrifice and who had not (for the main goal of the Passover sacrifice was deliverance from death through the blood of the lamb). For the most part, all of this was familiar to me. But I had never noticed what happened next. The Passover sacrifice did not stop with smearing the blood on the doorpost. The sacrifice was not completed until the Israelites ate the lamb. "They shall eat the flesh that night, roasted; with unleavened bread and bitter herbs they shall eat it" (Ex 12:8). In other words, the immolation of the lamb did not conclude the sacrifice. For the sacrifice to be complete, there had to be something like a "communion meal". Only the Israelites could eat the flesh of the lamb, for this was a sacred family ritual, a covenant feast.

The Passover sacrifice was not a one-time event, but a sacred rite to be observed until the end of time: "This day shall be for you a memorial day, and you shall keep it as a feast to the LORD; throughout your generations you shall observe it as an ordinance for ever" (Ex 12:14). Every spring, Israel was to celebrate the Paschal Mystery. Of course, over the nearly fifteen centuries between the first Passover and the Last Supper, the sacred rites had developed and changed. By the time of Jesus, the lambs had to be sacrificed in the Jerusalem temple and eaten in the city of Jerusalem. Only Levitical priests could pour the blood of the lambs on the altar. But it was still the "sacrifice of the LORD's Passover" (Ex 12:27; cf. Deut 16:5). Josephus mentions that the number of sacrifices offered at the temple during this feast was a staggering two hundred thousand lambs for nearly two million people! I was no Robin Hood. I had never witnessed the killing of any animal, let alone the blood of innumerable animal sacrifices. But one thing was clear: no first-century Jew would have forgotten that the Passover meal was also a sacrifice.

In fact, the annual celebration of the Passover was considered to be a *participation* in the first exodus. For a first-century Jew, the Passover meal was a "memorial" or remembrance (Ex 12:14) by which the members of the covenant family of God were able to make present the deliverance from Egypt. According to the Mishnah, the Paschal rituals were a way not only to remember the past but also somehow to share in the original act of redemption: "In every generation a man must so regard himself as if he came forth himself out of Egypt, for it is written ... *It is because of what the Lord did for me when I came out of Egypt"* (Mischnah, *Pesahim* 10:5; cf. Ex 13:8). Although Jews in Jesus' day lived centuries after the first exodus, at Passover it was as if the first exodus was something they experienced. In keeping the Passover, they *participated* in it, made it *present*.

And Jesus was the new Moses. Before his own "exodus, which he was to accomplish at Jerusalem" (Lk 9:31), he not only kept the Passover feast with his disciples, but transformed it into a new exodus for a New Covenant. In lifting up the bread and wine and saying, "Take, eat; this is my *body*," and, "Drink of it, all of you; for this is my blood of the covenant, which is poured out for many" (Mt 26:26–28; cf. Mk 14:22–24; Lk 22:19–20; 1 Cor 10:16; 11:23–25), Jesus was saying: "Look! I am the new Passover lamb of the new exodus! I am the new sacrificial meal!"

Just as the first Passover ritual sacrifice was a "memorial" (Ex 12:14), so also in the new Passover Jesus commands his disciples, "Do this in *remembrance* of me" (Lk 22:19; 1 Cor 11:24). In other words, the disciples were to perpetuate this new Passover sacrifice forever, not only to recall the new mystery but to make it *present*, to *participate* in it. And just as the old Passover of the first exodus was not completed with the death of the lamb who was slain but with the eating of its flesh, so also the new Passover of the new exodus was not completed with the death of the Lamb but with the eating of his flesh. "For my flesh is food indeed, and my blood is drink indeed. He who eats my flesh and drinks my blood abides in me, and I in him. As the living Father sent me, and I live because of the Father, so he who eats me will live because of me" (Jn 6:55–57).

Saint Paul saw it clearly: "Christ, *our Paschal Lamb*, has been sacrificed. Let us, therefore, *celebrate the festival*" (1 Cor 5:7–8). For Saint Paul, this feast was no mere symbol of the Lamb's flesh and blood—it was the real thing. "The cup of blessing which we bless, is it not a participation in *the blood* of Christ? The bread which we break, is it not a participation in *the body* of Christ?" (1 Cor 10:16). Communion, here, is *koinonia*, a real participation. Just as Jews in the Old Covenant saw their Passover rites as a real participation in the exodus from Egypt, for Saint Paul the Eucharist is a real *participation* in the Lord's Supper and the sacrificial death of Jesus.

But was the Crucifixion a part of the Last Supper? Did Jesus deliberately link the bread and wine to his own Passion and death? As I began to ask around, a fellow seminarian introduced me to a talk by Scott Hahn called *The Fourth Cup*. And I would have listened to it sooner, but my classes were demanding, I was editing *When Donkeys Talk*, and I wanted to spend what little free time I had talking to Brittany. Also, Guy and Sven had transformed a basement made of old stones and hand-hewn timbers into the "Pub of Saint Gambrinus", furnished with a bar and stools and a pool table.

And so after talking with Brittany I often stomped through the snow to the Pub of Saint Gambrinus to talk to Guy and Sven. We talked about Christology and made popcorn, drank beer, and wrestled. In a playful spat one night, I broke Sven's nose. The huge Swede would have destroyed me had Guy not interfered with desperate yelps. Unfortunately, that was the same night a German foreign exchange student rang the Saint Michael bell, and as 1:00 A.M. was no time for saying the Angelus, it was a transgression so verboten that the entire campus was assembled the following day. The merits of pubs and late nights were brought out for public inspection, and professors and students weighed in. It was the opinion of some that the campus ought to be quieter than it was, and it was already quiet. A great tumult broke out, and in the end it was determined that staying up late to argue about Christology was to be tolerated, but that no one should ever ring the Saint Michael bell except for the thrice-daily silent recitation of the Angelus. Sometimes seminary felt like being in a crowded elevator that got stuck between the twenty-second and twenty-third floors. In such a predicament, outbursts were perhaps inevitable.

By cramming students into a relatively small space and forcing them to do everything together at all times, Nashotah House taught many lessons. Indeed, the diversity of views on campus was as wide-ranging as the Anglican Communion itself—some believing women could be priests and others not, some availing themselves of seven sacraments and others only two, some saying they were Catholics and others Evangelicals, and so on—it was no modest achievement that we did not reenact the Reformation all over again. No one was drawn and quartered or locked in a tower. Such a toleration of views was called the *Pax Nashotah*. People came to the House from all over, everyone holding contradictory views about nearly everything, and still they managed to celebrate the eucharist together. Some held up the *Pax Nashotah* as a model for the Anglican Communion at large.

That winter I saw a mountain of Greek flash cards and Church history exams. Lent felt like it would never end. I couldn't seem to find the time to play guitar, and I was frustrated that I was losing my "chops". In those days I listened to a lot of Arcade Fire and PJ Harvey, which didn't improve my sedentary mood. Brittany talked about how she came home exhausted from standing at the chalkboard all day, but I was exhausted from sitting. I was tired of pacing my apartment while reading heavy tomes, or sitting on the couch with soggy ice packs leaking down my back. We both felt restless, waiting, suspended in the air. We were busy, yet life seemed to be on hold. In our busyness, perhaps our *acedia*, did we lose the meaning of what waiting can offer us?

* * * * *

But was the Last Supper a sacrifice? And was the crucified body of Christ in any way linked to the bread and wine of the table? It's no secret that baking cookies is a way to turn a manic, erratic seminarian into a satisfied and happy child of God. Measuring cups of sugar, flour, or butter for a recipe, cracking the exact number of eggs, kneading the dough or cutting out cookie shapes—it can transform even the dourest of M.Divs into a peaceful mystic lost in hesychastic prayer. While making cookies in the communal kitchen one afternoon, I finally got around to listening to Dr. Hahn's talk about the link between the Passion and the Paschal Mystery.[7] And it seemed almost as if he were combining covenant ingredients to show us how in the ugliness and pain of the world Jesus was creating something that was, in and of itself, goodness, love, and even beauty. In the Paschal Mystery, Jesus celebrated the banquet of the New Covenant, a banquet that culminated in his Passion.

Hahn described how the Passover meal in Jesus' day was organized around four cups of wine. The first cup was called the *kiddush* cup and was part of the introductory rite. After mixing a little water with the wine, the father of a Jewish family blessed the cup saying something like, "Blessed art thou, O God, King of the universe, who creates the fruit of the vine." The second cup was called the *haggadah* cup because here the father proclaimed and explained what God had done for his people, freeing them from Egypt. The third cup was the cup of blessing, the *berakah* cup. When it was mixed with water it cued that it was time to eat the body of the Passover lamb and the unleavened bread, but it was drunk *after* the meal. The father blessed it saying something like, "Blessed art thou, O God, who brings forth bread from the earth." The fourth cup was called the *hallel* cup, the cup of praise, and when it was drunk the Passover was complete. But first, Psalms 115–118, the "Hallel Psalms", were sung as a sacrifice of thanksgiving, a *eucharistia*. After singing the psalms, the fourth cup of wine was drunk. The question was, Did Jesus finish the Last Supper?

In Luke 22:14–20, Jesus refers to the meal as "this Passover" (v. 15) and takes two cups, one (most likely the *haggadah*, the second cup of proclamation, presumably following the *kiddush* cup) over which he gives thanks and then explains the good news of the *new* Passover and the other (the *berakah*, the third cup of blessing) "after supper" (v. 20), which he identifies with his blood. Saint Paul even refers to this cup as the "cup of blessing" (1 Cor 10:16). Like Jewish fathers in the Old Covenant, during the *haggadah* Jesus explains the meaning of the unleavened bread, identifying it with his body (Mt 26:26; Mk 14:22; Lk 22:19; 1 Cor 10:16; 11:24). Interestingly, in Matthew and Mark we see Jesus break from the ancient Jewish traditions. After identifying the third cup with his blood, he said, "I shall not drink again of this fruit of the vine until that day when I drink it new with you in my Father's kingdom" (Mt 26:29; cf. Mk 14:25). And then he doesn't drink the fourth cup! Instead, they sing a hymn (most likely Psalms 115–118) and go out to the Mount of Olives. Why did Jesus not drink the *hallel* cup, the fourth and final cup of the Passover meal? Instead, he vows not to drink wine again until the Kingdom was fully established. As far as the disciples were concerned, not only did Jesus focus the Passover liturgy on his own body and blood, but he never finished the Passover meal! As far as they were concerned, the sacrifice was incomplete.

As the aroma of baking cookies filled the kitchen, I listened as Dr. Hahn described what happened next, just after Jesus and the disciples leave the Upper Room. In the Garden of Gethsemane, Jesus prays: "My Father, if it be possible, let this chalice pass from me.... If this cannot pass unless I drink it, your will be done" (Mt 26:39, 42; cf. Mk 14:36). Was Jesus referring to the fourth and final cup of the Paschal liturgy? Was he linking the Cross to the completion of the Passover meal? Matthew and Mark go out of their way to emphasize that while Jesus was on the Cross he did not at first drink the fruit of the vine: "They offered him wine to drink, mingled with gall; but when he tasted it, *he would not drink it*" (Mt 27:34; cf. Mk 15:23). But as his last breath approached, one of the bystanders "took a sponge, filled it with vinegar [sour wine], and put it on a reed, and gave it to him to drink" (Mt 27:48). According to John, at the moment of his death Jesus even requested wine:

> Jesus, knowing that all was now finished, said (to fulfil the Scripture), "*I thirst.*" A bowl of vinegar [sour wine] stood there; so they put a sponge full of the vinegar on hyssop and held it to his mouth. *When Jesus had received the vinegar,* he said, "It is finished"; and he bowed his head and gave up his spirit. (Jn 19:28–30)

I sat at the kitchen table, mouth open, transfixed. Jesus' vow not to drink wine until the consummation of the Kingdom at the Last Supper, his prayer about drinking the "chalice", and his request for wine make sense of his last words, "It is finished." Not only was his Messianic mission consummated, but having finally drunk the fourth cup, so was the new Passover. It was a new sacrifice for a new Passover! Jesus united his sacrifice on the Cross into the Passover, and he united the Passover meal to his sacrifice. The Crucifixion was a sacrifice because it was part of the Passover meal.

I saw then that I had misunderstood what Catholics meant by "the Sacrifice of the Mass" because I had a blinkered understanding of what a sacrifice was. A true sacrifice ends not with the immolation, but with God the Father's welcome; for the root idea of sacrifice is not death (though in a fallen world the death of the victim may be necessary), but transformation, adoration, and reunion with God. In the Bible, sacrifice means not only "to kill" but also "to commune". On the Day of Atonement, for example, the animal was slaughtered *so that* the priest could sprinkle the lifeblood on the Mercy Seat, thereby bringing Israel into at-one-ment with God. The sprinkling of the blood was as much a part of the sacrifice as the slaughtering. In fact, the offering of sacrifice does not always require death or the shedding of blood. If it did, we could not offer ourselves as living sacrifices to God. But when there is an immolation, that death is pointed toward the heart of sacrifice, which is communion. In the case of the Passover, the meal *was* the sacrifice.

The pieces began to fit together. *Communion* and *sacrifice* are consanguineous. The table is an altar. Just as the Old Covenant sacrifice was not complete with the killing of the lamb, but culminated in the eating of the lamb, so also the sacrifice of Jesus is not completed with the killing of Jesus but culminates in the eating of Jesus. And just as the Passover meal made present the exodus, just as the rites made the Jews participants in what happened once hundreds of years earlier, so also the new Passover meal, the Eucharist, makes Christians participants in what happened once hundreds of years earlier. Christ is not "recrucified", but still it is "the sacrifice of the LORD's Passover" (Ex 12:27). The Sacrifice of the Mass not only makes present the Last Supper; it makes present the Crucifixion. And since we participate not only in Christ's sacrificial death (Heb 9:18) but also in his heavenly intercession (Heb 7:25), the Mass is heaven on earth.

I didn't realize that my cookies had burned until it was too late. But I didn't mind so much because I was inspired by just how unsedentary is the Kingdom of God. When the Jews celebrated the Passover sacrifice they did not just sit there. They *did* something, and the liturgical action was a real participation. The meal didn't come wrapped in plastic. They knew it was a sacrifice. So also, when Christians celebrate the Sacrifice of the Mass, they don't just sit there. The meal is not just a symbol. It's a miracle. It's a real participation, and Jesus is "known to them in the breaking of the bread" (Lk 24:35). When we "do this in remembrance (*anamnesis*) of Jesus" the past is not merely recalled, but relived. The event is made present, making it possible for us to participate in it today. The Eucharist is *how* Jesus is with his Church.

I dipped a blackened cookie into a glass of milk and chuckled at how silly I could be. But it was there, the old Passover and the new Passover. For a moment I saw them, and for a moment I saw just how unreal and wrapped in plastic was my old idea of Communion. Such a meal was to varying degrees abstract. I needed to stop sitting. I needed to give God everything, to hold nothing back. In order to "complete what is lacking in Christ's afflictions" (Col 1:24), I needed the Sacrifice of the Mass. I needed to *participate* in the sufferings of Christ. What if suffering, sacrifice, is a neglected grace?

When Jesus died, his sacrifice was sufficient. But he brings us in. He allows us to have a share in his suffering and in his mission for the world. "Christ also suffered for you, leaving you an example, that you should follow in his steps" (1 Pet 2:21). We get to pick up our crosses too. And in Mass, especially, we can join our sufferings to the Cross. In the Mass, the Crucifixion is made present—not a resacrifice of Christ, but a re-presentation of the once-for-all sacrifice of Christ. It happened millennia ago in time, but is brought through time and made present on the altar. You have to eat the Lamb who was slain. No wonder Saint Basil said the Eucharist was "the food of eternal life" and "necessary for life everlasting"![8]

By our Baptism, we are priests of God (1 Pet 2:9–10). While the ministerial priests offer up the sacrifice of Christ upon the altar at Mass, we nonministerial priests offer *ourselves* to God—our bodies, our actions, our labor, and even our sufferings. "I appeal to you therefore, brethren, by the mercies of God, to present your bodies as a living sacrifice, holy and acceptable to God, which is your spiritual worship" (Rom 12:1). In other words, we weren't made to sit around. We can put our suffering to work for salvation—our own, others', for the Kingdom. We can "do this in *anamnesis* of Christ."

* * * * *

If there is a neglected grace in waiting, it lies *within* those very moments. Even in the "in-between" moments of our lives, we must be present to the here and now. We must wait upon the Lord with vigilance and not spiritual drowsiness, listen for the footsteps of the Holy Spirit. When God speaks he seems not to interrupt but to wait until we're listening. So why do we fill our waitings with so much chatter?

For me, the seemingly endless waiting of that winter was nerve-wracking. Time itself seemed flexed and unyielding. Spring couldn't come soon enough, and I was stir-crazy. Even in the excitement of all I was learning, I still found the requirements of the seminary's Benedictine Rule stifling. Even the plainsong Psalter seemed plodding. The novelty of the black cassocks and copes and prayer beads had worn off. I was no longer awed by the sacred vessels and vestments, whether it was the Tiffany gold and porcelain enamel chalice and paten and the red and gold cope and chasuble worn by Blessed Michael Ramsey (my hero) or the simple, hand-carved altar candlesticks prepared for James Lloyd Breck in the 1840s (at a time when ritual candles were verboten in the Episcopal Church). I no longer felt a rush of devotion when I served as a torchbearer, lector, thurifer, crucifer, or subdeacon. Even my jobs in the sacristy, coordinating vestments or taking inventory of the sacred vessels, seemed dull. Even though all of these things exist to adore the Body and Blood of Jesus, my heart was not quick to bend a knee, and this caused me no small anxiety. While reading books like Bruce Metzger's *The Bible in Translation* or David Steinmetz's *The Superiority of Pre-Critical Exegesis* inspired me, and while Brevard Childs' *The Sensus Literalis* or Frances Young's *Exegesis and Formation of Christian Culture* or especially Richard Bauckham's *Jesus and the Eyewitnesses* made the Scriptures come alive, my studies brought with them an overwhelming sense of just how much I did *not* know, and I felt a little intimidated by the vast world of biblical scholarship. I missed Brittany so much it felt like I had been punched in the heart. And the assigned reading for my theology classes was overwhelming. In short, I was feeling depressed. Compared to Saint Paul's suffering—being imprisoned and stoned and half-starved—my suffering seemed scant and inconsequential. But that didn't mean I should just sit back and miss the opportunity for growth, for service to my Lord. Some give themselves to God out of a wealth of suffering; but why should I, out of my poverty, waste what little I had been given?

Pope Saint John Paul II said, "In the cross of Christ not only is the Redemption accomplished through suffering, but *also human suffering itself has been redeemed.*"[9] In suffering, Jesus showed us how to suffer. Even more, if we let him, he will suffer in us and we in him. Because Christ lived in Paul, he suffered in Paul (Gal 2:20). Because of Baptism, because of the Sacrifice of the Mass, the Paschal Mystery available only to those who live in communion with Christ is made present. For the baptized faithful, pain is not pointless. Sharing in the Paschal Mystery, suffering can be salvific, a compassion. And I didn't want to sit this one out. I needed to stop being so "busy". It was time to quiet my heart, to *rest* in the in-between time of waiting, and to lean into Jesus.

Talking with Brittany on the phone one night, she sounded a little depressed too. Many of her students did not respect themselves, or her, and she came home from work feeling defeated. Just that day one of her students shredded a classmate's entire year's notes, scribbling insults all over the binder because, well, that classmate had taken notes! And Brittany still had to teach them, both of them, and love them. She missed me. Her life seemed unresolved. Maybe setting her career in conflict with our marriage was too rigid a dichotomy? Why couldn't we just get married today? But mostly Brittany felt burned out. The long hours, the thankless tutoring, the grading, the school politics, and the fleas in the laundry room were beginning to take a toll. I felt awful for her and didn't know what to say. And then I remembered Robin Hood's tights and the Sacrifice of the Mass.

"Offer it up," I said.

"What?"

"I mean, don't waste your suffering. Make a good intention, in the Mass, along with Christ to God the Father. Or even tonight, simply ask God in the midst of all the suffering, to join your suffering to Christ's. Pray that God would use it for the good of his Church."

"But I thought Jesus suffered so we wouldn't have to."

"Well, aren't you suffering now?"

"That's true," Brittany admitted. "But what is it that I offer up?"

"Offer up your pain," I said, "in union with Jesus on the Cross. I will too."

"But I'm not really suffering, at least not really."

"That's no excuse. It's an incredible privilege that Jesus would allow us to unite our sufferings to his Cross for the salvation of the world. Let's use what little suffering we've got!"

And we did, or at least we tried. We offered up the hours of sitting and the ungrateful students and the depression and the waiting to get married. We offered up our small portion of suffering to the Cross of our Savior, and I believe he received it. He put it to work. And maybe the Eucharist became less abstract. Maybe I was becoming a more active participant in the Sacrifice of the Mass. In tiny ways, perhaps, I was filling up what is "lacking" in Christ's afflictions. Here was something specific I could do. I could offer it up. It's like Saint Paul said: "The bread which we break, is it not a *participation* in the body of Christ?" (1 Cor 10:16).

* * * * *

It cannot go without saying that in the spring of 2013, I foolishly opened my laptop and ceremoniously logged into Facebook to type a contentious utterance: "I am not Anglo-Catholic. I am not Roman Catholic. I am Catholic." What followed was a thread of high-strung comments and hours lost to the half light of my computer screen. And in the subsequent weeks, I began to suspect that my proclamation was not only impolitic and possibly erroneous; it was *forgettable*. From this foray into social media, at least one lesson was learned—mainly, *doing* social media is boring. All my storytelling needed more story and less telling.

No matter how interesting my life was, turning any given moment into a Facebook post actually diminished the moment. I had a life. But in always telling the story, I was losing the story. The *act* of social media is hunched, lethargic, fastidious. The gestures of a priest at the altar or the somatic rhythms of cutting carrots or folding the laundry are engaging, even graceful. The everyday routines of brushing teeth or turning the page of a book—this is the stuff of art. But the physical gesture, the living breathing moment, of posting something on Facebook is not worth painting or sculpting. The human form engaged in social media is a bent, reptilian thing.

The world I knew as a boy had been brimming with life, connected, and in many ways more real than the world of my twenties. I chewed Flintstones Vitamins every morning, purchased music I could touch (cassettes and later CDs), and passed notes to girls. There was no texting or snapchatting, no digital music, and the Internet was still a frontier. After homeroom, I hauled my twenty-pound backpack stuffed with Trapper Keepers, a graphing calculator, and Market Day orders to the library. We learned how to use microform, the card catalogue, and find periodicals using titanic indexes—skills that would soon be obsolete. Eventually, library sessions doubled as computer class. We sat in front of monumental desktop computers and the librarian demonstrated how to use a search engine.

Talking on the phone never happened on demand. I memorized friends' phone numbers. If my parents were late to pick me up, I had no way of finding out why. I had no idea what my friends were up to at any given moment. If I liked a girl, I had to call her parents' house. If no one was home, I would have to leave a message on her parents' answering machine. Photography was also slow, and our engagement with pictures was very physical. I remember flirting with girls in the dark room—the horrid smell of the chemicals, the red light, and the magic of watching an image appear on a blank sheet of paper.

A photograph was something you held in your hand, something for which you waited. Everyone brought disposable cameras on mission trips. It never occurred to me that these cameras, like landlines, would go the way of the busy signal.

When I was sixteen, friends pulled out Nokia cell phones with interchangeable faceplates, thirty texts per month, and unlimited minutes after 9:00 P.M. At first, the phones were relatively innocuous and even helpful for getting out of sticky situations. But soon they became invasive. I remember we had a Friday-night tradition of having a bonfire in the woods behind church—singing songs around the fire, throwing marshmallows at each other, peeing in the woods, staying up late talking on blankets by the dying embers of the fire. But soon, my friends were there, but half there, stealing glances at their new phones, wondering what they would do afterward. The phones made it possible for the entire bonfire to be spent arranging what we were going to do *next*. And how embarrassing if you were the one with no one to text.

Because we were in a long-distance relationship, Brittany and I depended on technology to stay in touch. A moment here, a moment there—cell phones, email, and Skype made the silence of being apart seem almost to sizzle with in-love-ness. Yet for all the conversation and sharing, we don't have many stories worth telling. To use a metaphor, our relationship was beginning to feel "spiritual" but not very "religious". It was illusory, disembodied. We had a lot of "faith", but very few "works". The accumulated months of online communication had the effect of making our love increasingly hypothetical, "out there" or "next"—not here, not now. We dreamed of the day we could get real, so to speak—get married and share a life of rhythms and tasks and things. Love, especially sexual love, seems to demand a home, a place to live a story. Stocking the fridge, taking out the trash, making a pot of tea—these tiny acts add up to a story worth telling. And marriage was meant to tell a story.

Now, some might have wondered at the small forays into biblical theology in these last two chapters, and I'm afraid to say there's more ahead. This is because during my time at Nashotah House, almost by accident, I became less interested in the inspirational quality of single-verse "devotions" and increasingly interested in the coherency of the Bible as a collection of books that tell the one true story of the world. Maybe you have too. In a fresh, bottom-up way, the Bible began to give *shape* to salvation history and where I fit in—but more on that in the next chapter. For now, it must be said that the modern historical-critical methods had always bored me; but I was discovering typology, the medieval "fourfold sense of Scripture", and the coherency of the covenants, and it made the Bible hum with life. It is often said that ideas have consequences, and during seminary my story became tangled up with Scripture in ways that would have frightening repercussions.

9

In Chevron Formation

No one comes to the Father, but by me.

—John 14:6

His father saw him and had compassion,
and ran and embraced him and kissed him.

—Luke 15:20

"Dearly beloved, we are gathered together here in the sight of God,
and in the face of this congregation, to join together this man and this
woman in holy Matrimony; which is an honorable estate, instituted
of God in the time of man's innocence, signifying unto us the mystical union that is betwixt Christ and his Church: which holy estate
Christ adorned and beautified with his presence, and first miracle that
he wrought, in Cana of Galilee ..."

And so the ceremony began.

Brittany and I just couldn't wait any longer. It was June 30; not
even six months had passed since I had proposed. She was passionate
about social justice and it was impossible to obtain a conflict-free
diamond, so I had given her an engagement ring with a pearl in a
medieval-looking setting. We didn't want our marriage to be about
"making it", a big show, or a grand exhibition of money. We also
didn't have any money. We bought the food for the luncheon at
the local grocery store, Brittany sewed the bunting herself, and our
wedding party helped cut fruit and hang decorations in the basement
of our small Anglican parish in the suburbs of Minneapolis. It was
a crisp June morning, and I had forgotten to pick up the donuts. A

groomsman raced me to the donut shop. We rushed back with the boxes just in time for me to put on my bow tie. I was sweating.

Everyone stood to sing the Magnificat when Brittany walked down the aisle, beautiful and radiant. Sunlight shone through the stained-glass windows. The parish priest, a dear friend, was officiating. Our family and friends were gathered around to support us, to celebrate this ancient ritual as old as time. I was terrified, but happy. At last, we stood before the priest, grinning shamelessly at one another. I was very aware that Brittany and I had chosen marriage as the path we were to walk toward heaven. But how does anyone, married or not, *approach* heaven? What is the shape or direction of salvation history?

And all at once an unexpected gust, a vision of a sea, rushed by me. I almost took a step back. I had the strangest impulse to cross myself, and quickly lifted up an Our Father. It was as if I saw heaven and earth collide. I saw God the Father look out from his eternal throne of justice across a raging sea at a combat fleet advancing its attack. I saw ships in wedge formation cut through the white foam breakers of his justice.

Our Father who art in heaven ...

It was only a second, but I saw it. Standing there across from my beautiful bride dressed in white, I saw the Church storming heaven like a great fleet of yore, like an innumerable fleet attacking a great king. I saw the saints crashing over the waves of God's anger, a fleet of freighters and galleys shaped like two hands joined in prayer, two hands shaped like a high Gothic steeple shooting straight into heaven. And God the Son was the first ship, the captain and head. The Father's only Son, laden with the sins of the world, led the Church to the Father in V formation. How can the Father defend himself? How can a Father refuse his only Son? His Son told them everything—these words seem to conquer him, the unconquerable:

Our Father who art in heaven ...

This was the maritime image of Charles Péguy's poem "A Vision of Prayer". Several years earlier, my friend Old Hickory read this poem to me before going to Mass. He read it, I nodded some vague approval, and life went on as usual. But the image never left me. While preparing for the priesthood, especially, I returned to this vision again and again, like a man who keeps coming back to the same painting in a museum, each time seeing something new. On our marriage day, it was like I saw the hands of a man and woman coming together in the sacred bond of marriage, forming a perfect architecture, a kind of cathedral that served as a physical reminder of Christ and the Church.

The priest continued, "Marriage is not by any to be enterprised, nor taken in hand, unadvisedly, lightly, or wantonly, to satisfy men's carnal lusts and appetites, like brute beasts that have no understanding; but reverently, discreetly, advisedly, soberly, and in the fear of God ..."

The liturgy had a way of making not only our marriage but all of life come into focus. The church quieted, the coughing subsided, and it seemed almost as if the whole world was paying attention. Brittany looked stunning and victorious. And again I saw the Church in chevron formation bounding over the wake of God's justice, like a bride running hand in hand with her husband to their new home. It was a picture not only of Brittany and me, our marriage, and our prayer to serve God by "planting" a church in Minneapolis, but also of the story of the ages, the story of God's romance with mankind.

For me, the vision illustrated the *shape* of salvation history. Péguy's "A Vision of Prayer" pulls back the curtains of the Trinitarian life at salvation history's most dramatic moment, the moment when the Son returns to the Father as both God and man, bringing all mankind with him. It is a picture not unlike that of Mont-Saint-Michel, that triangle of granite rising from the sea, turrets and bulwarks towering out of it, generations of churches built upon churches, a triangle that culminates, finally, in a steeple assailing heaven itself. Jesus leads the Church back to God, and he brings her in the triangular shape of the triune God.

* * * * *

It was meaningful for me that our marriage began with the celebration of the Eucharist. I felt unworthy—unworthy of Brittany and unworthy of the Eucharist. I felt this way because the Lord is utterly, unapproachably holy—and I knew that were it not for Christ I would not be able to draw near: no unclean thing may enter the presence of the all-holy God without being first cleansed and consecrated. Only the pure of heart can "see God" (Mt 5:8). Without holiness "no one will see the Lord" (Heb 12:14). The holiness of God is so excellent that even "the heavens are not clean in his sight" (Job 15:15) and "his angels he charges with error" (Job 4:18).

The essence of God's covenant with Israel was, "I ... will be your God, and you shall be my people" (Lev 26:12). But an all-holy God cannot dwell in the presence of sin, and so his Presence was accompanied with a command: "You shall be holy to me; for I the LORD am holy" (Lev 20:26). The tabernacle was the visible demonstration of God's communion with Israel that they would be "sanctified by [his] glory" (Ex 29:43; see vv. 44–46). The location, design, materials, and accessibility of the tabernacle (and later temple) symbolically communicated the fact that it was *dangerous* for an all-holy God to dwell in Israel's midst. Thus, the entire shape of the Israelites' covenant was a patterned triangular formation. God's awesome presence was "enthroned upon the cherubim" (Ps 99:1), inside the innermost sanctuary of the tabernacle, the Holy of Holies, just above the Ark of the Covenant. From this epicenter, the presence of the Lord in Israel's midst was borne out through the tabernacle and into the arrangement of the camp in degrees of holiness. From the Mercy Seat into the Holy of Holies, then into the Holy Place, from the tabernacle into the courtyard, and finally out into the camp. To be "outside the camp" (Num 5:3) was to be outside of the covenant, to be "unclean" (Num 5:2).

Only priests could enter the tabernacle, and only the high priest could enter the Holy of Holies to sprinkle the living blood of the victim that had passed through death (and represented the people) upon the Mercy Seat, "confecting" at-one-ment between God and his people, and only once a year, on the Day of Atonement. The priest was the first ship, the mediator, and behind him came the whole camp, approaching God's throne in chevron formation.

All of this, of course, would culminate in the death, Resurrection, and Ascension of Jesus Christ, who "became flesh and *dwelt* among us" (Jn 1:14). And the uncreated Son of God became the created Son of Mary and dwelt among us, not by the conversion of the Godhead into flesh, as the Athanasian Creed reminds us, but by the *taking up* of manhood *into* God! The waves of God's justice push sin away, but in Christ we are drawn into the merciful arms of the Father. We are no longer outsiders, but insiders.

"The kingdom of heaven has suffered violence, and men of violence take it by force" (Mt 11:12). From the rocky promontory of his justice, God the Father sees a fleet of ships, their wake growing wider and wider until it disappears against the horizon, more innumerable than the stars of heaven, what Saint Cyprian called "the bright army of the soldiers of Christ".[1] The Holy Spirit fills every sail, forcing each ship through the breakers of his justice, the breakers that push every unclean thing away from his holy presence. The Church is attacking heaven in V formation, a once unholy people daring to approach a holy God. And the Son is the first ship, the breaker ship. How can a Father refuse his only Son?

Our Father who art in heaven ...

We can approach God *as Father* because we are *sons*. When we are baptized into Jesus, we become full participants in his Sonship (Rom 8:14–17; Gal 3:26–27). In the early days of the Church, no unbaptized person was allowed to say the Our Father. "For how can they say the Our Father who are not yet born sons?" asked Saint Augustine.[2] He called the Pater Noster the "fraternal prayer" because the baptized faithful have been adopted into God's family and are "God's children" (1 Jn 3:2). By grace, we are "sons in the Son, from the Father and to the Father like him" (*Filii in Filio, ex Patre et ad Patrem*).

And this is why the fleet of ships flies in *triangular* formation: in heaven, the whole Body of Christ will gaze upon the face of the Father through the eyes of Jesus, who is our head, the first ship, our captain who has gone into heaven to bring glory to the Father and to intercede for us. The Church is in the shape of a triangle because she is in Christ's wake. Through the incarnate Son, we approach the Father. As Saint Augustine put it: "Since the Church is Christ's own body, she learns to offer up herself through him."[3] And when the Father sees us, he sees the Son. Why? Because in the waters of Baptism, the Holy Spirit remakes us into *sons in the Son*.

As I stood at the altar holding my bride's hands, the whole world seemed to grow still. To my wonderment, I was about to become Brittany's husband. Gone were the days of long-distance phone calls, of coffee-shop trysts, of saying goodbye. In a moment, in the twinkling of an eye, I would be all at once what she is. I wanted to draw her to me, she who was my equal and my likeness. No more twain, but one flesh.

Marriage reminds us that we are the *body* of Christ because we are the *bride* of Christ (Eph 5:31–32). From beginning to end, Jesus' ministry had a nuptial theme. His first miracle took place at a wedding where he turned water into wine (Jn 2:1–11), and the climax of the new heaven and new earth culminates in the "marriage of the Lamb", when Christ will receive "his Bride" (Rev 19:7), the Church. To enter God's heavenly temple, humanity needs a mediator. We need someone who belongs both to the world of God and to our own human world, someone who can bring the two shores together. As humanity's husband, as an Adam, Jesus is also our priest. He is *the* priest, the mediator of the New Covenant (Heb 9:15). He has ascended into the heavenly Holy of Holies to do what he has done from all eternity: offer *himself* to the Father. Except now, his offering includes his bride, the Church. The two have become one flesh. C. S. Lewis put it this way: "A cleft has opened in the pitiless walls of the world, and we are invited to follow our great Captain inside."[4]

When a man and woman come together in the self-giving love of Matrimony, they create a dwelling place for God. Within the sanctity of their bond, they offer an image, a sacramental icon, of the loving and creative union of the Holy Trinity. Self-giving love is an essential attribute of God's triune nature. And Jesus shows us the way.

The morning sun splashing into the sanctuary had a way of putting the moment in perspective. I was strangely aware that Brittany and I were besieging heaven with our prayers, that we were *living* a prayer. We were entering a covenant that God intended to be a reflection of *the* covenant.

"Wilt thou have this woman to thy wedded wife?" the priest continued, looking straight at me. "Wilt thou love her, comfort her, honor, and keep her, in sickness and in health; and, forsaking all others, keep thee only unto her, so long as ye both shall live?"

My knees were wobbly, but I could only give one answer. "I will."

The congregation was now very, very quiet.

"Wilt thou have this man to thy wedded husband," said the priest, turning to Brittany. "Wilt thou obey him, and serve him, love, honor, and keep him, in sickness and in health; and, forsaking all other, keep thee only unto him, so long as ye both shall live?"

Brittany's red hair was angelic in the sunlight. Her face couldn't contain her joy.

"I will."

* * * * *

I knew of no other way to think about my marriage to Brittany except to map it out in terms of the big picture, "the Church in chevron formation". As I was preparing for Holy Orders, especially, this overarching shape of the universe, the direction of history, mattered a great deal. And it all begins with God.

The Trinity is often drawn in the shape of a triangle, with God the Father at the top and the Son and the Spirit below. To the classical mind, the triangle represented perfection: having three lines, a triangle has the lowest possible number of straight lines needed to make a geometric form that is constant. There is the most basic human triangle: man, woman, and child. Pope Saint John Paul II once said that "God in his deepest mystery [the Holy Trinity] is ... a family".[5] God is a communion of Persons that are equally God yet differentiated in their relations—Father, Son, and Holy Spirit.

From all eternity, the Father generates the Son in self-giving love. The Son, in imitation of the Father, pours himself back to the Father in self-giving love. And the bond between them is the very Person of the Holy Spirit. Although all Persons of the Trinity are equally divine, the Father is "first" because the Son and the Spirit proceed from him, but he proceeds from none. The Father alone is the source and summit of the Godhead, and everything the Son does through the Holy Spirit he does for the glory of the Father. In other words, the inner life of the Trinity is in chevron formation.

Only *in Christ* can we dare to approach this all-holy God. The Church is in bridal procession, as one caught up into the self-donating love between the Father and the Son; and this is, of course, the Sacrifice of the Mass. As George MacDonald put it, when Jesus sacrificed himself, he did "in the wild weather of his outlying provinces" that which from all eternity "he had done at home in glory and gladness".[6] *This* is the eternal sacrifice in which every Mass participates: in Christ, as his body and bride, we can offer God to God! The only gift worthy enough for God is God himself. And in Christ, we can offer the Father nothing less than his only Son!

Salvation history is oriented toward the Father. This is expressed symbolically when the ministerial priest (who is the icon of Christ) offers the Mass *ad orientem*, facing liturgical east. As one looks to the east for the rising sun, the ordained Catholic priest leads the people in looking east as they await the one true Son of God. Acting *in persona Christi*, he offers the Father the sacramental Body and Blood of the Son, with the congregation in his wake. Everyone looks to the east, toward Jesus, and Jesus is looking toward the Father. Everyone is connected in the Holy Spirit, and moves as one Mystical Body and offers one sacrifice, the sacrifice of Christ. Here we tread the dawn.

Suffice it to say, with a growing sense of God's holiness and my unworthiness, with a clearer understanding of the *direction* of the Mass—to the Father through the Son, in the bond of the Holy Spirit—I had become one of the many cassock-wearing, High Mass, Communion-on-the-tongue, kneeling-to-receive, Rite 1–loving, young seminarians that have passed through the halls of Nashotah House.[7]

Alas, Brittany and I were the only people at our wedding who believed the Communion meal we shared that day was a sacrifice. The Roman Catholics in attendance did not believe it was a valid Mass, the Anglicans did not believe in transubstantiation, and the Evangelicals thought it was a memorial (in the modern sense of the word), as did the atheists and agnostics in the room. When we asked our parish priest if he would face liturgical east for Mass, he very gently refused. He felt it would only make people feel excluded. Even so, that morning I saw the Church making an organized assault on heaven.

An image of the Trinity, the Church moves in triangular formation. Our eucharistic oblations here on earth *participate* in Christ's glorified oblation in heaven. In worshiping God now, the Church is in the early stages of her participation in the Trinity's eternal blessedness. Love, when properly directed, always moves through the creature to the Creator, through the divine processions within the Trinity, toward its final goal: God the Father Almighty.

I felt unworthy and inadequate, but standing before the altar on my wedding day was a kind of summons. Marrying Brittany was, in a sense, the beginning of the end of my spirituality. It was the first real vow I had ever made. I had chosen one woman and forsaken all others. Forever.

This singular act, the act of making a real commitment, was in fact *religious*. I put something (marriage) and someone else (Brittany) before me; from then on, I would have to deny my own desires, live for more than my natural instincts, and serve Brittany and our marriage. The modern era privatized marriage, taking it out of the public sphere and redefining it not as a *covenant* for the fulfilment of God's purposes, but a *contract* between two consenting adults for their own personal fulfilment. But Christian marriage is meant to tell a public story, a story of covenant. Now I belonged to a mission that was quite naturally much bigger than myself: marriage, the "domestic church", an image of the Holy Trinity.

*****

When Brittany studied abroad in Paris, she found a pair of red glasses in a small shop in Saint-Germain-des-Prés. With the outer edges pointed slightly up and the bottom gently rounded, they gave her an aura of femininity, culture, even intellectual achievement. Because she was sharp-witted and vivacious, I considered these very French-looking glasses to be iconic of Brittany's personality. The way the glasses ended was iconic enough.

The great advantage of having your wedding in the morning is that you have the whole day ahead of you. After we said our vows, we sped off to an old stone inn on the Mississippi in my red Ford Ranger. Hours later, we rendezvoused with friends and family at a swanky bar down by the river to drink and laugh. We then honeymooned at my uncle Tim and aunt Lisa's cabin on a lake in Wisconsin. The July heat was so overpowering we spent the first morning on the lake.

Brittany sat on the front of the pontoon signaling where she wanted to go while I steered. At last we dropped anchor in a secluded bay. With happy shouts we dove into the clear water, but a moment later Brittany was yelping.

"My glasses!"

She was not wearing them.

"I forgot to take them off! They're gone!"

I dove and dove, but could not find them. Eventually, we climbed out of the water.

"I can't see," Brittany said, sitting on the edge of the pontoon.

I looked over at her, stunned. Brittany was practically blind, and we had seven days of honeymooning left. We couldn't buy another pair—no one would be open on Independence Day weekend. She had a backup pair that were her prescription back at her parents' house. We would have to go back.

With heavy hearts and with finger paintings—"Just married!"—decorating my red truck, we drove the four-hour drive back to Minneapolis, to the cul-de-sac on which her parents lived. They weren't home. Brittany found the hidden key, and then ruffled through her childhood dressers to find the old pair of glasses. Thankfully, she found them. They were very plain; they were not from Paris, but she could see. Then we drove the four-hour drive back to the cabin. On the way, we stopped at Taco Bell and ate chili cheese burritos.

"I've never been happier," Brittany said, looking at me from across the table through her old glasses.

"Really?" I asked.

"This isn't at all what I thought the first day of our honeymoon would be like ... but I'm just so happy to be married to you. You're my man!"

And as we unwrapped our burritos, I had to agree with her. The day hadn't turned out to be anything like what we had planned, but we were married. I had never felt more free.

Losing Brittany's glasses and a whole day of honeymooning had a strange effect on us. We felt unrestrained by our plans, on the loose. We were on our own, and we didn't have to think about children because, of course, Brittany was on the pill. After the cabin we spontaneously decided to take a few more days and head up to Grand Marais, Minnesota. It was a whim, and a long drive, but we were unheeding. Besides, we wanted to see the Sawtooth Mountains, a range of low, serrated ridges situated on the North Shore of Lake Superior, and eat at the World's Best Donut Shop, a red-colored shop that serves nothing less than the world's finest donuts.

Brittany and I talked the whole way, her feet up on the dash, following Highway 61 as it snaked along the rocky shores. We listened to Vivaldi and Tom Petty. Dark pines cut at the horizon line, tall and green, every one of them a monument to freedom.

We didn't have much money, but thankfully we found a cheap motel. It was our castle. The next morning we rose before dawn, wrapped ourselves in warm flannels, and drove into town to get donuts. Seagulls circled high overhead the small red shop, which was couched on the shoreline of Grand Marais Harbor.

We were the first in line, clutching our paper cups of coffee to warm our hands in the brisk predawn. As we placed our orders, the shop owner regaled us with a colorful account of her methods and the quality of her fryers. Carrying our treasures down to Cobblestone Beach, we walked the shoreline until we found a good spot to watch the rising sun. The cake donuts were still warm. Brittany shivered with pleasure.

"It's all about those fryers!" she crowed, stuffing a donut in my already full mouth.

After we guzzled the last drops of hot coffee, we clambered over the cold rocky outcroppings until we were face-to-face with Lake Superior. The rock plateaued level with the water, and we crouched to watch the blue waves undulate in the early light. We were so happy in Grand Marais that we impulsively booked our room for the whole week. We hiked Cascade Falls and explored Devil's Kettle. We went cliff jumping at Baptism River, picnicked at Split Rock, and looked up at stars on Pincushion Mountain. And every morning we rose before dawn and made our way to the donut shop.

It was the quiet before the storm. The air was clear and cool, and we had plans to build something beautiful, plans to organize an Anglican church in Minneapolis, plans to start a family, and on the North Shore it seemed like we had all the time in the world to talk and pray together. With these plans in view, I did not want Brittany to "accept me just as I am". In my heart of hearts, I knew that I was not perfect. There were many things about me that needed to be changed. And as I allowed Brittany to get to know me, I saw that I wasn't the only one with needs, deep needs, and flaws. From the start, our marriage sent us on a journey of transformation, which makes sense if marriage is more than "just a piece of paper".

Again, what if marriage is meant to tell a story? Saint Paul says the one-flesh union between husband and wife is a "great mystery" (Eph 5:32) that gives us a glimpse of the union between Christ and his Church. The Church and marriage explain one another. The Bible begins with a wedding (Adam and Eve) and ends with a wedding (Christ and the Church). Marriage was designed to be a reflection of God's love for us in Jesus. Marriage only "works" to the degree that it tells this story, the story of the wedding of heaven and earth.

Brittany and I wanted our marriage to be a *sacrament*. But, as we would come to see, the difficult thing about sacraments is that they do not exist apart from Church. In Ephesians 5, when Paul speaks of the Church's need to "submit" to Christ—as a wife submits to her husband, as Christ submits to the Father—the word he uses for submission (ὑποτάσσω) means to subject oneself, to place under. It has its origin in the military, denoting a soldier submitting to an officer. The idea is that when you join the military you lose control over your schedule, over when you go on vacation, over when you're going to eat, what you eat, how you eat. To be part of the fleet, the greater unity, you have to yield your independence. You cannot stand on your rights. Rather, it seems you must put the good of the whole over your own. Paul says that this ability to relinquish one's rights is the knot between Christ and his Church. Jesus *gave himself up* for us. Though equal with the Father, the Son gave up his glory and took on our human nature (Phil 2:5). He willingly went to the Cross, and his sacrifice brings us into a conjugal union with himself. Saint Paul paints a picture: brides submit to their husbands, husbands lay down their lives for their wives, the Church submits to Jesus the Son, and the Son submits everything to the Father. Unselfish service is the *shape* of love in the Trinity, the shape of the covenant, the shape of religion.

Salvation history is going somewhere. And the crashing of the salt-spray, white-crested waves of God's justice, the course along which the plot moves, advances inexorably to the Father. This is no time to toot your own glorious bugle. You need to get in line, to find your rank in the Church's formation as it advances toward heaven. To join the dance, you must learn the steps.

Our Abba is attacked. He is disarmed. And he is happy. "See what kind of love the Father has given us, that we should be called children of God; and so we are" (1 Jn 3:1).

But would we tell the story? Brittany had generously given up her plans to teach with Teach for America, shortening her two-year plan to move to Wisconsin right away. She was hired to teach at a nearby military academy for high school boys, which would be a new sort of adventure. But we knew that ultimately, God was calling us to start a church in Minneapolis, and we knew our marriage would be an important component in ministry. It was too late to back out now, even if we wanted to, which we didn't. We were all in.

I was ever more awake to just how much more sinful and flawed I was than I had ever dared believe, yet at the very same time I was more loved in Jesus Christ than I ever dared hope. Love without truth is sentimentality. The truth of Christ's love, even with all that it demands, was strengthening me to seek the truth with more honesty, and to repent. And before I had ever heard of the Divine Mercy Chaplet, my heart began to pray something like: "Eternal Father, I offer you the Body and Blood, Soul and Divinity, of your dearly beloved Son, our Lord, Jesus Christ, in atonement for our sins and those of the whole world."

10

Priestcraft

When there is a change in the priesthood,
there is necessarily a change in the law as well.

—Hebrews 7:12

The priesthood is a matter, not of a profession,
but of a participation in the redemptive work of Christ.

—Hans Urs von Balthasar[1]

During my first year of seminary, I had believed with unusual zeal that women should be able to be ordained priests. It was a matter of rights, equality, and social justice. And the fact that almost all Anglo-Catholics believed otherwise was for me biblically suspect and downright embarrassing. When a seminary friend called me an iconoclast and a clericalist and accused me of submitting to a "transgender priesthood", all the while referring to women priests as "priestesses", I was so appalled I declined to sit next to him in the refectory for weeks.

Before the summer Brittany and I were married, I had sought the advice of a professor I respected, Father Willard. He still wore a biretta, looked like J. R. R. Tolkien when he smoked his pipe, which was constantly, and had known Michael Ramsey personally. When I stepped into his quiet office, I was instantly seduced by the books crammed into every corner, the old maps tucked between jars of pencils and packets of tobacco, and the small prie-dieu in the corner for his private devotions.

"I'm in favor of women priests," I said firmly.

The old man smiled sweetly, surprising me. I had expected him to make a biting remark or perhaps an exclamation of astonishment.

(Priests like Father Willard tended to be scandalized by any break from tradition.)

"I quite agree!" he said, his eyes twinkling with mischief and intelligence. "If I were you and had to become a priest in this day and age, I would stand up for women's rights. Men aren't more Christlike just because they're men. Many women can do the job better than their male colleagues—they're better public speakers, counselors, and scholars. We're not cavemen anymore."

Father Willard had a unique gift for being sarcastic without also being insulting. I nodded benignly, glanced at my watch, and excused myself. We obviously disagreed about whether women could be priests; but if we *were* to agree, he pretty much summed it up. So why did I suddenly feel adrift?

I took solace from the fact that I did not need Father Willard's approval. I had the Bible. I no longer believed in *sola scriptura* in theory, but in practice I still used the Bible to break camp with tradition when I deemed it necessary. And although ordaining women was contrary to tradition, both in the East and the West, I believed that a female priesthood was *biblical* because of contemporary scholarly consensus. (I could safely abrogate Catholic or Orthodox scholars because my presuppositions tacitly determined *which* scholars and *which* consensus was truly biblical; and it was an obvious fact that denying Holy Orders to half the human race was sexist.)

I became so passionate about a woman's right to be a priest I wrote an essay about it, even though it was not assigned for class. I stayed up late into the night in research, and especially appreciated the arguments of R. T. France in *Women in the Church's Ministry* and Kenneth Bailey's essay *Women in the New Testament: A Middle Eastern Cultural View*. France suggested that priesthood is functional, not ontological, and made the case that the Bible does *not* teach that women should not teach or hold authority over men. He held up Galatians 3:28 (there is "no male and female" in Christ) as an early challenge to patriarchy and a foreshadowing of an egalitarian society. Jesus' exclusion of women from being numbered among the twelve apostles was only "a historical provision of limited duration, not an ideological statement about the permanent values of the kingdom of God".[2] Kenneth Bailey suggested that there is no "creation principle" (Adam and Eve) that suggests women cannot do ministry.[3]

Women spoke in church and even taught. Jesus had women disciples. Phoebe was a deacon. Junia was an apostle. The reference to "older women" in 1 Timothy 5:1–2 conceivably describes women elders. Thus, in Scripture we see "women as disciples, teachers, prophets, deacons, (one) apostle, along with the possibility of women elders".[4] My essay was watertight. The matter was clinched. Women could be priests.

But it is said, "Know your enemy." So when I packed for my honeymoon, I packed what any normal newlywed would pack, and then threw into my suitcase a small pamphlet that Father Willard had given me, called *Women Priests?* by the late Anglo-Catholic priest E. L. Mascall. And whether we were tucking in for the night at the cabin of logs or stopping to rest on a high outcrop over Lake Superior during a hike, Brittany would roll her eyes as I pulled out *Women Priests?* to learn better the enemy's strategies.

"You're so romantic," she said, when I pulled out the pamphlet during a water break while hiking in the woods.

"Really?"

She looked at me like I was one of the delinquent students in her math classes. I tucked it back into my pocket. It was understandable that not *everyone* saw the romance in defending women priests.

Now, while I had been defending women priests to everyone on campus the previous year, I had also been learning that the very essence of the priesthood is *Christ*, the last Adam who offers himself (and his bride) to the Father in the Holy Spirit.

I had also been learning that we were not made in the image of garden snails. Male and female human nature is the created expression of the uncreated nature of God, and the Godhead is a perfect unity and community, a *Trinity* of Persons who are equally God but with different roles, or "missions". Thus, it was not good for the image of God that Adam be alone, and so God made Eve. Together with their children, Adam and Eve reflect the triune God. Unlike androgynous mollusks, people do not have interchangeable sex organs; and, made in God's image, people do not have interchangeable roles. Equal does not mean same, and our different vocations are inexorably linked to our being male and female. These differences are not about capacity or competence, who is smarter or stronger, but rather about communicating and sharing the life of the Trinity.

And so I was struck by E. L. Mascall's observation that some religious symbols are not culture-bound or plastic. God might use feminine metaphors to speak of himself, but he has indelibly revealed his *name* as "Father", "Son". Because male-and-female humanity is an icon of the Godhead established in the creation of the world, its *religious symbolism* is ineradicable. Did it follow that Christ being a *male* human is not incidental to his being *priest*? Christian humility seemed to demand the admission that an unbroken and universal practice in the Church is almost certain to have some profound theological basis, even if we have forgotten what it is. "When we find our Lord and the primitive Church restricting the ministry to males in spite of the emphasis laid by both alike on the absolute equality of men and women as members of the New Israel which is the Body of Christ, is it not prudent to assume that there must be some very deep and significant reason in the nature of things for this restriction?"[5]

While Brittany and I explored the North Shore, the spooky realization came upon me that perhaps I had been pursuing ordination without ever really stopping to ask what Holy Orders were. And although I was happy, the drive back to Minneapolis was haunted by a looming question: What *is* a priest?

Brittany and I stayed a night at my parents' house. The next day we went shopping for a bed.

"I want a full mattress," I said.

"Are you serious?" Brittany said.

"I want to be close to the woman I love!"

"I want a king."

"But—"

"But I'll settle for a queen," Brittany said, and I could tell that she would budge no further. With that, we piled our possessions into a U-Haul and drove to Nashotah House. The first thing we unpacked was a bottle of red wine and a record player. Over the wails of Ray Charles and James Brown, we sorted our clothing and kitchenware and argued about where to hang the pictures on the wall. Later, when we were able to laugh about it, we realized that this was our first real fight—raised voices, rouged faces, slammed doors, and all over a few picture frames!

Married student housing was clean but cramped. The July weather didn't help. The air was sticky, and the open window seemed only to let in more heat. But did any of it matter? We had thrust a stake in the ground. This was *our* home, our fence post, and we were jubilant and proud. Brittany unpacked her library and I unpacked mine, and we realized we did not have enough bookshelves. The next morning, our mattress on the living-room floor, our little apartment crowded with stacks of books, Brittany rolled her eyes when the mailman arrived bearing gifts: Dulles' *The Priestly Office*, Balthasar's *Priestly Spirituality*, Pope Saint John Paul II's *Ordinatio Sacerdotalis*, and an anthology on the subject with essays by Thomas Hopko, Alexander Schmemann, and Kallistos Ware.

"Do we need more books?" Brittany said.

"Think of it as we *get* more books," I said.

"Well, just don't forget the budget," Brittany said. "You pay for what you get."

"And you get what you pay for?" I said sheepishly, but a pillow was already flying straight at my head.

* * * * *

In those days I made coffee and read about the priesthood before sunrise. I was so hungry for answers, I often forgot to eat breakfast: I had been claiming that God was calling me to be a priest, and yet I didn't even know what a priest was! How had I not asked this most basic question? The days went by, and I soon realized that a possibly gaping hole in my impenetrable argument for a female priesthood was that I was concerned firstly with rights. Can anyone claim a "right" to the priesthood of Jesus Christ? Certainly not me!

I also saw that the priesthood is not a question of sexual equality. For if the Trinity is a community of Persons equally God but with *different* roles, wouldn't we expect Adam and Eve to be equally human but with different roles? As the Son does not have the same "mission" or "procession" as the Father while remaining fully God, wouldn't Eve not have the same vocation as Adam while remaining fully human? No, equal could not mean identical.

But then I also saw that the priesthood couldn't be a matter of social justice, because the ordained ministry is not about capacity or competence or power, but is an office that the Lord freely entrusts to those whom he chooses. All the passages defending women speaking publicly or prophesying or leading were simply not apropos to the discussion because the ministerial priesthood is not reducible to a

ministry of leadership or preaching or administration and is by definition distinct from the "priesthood of all believers". A priest is not
the professional possessing the best qualifications for the job. He is the
sacramental sign and presence of Christ in the Church, and his office
belongs to the economy of salvation. Therefore, at least in theory,
excluding all women and most men from the ministerial priesthood
would not be, as I had been arguing, unjust.

I returned to the Scriptures to take a second look, except this time
I didn't just go to the contentious texts about women. I wanted the
"big picture", so I went back to the beginning, to Genesis, to Adam,
asking: What *is* a priest?

I learned that priesthood began with digging in the dirt. First, God
formed Adam from the soil; then he planted a garden and put Adam
in it (Gen 2:8). As if to highlight that man is closely linked to the
ground, Genesis 2:7 and 3:19 involve a wordplay between "Adam"
and *adamah* ("ground, earth"). This garden was the first Holy of
Holies, the room in the temple only the high priest could enter, the
special place where Adam walked with God (cf. Gen 3:8). And as
soon as God put Adam in this sanctuary garden, he told him "to till
it and keep it" (Gen 2:15). Adam's charge was, in fact, his ordination.
These two Hebrew words are only used together elsewhere in the
Bible to describe the jobs of the Levite priests in the tabernacle (Num
3:7–8; 18:7). "To till" (*habad*) means to serve or to minister, and "to
keep" (*shamar*) means to guard. Adam was to maintain the sanctity of
the tabernacle of the living God. The manual labor of gardening was,
like the maintenance and upkeep of the temple furniture, a priestly
job. Adam was the high priest of creation, and Eden was the first holy
of holies. Adam was to lead his family in a life of praise.

Adam was a priest, and as such he was a *father*. Throughout salvation history all priesthood belongs to spiritual fathers. As *fathers* Noah
and Abraham and Jacob were priests, offering sacrifice, building
altars, blessing children, planting trees, erecting pillars, and sometimes
even announcing curses. Job "would send and sanctify [his children],
and he would rise early in the morning and offer burnt offerings
according to the number of them all; for Job said, 'It may be that
my sons have sinned, and cursed God in their hearts.' Thus Job did
continually" (Job 1:5). In the Old Testament, *fatherhood* and *priesthood*
seemed to be linked.

And then there was the glaring fact that all the Old Testament priests were men; only pagan religions had women priests, or "priestesses". The priest-king of Salem, Melchizedek, offered the fruits of the earth ("bread and wine" [Gen 14:18]), which makes sense because the first priest, Adam, was a farmer and a father and a king given royal prerogatives: "Be fruitful and multiply, and fill the earth and subdue it; and have dominion" (Gen 1:28). And Adam himself is the "type of the one who was to come" (Rom 5:14). Jesus is the "last Adam" (1 Cor 15:45), a priest forever according to the order of Melchizedek (Heb 7:1–28). He is the "one mediator between God and men, the man Christ Jesus" (1 Tim 2:5). As *Adam*, Jesus presents God to the Church and offers the Church to the Father.

"Adam" is the appropriate *matter* for the Sacrament of Holy Orders. And the ministerial priesthood participates in Christ's priesthood. In the words of Blessed Columba Marmion, "The priest carries on the work of [Mary's] Son by the ministry of the Word, by the administration of the sacraments, and especially by perpetuating the divine immolation under the veil of the sacred species."[6]

The priest is not the holiest member of the congregation. He is not the smartest, the most talented or charismatic, of his flock. But he has been ordained into the priesthood of the New Adam, the priesthood foreshadowed in creation, prefigured in the Old Testament priesthood, and fulfilled in Christ. He is the sacramental *sign* of the eternal Son-made-man's offering up to the Father nothing less than the transubstantial Body of Christ, with the Church in his train. Being male and female is meant to tell the story of the wedding of heaven and earth, and the priesthood is no exception. By ordination, the priest acts in the Person of Christ, and this applies primarily to the bishop, who has the fullness of priesthood, but also to the presbyter who participates in that same priesthood. Gender, marriage, sex, priesthood, Church—all of it is meant to tell the story of the New Adam and the New Eve. As Saint Ignatius of Antioch put it, "Where the *bishop* appears, there let the people be, just as where *Jesus Christ* is, there is the catholic Church."[7]

"Agh!" I said, pushing the stack of books away from me. I was not afraid, but the sensation was like being afraid. With no women priests in Church history, no women priests in the New Testament, no women priests in Israel's history, what had I to go on? The exegetical arguments of my favorite late twentieth-century scholars defending a female priesthood had failed to address what a priest is. But was it just a coincidence that the first women priests in salvation history appeared shortly after the sexual revolution? Was the Holy Spirit really doing a new thing? It still felt sexist, but I could no longer honestly believe gender was irrelevant to the priesthood of Christ.

Sharing my concerns with Brittany, I was surprised that she wasn't bothered in the least.

"Of course," she said. "A woman can't be a priest."

I coughed. I was hoping she would give me a good reason not to join the ranks of the sexist bigots. "But in Galatians 3:28, Paul says there is neither male nor female," I said.

"Baptismal equality doesn't mean we all get to be priests, though," Brittany said. "God saves us from sin, but not the way he made us. Gender is meant to tell a story, and the priesthood is a big part of that story."

I blinked. I guess she had been listening to my ramblings over the past few weeks, after all. Brittany and I were aware that our marriage was momentary: in heaven, we will "neither marry nor are given in marriage" (Mt 22:30), because we will have the real thing. We won't need the parable anymore; we will be married to God. In heaven, earthly marriage will cease—but we will still be men and women. God does not save us *despite* our being male and female. He saves us *through* or *within* our being male and female. "Grace does not destroy nature," says Thomas Aquinas, "but rather perfects it."[8] The new creation will not be a great androgynous blob. The male-and-female icon is forever.

"Aren't you offended?" I asked.

"You guys can have the apostles," Brittany laughed. "I've got the Virgin Mary!"

I chuckled nervously.

"Mary, huh?"

That night I opened Pope Saint John Paul II's *Ordinatio Sacerdotalis*. He said that the Church does not have the *authority* to admit women to priestly ordination. The apostolic tradition of reserving priestly ordination to men traces back to the will of Christ himself: Jesus instituted the Sacrament of Holy Orders by way of the mission he gave the Twelve; it confers on the person ordained a unique ministry in relation to the rest of the baptized; and this office is passed on in apostolic succession. No new revelation can replace what Jesus Christ did "when the time had fully come" (Gal 4:4).

While women followed Christ as disciples and co-workers, we cannot change what Christ *did* when he only freely chose twelve men to the apostolate. Jesus' call of the Twelve ought not to be considered a caving to cultural norms, but a Trinitarian event in which the Son chose those whom he willed in union with the Father and through the Holy Spirit. Thus, *in imitation of Christ*, from the beginning, priestly ordination has always been reserved to men alone.

I humphed and looked over at Brittany, but she was sleeping. Outside, crickets were singing. I turned off the light, fluffed up my pillow, and humphed again. I no longer believed women could be priests—and, strangely, I didn't feel sexist. In fact, the whole *in persona Christi* thing had me second-guessing if God was really calling *me* to be a priest.

* * * * *

Brittany liked her new job, and the cadets at the military school were much more disciplined and respectful than her students had been in Mississippi. She met the change with some relief but missed the challenge and deeper sense of purpose she had previously had. Our new home was slowly coming together—curtains were hung, books shelved, clothes organized, and we set out our white Kitchen Aid stand mixer as a kind of monument to domesticity. Every afternoon we went for long walks. We wandered hand in hand through campus, spying birds and taking note of trees that had the look of an old soul.

"Just wait," a middle-aged neighbor couple loved to call out to us with wizened smiles. "You are doe-eyed lovebirds now, but you'll see."

"Haha," we would stammer, and pick up our pace.

This exchange happened so often that we called them and other older couples on campus the "Justwaiters". They meant to tease, but we took it as sacrilege, an offense against marriage itself. It was summer and we were green and the whole world seemed to spin in a never-ending victory dance. We grilled and drank bourbon and listened to Iron & Wine, Jose Gonzales, the Dave Brubeck Quartet, and Tchaikovsky. It was unbearably hot weather, and I quickly

realized that it was unrealistic to spoon with one's wife every single
night. In the stuffy heat I thanked God that my wife had the wisdom
and foresight to talk me into getting a queen mattress. At night, I was
afraid I would wake her up every time I moved; I had never noticed
just how much I tossed and turned in bed. By late July, the bullfrogs
in the woods behind our apartment were so loud I caved and shut the
windows. Brittany promptly turned on the air conditioner. We did
not believe in air conditioners, but that was before bullfrogs and a life
of cramped, shared spaces.

All the while, I was feeling unworthy of Holy Orders and was
second-guessing my "call". There were moments, quite unexpectedly, when something inside me raced with panic. To swear obedience to the bishop, to kneel before the bishop as the congregation
sings *Veni Sancte Spiritus*, to have the bishop lay hands upon my head
and to receive the Sacrament of Holy Orders, to be vested according
to the order of priests and to fashion my whole life according to the
precepts of the Church, to preach, to declare God's forgiveness to
penitent sinners, to pronounce God's blessing, to share in the administration of Holy Baptism and in the celebration of the mysteries of
Christ's Body and Blood, and to perform all the other ministrations
of the sacred priesthood—just thinking about it made me tremble. I
kept swallowing. I couldn't fall asleep at night.

I talked with Brittany about this, and we prayed together. Brittany
encouraged me to follow and obey the Lord, and not to rely on my
sense of worth.

"What is impossible with man is possible with God," Brittany said.

"I just feel like it's so improper," I said. "I feel guilty for wanting
to be a priest."

"I think God has given you a burden to reach the unchurched.
You have a holy discontent. Trust in Jesus, not your strengths and
weaknesses."

As the days passed, I sought Godly counsel. I also spent long hours
in the chapel on my knees. And I began to feel a desperate *need* for
priests. The world was starving for holy priests to present Christ at his
holy altars, to confect the sacrament, to preach the Word of God, to
absolve sins, and to continue the apostolic ministry.

One night we opened a bottle of Saint Germaine, a wedding gift
we had been saving, and laid out a huge sheet of white paper over the

entire dining-room table. Colorful crayons and chalklike pencils and Bible verses slowly began to fill the blank space as we drew our prayer for planting a church in Minneapolis. We gave ourselves over to planting and nurturing love, to "make love [our] aim" (1 Cor 14:1). The church plant would be a hospital for sinners, not a museum of saints, a place where the Gospel is proclaimed in the heart of the city. We trusted that our vision and mission for Minneapolis would be like "a tree planted by streams of water, that yields its fruit in its season, and its leaf does not wither" (Ps 1:3). We drew a parish with a towering steeple with light bursting from it, drawing people in from even the darkest corners of the city.

When I wrote our fundraising letter for the year, we invited others into this vision of fruitfulness. God willing, we would start a church in Minneapolis by 2015, and we were prayerfully committed to follow the call to lead this ministry. Parishioners were invited to come along with us, to join a confident, joyful, and hope-filled ministry. We asked them to invest themselves in this work to which God had called us—through the resources God gave them, their energy, their prayers, their money. "Help us invest in the Kingdom by investing in our preparation at seminary. With patient care, these early seeds can yield a great harvest."

Later that summer, we traveled back to Minneapolis to visit with our sending parish in order to discuss fundraising and make preliminary plans for the "church plant", and also for Brittany to check out a few schools she was interested in teaching at. We asked a focus group what they would love to see happen in Minneapolis. What were their fears and hopes? Had God given them a vision? We wanted to make sure that our calling was confirmed by others. We also wanted to seek God's will about *where* in Minneapolis he wanted us to go. We felt very strongly that cities were crucial to the Christian mission. The people of the world are moving into urban areas many times faster than the Church is, and I felt strongly that there was an urgent need for *priests* to minister to them.

We soon discovered an old church building that was for sale in South Minneapolis. It had traditional architecture, a beautiful lawn, and was couched in a diverse neighborhood. Because I was quite taken with the idea of a parish being not only a building or a congregation but also geography, a spiritual district with clear boundaries, we gathered friends together for a prayer walk. In my mind, it was a kind of "beating the bounds", the old tradition of a priest walking the boundary of his parish with a crowd of boys armed with green boughs so as to beat the parish boundary markers with them, reminding us all of our duty to care especially for the souls living within these borders. The prayer walk was a way for us to pray for that neighborhood and also to ask God if this was where he wanted us to start a new Anglican church from scratch.

Although we were stepping out in trust, the prospect of being a priest still scared me almost witless. I wrestled with a mixture of fear and excitement and sheer awe that God may actually be calling me to such a task. Our desire to learn all we could about church planting led Brittany to order *The Church Planter's Wife* one day. Much to our mutual surprise, it made her cry. By the time she finished it, she confessed that she also was second-guessing if this was truly the right fit for us, if this was our true calling. This gave me pause because it was important to me that Brittany was fully heard and involved in this mission. I did not want to move forward without her. I felt a responsibility to understand my wife's call, to listen to her.

To our relief, we were learning that *everyone* who plants a church gets overwhelmed. So, as our plans progressed, we chalked up our apprehension to a case of cold feet. We also learned that there is not one right way to start a church, but books like Rick Warren's *The Purpose Driven Church* and Timothy Keller's *Center Church* and *Church Planter Manual* helped us draw up our own road map of how to pray, strategize, raise funds, structure the early staff and volunteers, orchestrate the launch, and make the congregation grow. I taped a note on our fridge: "Commit your work to the LORD, and then your plans will be established" (Prov 16:3).

I could see it, but not yet; I could behold it, but not near. A parish would rise out of Minneapolis, rooted in Word and sacrament, her spire's gilded vane scratching heaven, her pipe organ roaring, and the perfume of her incense billowing through the narthex out into the streets. It would have just enough racial diversity to break the U.S. trend of Anglican churches consisting of wealthy, more educated white people. I was embarrassed by the yuppieness of the history of the Episcopal Church, as it contrasted with Baptist churches or even Catholic ones. For example, when the Anglican Christopher Dawson told his mother that he was converting to Roman Catholicism she replied: "It's not so much the doctrines that concern me; it's that now you'll be worshipping with the help!"[9] And still, however multicultural our parish would be, I secretly hoped that the core launch team would be college-educated artists and urban crawlers covered in tattoos and into liturgy, but also really into bands like Neutral Milk Hotel, Wilco, and Modest Mouse. The Sunday worship music would be at once traditional and cutting-edge, hymns sung to the pitch of Mumford & Sons, Bon Iver, or Belle & Sebastian. I would wear traditional vestments, but with Converse sneakers and torn jeans and would help spearhead mighty feats of social justice. I saw myself racing through Minneapolis on an old motorcycle, wearing tweed and my clerical collar, the wind in my hair and the Book of Common Prayer in my pocket, on my way to administer Last Rites to some poor hipster on the south side.

As we brainstormed and sought wise counsel, there was no shortage of Justwaiters.

"Just wait," someone would say. "Ninety percent of all church plants fall apart after just one year."

"Just wait," said another. "Church planting ruins your life."

"Haha," we said, and tried to put our best foot forward.

And as we grew in trust on this journey, perhaps God was also growing us. He was slowly preparing us for taking big risks for his sake. We were learning to put ourselves second to this mission. Reaching the lost, helping the baptized to grow in their faith, caring for the poor and the sick, living a life of sacrament. As we prayed and developed our strategy, God seemed to be honing the vision, providing focus. Blessed Columba Marmion's *Christ: The Ideal of the Priest*, especially, roused me to take action, no matter how unworthy I felt. And when I doubted my call, I remembered how insane it was to be a Christian in the first place: "We are children of God, and if children, then heirs, heirs of God and fellow heirs with Christ, provided we suffer with him in order that we may also be glorified with him" (Rom 8:16–17).

* * * * *

Chastened by what I was learning about the priesthood, and being generally nervous about preaching, I became particularly concerned about a priest's responsibility to teach "the faith which was once for all delivered" (Jude 1:3). The matter was more complicated than I had originally assumed. For although I believed the Church was apostolic, the very idea of a *teaching authority* still provoked misgivings. I granted that the Church is commissioned to bear authoritative witness to God's revelation in Christ, but I also felt that, in the end, people had the right to make up their own minds, even on matters of morality and religion. But would I someday preach with the authority of the Church, or would I merely be offering spiritual advice and moral suggestions? Could I really expect members of my congregation to surrender their personal opinions to the authority of my teaching, just as I tried to surrender my teaching to the authority of the Church, or would everyone have a right to his opinion?

It didn't add up. I took to heart the Vincentian Canon, and took care to hold only "that which has been believed everywhere, always and by all" (however small the resulting body of teaching would be). At the same time, however, I believed people had a right to their own opinion, even if that opinion were contrary to Scripture and Church teaching.

But when the Ethiopian eunuch was asked by the deacon Philip, "Do you understand what you are reading?" he didn't reply, "Does it matter? I have a right to my own opinion!" Instead, he replied, "How can I, unless some one guides me?" (Acts 8:30–31). Perhaps in establishing the "magisterium" Christ was responding to a real human need? People cannot discover God's revelation by their unaided powers of reason and observation. Even the most learned of scholars disagree about matters of faith!

No, I could see that I had to change my mind: perhaps Christians didn't have a right to their own opinions, even if they had read the Bible with the help of scholars. The faith must be taught by people authorized by Christ himself to teach what God deemed important to reveal in the first place. Jesus conferred on his apostles and their successors the authority to teach doctrine in his name so that God's revelation would not get confused with human speculation. "He who hears you hears me, and he who rejects you rejects me, and he who rejects me rejects him who sent me " (Lk 10:16). Jesus promised to remain present with those in apostolic succession to the end of time, sending his Holy Spirit to lead them into "all truth" (Jn 16:13). And it hit me with an unexpected force: when it comes to matters of faith and morals, Christians do not have a right to their own personal opinions.

Saint Paul did not mince words: we must "destroy arguments and every proud obstacle to the knowledge of God, and take every thought captive to obey Christ" (2 Cor 10:5). We must have the "mind of Christ" (1 Cor 2:16). The Christian faith was not a collection of personal views but the very revelation of God. The apostolic ministry's teaching authority called for a free, internal assent without which the "believer" excludes oneself from full participation in the Church. I began to wonder if the baptized faithful *must* profess the same body of revealed truth as expressed in creeds and dogmas. The fact of the matter was no one will get to bring his personal opinions with him into heaven, least of all me.

In view of heaven, I asked: What is a "right"? If Jesus was my Creator and King, then it seemed that I had a right only to do that which is pleasing to God. Just because I *could* steal didn't mean that I had the "right" to steal, because theft is forbidden by God. Jesus is King of the universe, and therefore I could not claim a "right" to choose what is evil or false, but rather only that which is good and true. And to insist I had a right to my own opinion seemed to imitate Lucifer's *Non serviam*, "I will not serve." It seemed selfish, almost idolatrous.

The teaching authority of the apostolic Church made sense, but it still made me uncomfortable. It was one thing for me to submit to the authority of Christ's Church, but it was quite another to expect my congregation to do the same. Clearly the bishop (in whose ministry my potential priesthood would participate) was in the uncomfortable position of reminding the flock that they do not get to decide what reality is. His apostolic office demands that he not teach sentiment and speculation, but proclaim with *the authority of Christ* that which is necessary for salvation. Monsignor Robert Hugh Benson put it this way:

> It is only a dead religion to which written records are sufficient.... The Teaching Church must know her own mind with regard to the treasure committed to her care, and supremely on those points on which the salvation of her children depends. She may be undecided and permit divergent views on purely speculative points ... but in things that directly and practically affect souls—with regard to the fact of grace, its channels, the

things necessary for salvation, and the rest—she must not only know her
mind, but must be constantly declaring it, and no less constantly silencing
those who would obscure or misinterpret it.[10]

In other words, the Church may permit divergent views on purely
speculative points, but when it comes to the means of grace, the
things necessary for salvation, "the way", she must be certain.

I was reminded that when Jesus ascended into heaven he did not
leave behind a Bible so that every man could fend for himself. He
left behind a Church, and the Bible is the Church's book. But how
is the Church to proclaim without confusion what is necessary for
salvation, if she does not "have unity of spirit" (1 Pet 3:8)? And how
is she to speak with the unerring and articulate authority of Christ to
every generation, if she isn't even identifiable, with a visible hierarchy and unity?

What must I do to be saved? As I came better to appreciate the
mission of the apostolic ministry and the sacred priesthood, I came to
the sobering conclusion that every sermon needed to come back
to this one question. There was no short list, no "one thing" to get
off the hook. All Christians have to give God *everything*. And clearly
part of that "everything" included repenting of my private opinions
and submitting to the authority of the bishops in the apostolic succession of Christ. And if I was going to be a priest, I would have to
swear obedience to the bishop "as to the Lord himself".[11] This was
the only way to make sure that what I preached was not just my brilliant speculations but in fact the Gospel.

I saw then that my long-held theory of "pneumatic unity" did
not allow for many sects to go their separate ways claiming self-
contradictory truths and still be "one in Christ"; to admit pneumatic
unity does not excuse schism or heresy, but rather exposes the gravity
of these sins, for they profane the Mystical Body of Christ.

Jesus prayed that his Church would be *one* and provided every
means to ensure that it would stay one, "consecrated in truth" (Jn
17:19). Simply to leave the apostolic Church and start another one—
even if I took my congregation with me, even if I were a bishop
and I took my whole diocese with me—would be *diabolic* ("to tear
apart", "to scatter"). Jesus was clear: "If he refuses to listen even to the
Church, let him be to you as a Gentile and a tax collector" (Mt 18:17).

That very week my parish priest called me from Minneapolis.

"Tyler, I'm sorry to say that our diocese has left AMiA," he said.[12]

"Didn't we just leave TEC?"[13] I asked.

"Yes, and now we're leaving AMiA—too many disagreements," my priest said. "I know this is unfortunate, but we won't have a bishop for a while."

"How can we not have a bishop?" I asked, alarmed.

"We're looking for a new one," my priest assured me. "But in the meantime, as you pursue postulancy, you'll need to find another bishop."

And so it came to pass that as the summer of 2012 diminished, with a prayer for unity on my lips and gloomy thoughts for company, I went bishop shopping. Although I would not miss the insouciant care of the AMiA bishop who had liked my long hair, the task of finding and convincing another bishop to take me under his wing not only felt daunting but perhaps a little too clever. Pursuing Holy Orders in Anglicanism suddenly felt like a chess move whereby one takes the bishop but loses the match several moves later.

Meanwhile, Brittany and I were settling into the rhythms of married life. We listened to *The Chronicles of Narnia* on tape while drinking iced tea. We hiked the kettles and moraines of the surrounding countryside. We walked to chapel hand in hand, careful to avoid eye contact with the Justwaiters. Every Tuesday night we rubbed elbows with bikers at Stolley's Hogg Alley, a hole-in-the-wall bar known for its hot wings. Slowly, our new home was taking on a definite shape. We spied a ragged Victorian couch at a thrift store and used it to furnish our living room, and eventually addressed our book problem. Books seemed to be everywhere and always in the way. After countless hours of deliberation and measuring and a brief reconnaissance of the various markets, we packed a Stanley thermos and peanut butter and jelly sandwiches and made a holy pilgrimage to Ikea in order to procure a dozen very tall, very sturdy bookshelves. And on the night before classes began, books neatly shelved, couch in place, a few candles burning, we sprawled on the floor of our living room. We turned off the air conditioning and opened the windows so that we could listen to the bullfrogs lulling in the brown heat of August.

"Why are you always wearing that?" Brittany said, pointing to my scapular.

"It reminds me to pray," I shrugged.

"But you wear it *all the time*," Brittany said. "Even in the shower."

"I pray in the shower?" I lied.

"No, seriously," Brittany said. "You're probably the only Protestant who wears a scapular."

"I'm Catholic," I said.

"You know what I mean," Brittany sighed.

I was very sorry to admit it, but I did.

God Is an Artist

Never say, "What great things the saints do!"
but, "What great things God does in his saints!"

—Saint Philip Neri[1]

Christ loved the Church and gave himself up for her,
that he might sanctify her,
having cleansed her by the washing of water with the word,
that he might present the Church to himself in splendor,
without spot or wrinkle or any such thing,
that she might be holy and without blemish.

—Ephesians 5:25–27

Not long after classes picked up again, I received a formal invitation stating that the Society of Mary would be delighted if Brittany and I would attend their next meeting, to be held the following Friday after Evensong. Normally I would have thrown the invitation in the trash. Devotion to the saints was idolatry, and the reverence Catholics had for Mary was downright shameful. But when Brittany saw the beautiful embossed image of our Lady, she hung the invitation on the fridge. I still wore the brown scapular and remembered that Mary was my mother in trust, and I was curious.

When we made tacos that night I couldn't stop staring at the Blessed Virgin on the fridge.

"Why don't I pray to the saints?" I asked.

"How should I know?" Brittany sighed, putting down her knife and wiping her eyes. I washed my hands and took the knife from her.

"But should I talk to them, 'seek Mary's intercession', and all that?" I said, busying myself with the onions. A breeze blew in through the open window.

"I suppose that depends," Brittany said, after a moment. "Why do you pray in the first place?"

"Because God listens," I said. "Prayer makes a difference."

"Why?"

I dropped the onions into the skillet before speaking. "Because God loves to bless his people," I said. "And he especially loves to do it in answer to prayer. He wants us to join him in his mission. You know all this."

"By what principle, then, would the saints in heaven be left out?"

"That's what I mean," I said, brightening. "What if they're not left out?"

"So pray to the saints," Brittany said. "If you would ask me to pray for you, why wouldn't you ask Mary to pray for you?"

"Because," I said, "Christ is our only mediator. Why would I talk to a human when I could talk directly to God?"

"You're talking to me."

"That's different."

Brittany sighed, and began cutting the tomatoes. "Look, I don't know. Maybe praying to the saints isn't a game of telephone." She took an onion out of the skillet and nibbled it. "Maybe the living and the dead can talk to each other because they are together in Christ."

"By his light we see light," I said, deep in thought.

"Right," Brittany said, "like the way this conversation is happening in this kitchen: maybe all prayer happens *in* the Holy Spirit?"

At this, we both fell silent.

That night I lay awake in my pajamas wondering why I had always thought the saints were "asleep". It was a remarkable feature of my imagination that I had simply assumed, without any substantial argument, that when Christians died they remained unconscious until the resurrection of the body at the end of time—and therefore they did not intercede for us. I assumed that death put the communion of saints on hold, temporarily, and I had erected a large and increasingly rational-looking edifice of theological reconstruction on this assumption. But I was beginning to suspect that it was all wrong. Even atheists believe the dead are dead. Shouldn't Christians be different?

I knew that my "sleeping saints" theory was contrary to tradition, but was it also missing in Scripture? If anything, the Bible is clear that when a Christian dies, his life is changed, not ended. Our bodies may die, but our souls live on in Christ. In a sense, the faithful departed are more alive than we are. So why did I act as if they didn't exist? In the words of C. S. Lewis, "Christians never say goodbye!"[2]

* * * * *

The headquarters of the Society of Mary was, of course, the Bethlehem altar in the Chapel of Saint Mary the Virgin, but this was not the usual 7 A.M. Tuesday meeting for (as they put it) the recitation of the Most Holy Rosary. This was a dinner party, and the host, a student named Justin, had hinted that we dress up.

"I'm delighted you're here." Justin greeted us with a smile and ushered us in.

We slipped out of our shoes and looked around. The small apartment was crowded with rosy-cheeked children, students and spouses, and the aroma of baking bread filled the air. Candles flickered on a table that was far too small to seat even half the crowd, casting a warm glow on a wall of bookshelves cluttered with old missals and museum-quality statuary. Every square inch of the apartment seemed to be covered with tattered prayer cards, ancient thuribles, miniature triptychs, and an impressive collection of Tridentine-looking candlesticks and altar crucifixes.

"Where did you get all of this?" I said in quiet awe.

"Paris, mostly," said Justin. "It breaks my heart that such holy things were even for sale."

Justin excused himself, and very quickly we found ourselves settled into the room, holding glasses of wine. Justin's voice rose above the hubbub.

"Friends, dinner is ready. Let's pray."

Guests crossed themselves and joined in as Justin prayed: "Bless us, O Lord, and these thy gifts, which we are about to receive from thy bounty, through Christ our Lord. Amen."

I was just beginning to cross myself, but everyone kept praying: "And may the souls of the faithful departed, through the mercy of God, rest in peace. Amen."

"Amen," I said, and crossed myself. But we were not done praying.

"Lord, have mercy," said Justin.

"Christ, have mercy," said everyone.

"Holy Trinity, one God."

"Have mercy upon us."

"Mary, most holy."

"Pray for us."

"Holy Mother of God."

"Pray for us."

I glanced sideways at Brittany.

"Holy Virgin of virgins," continued Justin.

"Pray for us," said everyone.

Finally, the litany concluded. Soon everyone had bowls of soup and chunks of homemade bread and was nestled into chairs or on the living-room floor. The laughter of children playing in the other room floated through the walls. The chairman opened the meeting.

"The first matter to address is the calendar," began Alex, a postulant for Holy Orders. "Since we don't have enough time to plan an event for the Nativity of our Blessed Virgin, the motion that I propose to the Society is that we host an autumn procession and celebration in honor of Our Lady of the Rosary on October 7."

A murmur of approval went around the room.

"The second matter," continued Alex, "concerns the advisability of announcing our Tuesday morning recitation of the Most Holy Rosary."

A few students nodded in understanding.

"There has been yet another complaint that our weekly invitation is offensive to some, and the dean has asked if it is necessary to speak of our devotions during campus chapter meetings. We seem to go through this every year. To be honest, I think the only appropriate response is to continue to invite students to join us. To be silent out of respect for a difference in beliefs would not, in the end, be truly respectful."

Applause accompanied by a tinkling of spoons on teacups greeted the chairman's words.

"With that said," Alex continued, holding up his hand, "I'm well aware of the teasing and insults against the Society and even against the Blessed Mother, but I want to encourage you always to respond in charity."

More applause.

"The third and final matter to be addressed is the question of whether Mary was preserved from the stain of original sin. Justin has kindly accepted our invitation to share his presentation, titled ..." He looked at Justin.

"Mary and the Grinch," Justin said.

The room grew still and Justin stood to speak, shuffling his notes. "Again, thank you for allowing me to host this year's first meeting," he said. His voice was clear and bright. "The question I'd like to pose to you tonight is, Was Christmas necessary? In order to save us, did God *have* to become a human being? If sin had not entered the picture, would the Son have become incarnate anyway? According to tradition, the answer is yes. When God made the universe, he intended from the very beginning to become a part of his creation. The Creator planned on becoming created. One could even say God made humanity *in order to become human.*"

Sitting on the living-room floor, Brittany settled into my arms. It was more than Justin's almost old-fashioned hospitality, the delicious soup, or the honest joy of the Society—I couldn't quite name it, but I knew I was glad I had come.

"The Incarnation was God's plan all along," Justin continued. "And that's why Adam *was a pattern of the one to come* and Jesus is the *Last Adam*," said Justin. "The creation story was the beginning of Christmas."

I couldn't help but listen.

"But every Christmas has a Grinch," Justin said. "In a sense, Christmas is *why* Lucifer rebelled against God. When God announced his plan to the angels, just the thought of Christmas turned Lucifer green. It's one thing to bow to the Creator, but for the Creator to become a creature—that was entirely different! So the Grinch tried to steal Christmas, and he attacked the best of God's creation, his masterpiece, *Eve*."

I felt a shiver, a kind of tingling.

"Horribly, Eve was tricked by the serpent. And for a moment, it looked like the Grinch might have stolen Christmas ... but God wouldn't let him. Genesis 3:15 is the first announcement of the Gospel: 'And I will put enmity between you and the woman, and between your offspring and hers; he will crush your head, and you will strike his heel.'"

The room was very quiet.

"The Virgin Mary is *the* woman," Justin said, leaning in. "We read in Revelation 12 that she was the one who gave birth to the 'man-child' in this great battle against the serpent. Revelation depicts Mary as a queen crowned with stars, seated, as all Christians will be someday, higher even than the angels. And this is why Satan rebelled: he didn't want to bow to Christians as they 'judge angels', to be a second-class creation to the Immaculata! She is in the Eastern hymn, 'higher than the Cherubim, more glorious than the Seraphim.' "

Barnacles! I couldn't help but inwardly gasp. This was an unexpected twist in the story. Mary was not "immaculate"!

"Now, we all know that Mary was preserved from the stain of original sin by virtue of the merits of the Cross," Justin continued. "As the ark and the furniture of the tabernacle were *purified* so as to endure the all-holy presence of God, Mary was purified so that she could survive the eternal Son taking his human nature from her person, dwelling in her womb, and becoming man. She was made clean so that she could become one with God."

I sighed with dismay, perhaps louder than necessary, and everyone looked at me. Justin smiled affectionately, gesturing for me to speak.

I hesitated. "The Bible clearly says that *all* have sinned and fallen short. Why is Mary an exception?" I looked around, worried that I had spoken out of turn and was relieved to see everyone smiling patiently at me.

"If I may," Alex cleared his throat. "When my daughter was born *everyone* waited outside—everyone *except* my wife. She was inside giving birth to our daughter. Saint Paul meant it when he said that '*all* have sinned', but there was an exception, a New Eve whose body and soul cooperated with the Holy Spirit to produce the New Adam."

I raised my eyebrows.

"The Incarnation is the climax of creation, the reason why God made the world in the first place—and his new creation is *immaculate*. God is an artist and Mary is his magnum opus."

"But the Immaculate Conception is unbiblical," I objected.

"Not unbiblical," Alex mused, "just not explicit."

"Think of it this way," Justin said. "God had a plan of humanity *before* he made us, and from the beginning that plan included the Blessed Virgin Mary. We were destined to become one with God,

but sadly many of us will not fulfil that hope. Sin has blurred the original blueprint. Our music doesn't line up with the score, so to speak."

I nodded benignly.

"But what if there was someone who played the score God wrote
in the beginning?" Justin asked. "What if there was a creature with
whom the Creator could become *one*, someone through whom God
could see his original plan for creation become a reality? What if that
someone is the Blessed Virgin Mary?"

I pursed my lips. Everything they said made sense, but it disturbed
me.

"What I mean to say is," Justin continued, "God had Mary in mind
from the start. Before he made the world God knew that in order to
become a Son of Adam he needed a Daughter of Eve. Christmas is
the new creation story and Mary is the New Eve."

Alex served more wine, and Justin continued his presentation, sharing with us how Eve believed the serpent and gave birth to sin but
Mary believed Gabriel and gave birth to salvation. As Eve was the
"mother of all living", Mary is the Mother of "the way, the truth,
and the life". The Church traces its reality back to the moment when
the Word took flesh in Mary's womb. As the Mother of Christ, Mary
is also the Mother of the Church, which is Christ's Body, the living
organism of Christ's glorified human nature. By our Baptism, we have
been incorporated into the human nature of her Son, Jesus. And one
of the best ways to praise Jesus is to venerate the work of his hands—
especially his own Mother. Christ is redemptor, not co-redemptor;
Mary is co-redemptrix, not redemptrix. What Mary is we are to
become: God's co-workers, his co-redeemers. And by the end of it
I was surprised at how clean, almost elegant, the whole theory was.

Brittany and I walked back to our apartment in the September
dusk.

"I like them," Brittany said, squeezing my hand. "A lot."

"Me too," I said, the warmth of the candlelight conversation and
the Society's impeccable manners lingering with me.

"I think I believe," Brittany said.

"Believe what?"

"The Immaculate Conception, the perpetual virginity, the Mother
of the Church, the Queen of the Universe, all of it," Brittany said.
"It's biblical."

"Biblical?" I peered down at her, dumbfounded.

She poked me in the ribs. "You just have baggage."

"Baggage?"

"Confirmation bias is a real thing, dear," Brittany sighed. "You received a Protestant version of Christianity first, so it's understandable that you find anything Catholic suspicious."

"Don't psycho-analyze me."

"I'm just saying you have baggage," Brittany said. "I wasn't raised in a Baptist home. In just two short years I went from being a pro-choice LGBT activist and Derrida-thumping skeptic to a Christian convert who married an Anglo-Catholic seminarian."

"And I'm the one with baggage?" I said, opening the door to our apartment.

"Yes," she laughed. "You get so excited about typology and the Fathers and the communion of saints, and yet you can't admit this one obvious thing."

"This one obvious thing being nineteenth-century papal inventions about a woman in Nazareth?" I said, looking at my wife in dismay.

"Baggage," Brittany shrugged, shoving me through the front door. "Like I said, you guys can have the apostles; I've got the Virgin Mary!"

* * * * *

The next morning, I went on a hike at a nearby state park, Lapham Peak. I needed to clear my head. The forest floor was dusky, mysterious, and wet, and the trail was fringed with a lace of shadows from the trees high above. I paused to take in the creaking of the pines, the whistle of the wind in the boughs, and the azure sky spotted with heaps of white cloud overhead. Ever since my childhood, I had seen God in the beauty of the natural world. I praised him in his creation. The air was sweet with incense of the unseen and I breathed it in with a whisper: "I love you, Lord!"

And yet I couldn't stop thinking about Mary and the saints. Like a master artist, God made the world and "saw that it was good" (Gen 1:10, 12, 18, 21, 25). When he made Adam and Eve, in admiration he "saw everything that he had made, and behold, it was *very* good!" (Gen 1:31). I was struck by the idea that the best thing God made was not the sky or a forest but people, men and women—and he praised them! And I remembered Justin's idea that God is an artist and Mary is his masterpiece. Maybe he had a point. After all, Mary was the beginning of the Church and the Church is Christ's *new creation*, " 'clothed with fine linen, bright and pure'—for the fine linen is the righteous deeds of the saints" (Rev 19:8). Was it right to *venerate* (to love and respect) the saints?

As I hiked the trails of Lapham Peak, I figured that if you love an artist, you praise his art. To look up at the Sistine Chapel and say, "This is beautiful!" is just another way of saying, "Michelangelo is amazing!" If I loved God in the beauty of the natural world, why wouldn't I love him in the beauty of his saints? I wasn't a superstitious man, but I couldn't help sensing a kind of love—however simple, clumsy, or domestic—in the way Catholics *adored* the saints.

Love? The thought of *loving* the saints was almost frightening. Could I love the saints, especially the Blessed Virgin, and love God at the same time? Sighing, I tried to push these thoughts out of my mind. The trail came to Brittany's favorite spot, where the forest opened to a meadow. I remembered how we had spread a blanket there and listened to the crickets in the fragrant breath of sun-warmed grasses the color of ripe wheat. Oh, how I loved her.

And then it dawned on me: loving people *less* would not help me love God *more*. No husband in his right mind ever said he needed to love his wife less so that he could love God more. Love doesn't work that way. The first and second commandments are not in competition: the more we love God, the more we love our neighbor; the more we rightly love our neighbor, the more we love God. What we do to people we do to him (Mt 25:40). Saint John says that if a man claims to love God but does not love his neighbor, he is a liar (1 Jn 4:20). Clearly, love of God and love of people went hand in hand. So why had I thought that in order to love God *more* I needed to love the saints *less*?

According to C. S. Lewis, the whole philosophy of hell rests on the axiom that you cannot love two things at the same time.[3] You cannot love yourself and someone else, for example. Yet the triune God aims at what seems to be a contradiction: the communion of saints. The peculiar idiosyncrasy of Christianity is that things are to be many, yet somehow also one. "The good of one self is to be the good of another," Lewis wrote in *The Screwtape Letters*. "This impossibility [God] calls *love*."[4]

Over seventeen miles of trails loop around Lapham Peak's center hill, on top of which is built a high wooden observation tower that overlooks the entire county. I climbed the wooden steps, my head turning in a spiral of meditations. And as I looked out over southeastern Wisconsin, I was able to admit that the "cult of the saints" did not entirely repel me. God is an artist and the saints are his masterpiece—but people aren't lifeless mountains or paintings on a ceiling. The Church is the family of God. If I loved God, wouldn't I love his family?

I had always thought that praying to Mary was, at best, a waste of time. Why would Mary listen to our prayers? Surely in heaven the saints are so busy loving God they don't notice anyone else— certainly not listening to the prayers of people on earth! But *even in heaven, the second is like unto it.* Jesus loves the Father with all his heart *and* he loves his neighbor as himself. And if the baptized faithful who have passed through death are *alive* in Christ, wouldn't they do what Christ does? Wouldn't they join the Son in bringing glory to the Father *and* interceding for man? In Revelation, John saw the saints in heaven offering to God the prayers of the saints on earth (5:8; cf. 6:9–10). The righteous in heaven can and do intercede for us, and "the prayer of a righteous man has great power in its effects" (Jas 5:16).

Even in heaven we will have neighbors—but then we will see them for who they really are. As C. S. Lewis put it:

> It is a serious thing to live in a society of possible gods and goddesses, to remember that the dullest most uninteresting person you talk to may one day be a creature which, if you saw it now, you would be strongly tempted to worship.... You have never talked to a mere mortal.... It is immortals whom we joke with, work with, marry, snub, and exploit— immortal horrors or everlasting splendors.[5]

In other words, God is an artist, and the saints are his "workmanship" (Eph 2:10). One of the best ways to make much of God is to make much of his new creation—those saints in whom God has glorified himself, especially Mary. God himself has exalted her above all his other creatures because she is *the* woman, the bearer of the Word incarnate.

I remembered the liturgy from our wedding day. "With this ring I thee wed," goes the marriage rite, "with my body I thee worship." To *worship* is to ascribe worth. Why was it okay for me to "worship" Brittany but not to "worship" those saints in whom God has glorified himself?

Then and there, on the high deck of the observation tower, I believed in the communion of saints. I would like to say the clouds parted, the sun shone, and little cherubs and saints with halos circled above my head. Maybe they did. All I remember is that the world cohered, and I couldn't wait to get back home to my wife.

Mathematicians and physicists talk about the "elegance" of a theory. The beauty of the form, the inner consistency, the harmony—the idea is convincing, but also beautiful. For a theory to be "elegant" it must not only serve some utility, but strike a chord, complete what would otherwise be an incomplete gestalt.

From childhood, my whole world had been charged with the grandeur of God—the sunsets proclaimed his glory, the angels declared his praise, the Kingdom of God was at hand, and even the stars aligned to ring in the first Christmas in Bethlehem. But my version of the story had been an incomplete gestalt. There remained a gaping hole in the tapestry, a missing piece without which the story could never be complete: the saints, Mary, the company of heaven, and the wedding of heaven and earth.

The *elegance* of what Saint Edith Stein called "the science of the saints"[6] is the universal story of Jesus and the Church. Heaven and earth are getting married, and everything about being human was meant to tell this story. From creation to consummation, *this* was the story of the universe: in Christ, God and man have met together, heaven and earth have kissed, and that which God has joined, let no one put asunder.

* * * * *

Around this time, I resolved to grow my beard as long as I possibly could. My goal was to look as Eastern Orthodox as possible, and growing a large fluffy beard became a symbol of the kind of faith I wanted: gnarly and unclipped, steeped in the hairy lore of Church history, in love with the saints. Like the bearded patriarch of the Bible, I wanted yet again to step out in faith not knowing wither. There was much I did not understand, and I still had a lot to learn. But to understand you must first believe. *Credo ut intelligam.* All I knew was that I needed to follow the example of Mary, who reversed the disobedience of the first Eve, and step out in trust.

What was the truth about Mary? I had to confess my ignorance on the matter. I went racing back through the Bible with new commentaries, Catholic commentaries, my mind humming with questions. I ordered more books, books with Marian-blue covers and titles like *Redeemer in the Womb, All Generations Shall Call Me Blessed,* or *Mother of Christ, Mother of the Church,* and Brittany reminded me about the budget. I discovered the typology of Mary as the Ark of the Covenant, as the New Eve, as the Mother of the Church, and the experience was not unlike what it must feel like to be ripped from Plato's cave of shadows and thrown into the light of day.

In the end, I decided to join the Society of Mary. I still had questions, but I was hungry.

Early in the morning, while mists still cloaked the surrounding fields, I attended the recitation of the Most Holy Rosary. At first, I fidgeted through the repetitious prayers. But the Rosary was so *biblical,* and the Kingdom of God was so much bigger, and after a few weeks I was surprised to find my heart singing Mary's praises. When you love an artist, how can you not praise the work of his hands?

Over time, I grew more aware of the saints' presence. They were more present to God than I was, and I felt connected to them in a real and vital way. My prayers became a conversation that included them. I asked the Blessed Virgin to assist me by her powerful intercession and obtain for me all spiritual blessings from Jesus. I sought the intercession of Saint Joseph, patron of the Church, as I pursued Holy Orders. I even fled to Saint Anthony when I lost my Greek homework. Acknowledging the three states of the Church (militant, suffering, triumphant), the Kingdom of God seemed to pulse with life. The saints, "so great a cloud of witnesses" (Heb 12:1), were cheering me on as I stumbled after Jesus, through my share in his Cross.

Meanwhile, I joined a confraternity on campus that existed to help students become better preachers. For the next two years, students and professors would suffer through my homilies, offering criticism and encouragement as I perfected the craft of preaching. I also partnered with a fellow seminarian, Gabriel, in his prison ministry. Every Friday afternoon we drove two and a half hours through beautiful countryside to a medium-security correctional institution so that we could lead a Bible study for thirty minutes before turning around and driving two and a half hours back. I found the experience of going through security, being escorted to the basement of the prison chapel, and then left to manage twenty inmates with disparate views about the Scriptures so alarming I almost quit. But the men were so thoughtful and sincere, and so grateful that Gabe and I took the time to open up the Bible with them, that I couldn't bring myself to give it up.

Prison ministry forced me to address *sainthood* from another, less rosy perspective. Moral questions are often left unanswered in everyday conversation by dividing the population into good people and bad people, where bad people go to prison. But every Friday afternoon I was surrounded by inmates who claimed to be Christians and were "basically good people". Being a "good person" was obviously not good enough. We were all sinners in desperate need of God's mercy—yet in Jesus, we were also somehow saints.

"It doesn't add up," I said, driving home from the prison one afternoon. "How can you be born again and then sin so bad you get sent to prison?"

"That's why prison ministry is so refreshing," Gabriel said. "Most of us can convince others, even ourselves, that we're basically good Christians. But in prison, no one's fooled. You have to drop the act."

"It's too bad none of them are Anglican," I said. "Wouldn't it be great if these men could receive the Sacrament of Reconciliation?"

"The priest who runs the Catholic Bible study offers Confession and Mass," Gabriel explained. "But we lead the Protestant Bible study."

"But we're more Catholic than the Catholics!" I said. "Why can't we have Confession?"

"Would anyone go?" Gabriel asked.

I sighed, and looked out the window, my thoughts turning back to sainthood. Prison ministry brought into focus the scandal of the Gospel. The fact of the matter is, only God is a saint. In the Gloria, we sing to God: "You alone are the holy one!" In Latin, *Tu solus sanctus,* this could read: "You alone are the saint!" In the Old Testament, the people of Israel were "set apart" for God and therefore considered *kodesh*, holy. But no individual person was described as "holy" because holiness was God's essence. God alone is a "saint", yet Saint Paul does not hesitate to apply the term "saint" (ἅγιος) to man. Why? Because Jesus, "the Holy One of God" (Jn 6:69), *shares* his holiness. Christians are "saints *in Christ*" (Phil 1:1). The eternal Son of God became the Son of Man so that we could become "sons of God" (Lk 20:36; Rom 8:19; Gal 3:26). Because God shared our human nature, we share his divine nature (2 Pet 1:4). What Jesus is by nature, we are by grace, "children of God, and if children, then heirs, heirs of God and fellow heirs with Christ" (Rom 8:16–17). Jesus doesn't just save us *from* sin; he saves us *for* sainthood.

Does this mean we can go on sinning? Not at all. The stakes are even higher now because sin contradicts our new life in Christ. We are in him, and he is in us. We have been made a "temple of the Holy Spirit" (1 Cor 6:19). If a saint were to sin, he would quite literally be *desecrating* God's temple. Holiness is shared, but it must be lived. We must not only be "born again" (cf. Jn 3:3) into Jesus, but we must "grow up" into the full stature of Christ (cf. Eph 4:13).

Michelangelo's writhing, unfinished statues of slaves, struggling in their prisons of stone, are a picture of the Christian life; broken and banished from Eden yet baptized and brought back into the family of God, we are an unfinished product. But our Lord is making all things new; he is making saints.

Suffice it to say, prison ministry helped me sort out my mixed feelings about purgatory. I could see quite clearly why the Church has always taught that before the baptized faithful can enter the all-holy presence of God in heaven, souls must undergo some kind of purification. Unlike those "saints in light" (Col 1:12) who have passed through death and "see [God] as he is", the pilgrim Church is not yet perfected (1 Jn 3:2). "For now we see in a mirror dimly, but then face to face" (1 Cor 13:12). The saints on earth need a chance to wash up before we could join the "saints in light" and enter the throne room of the God who "dwells in unapproachable light" (1 Tim 6:16). We must be purified like gold through a fire (1 Cor 3:15).

For the next two years, Gabriel and I led the prison Bible study, talking and praying and planning our sessions during the long drives.

The task was difficult. The men spoke differently, thought differently, prayed and even argued differently. The prison ministry challenged me to take all that I was learning in seminary and to distill it into simple, practical "takeaways". Huddled in a circle in the basement of the prison's chapel, everyone reading a different translation of the Bible, everyone coming to the Scripture with a different story, I learned to love Christ in my neighbor. God had brought us into one another's lives not only so that I could pray for them, but also so that they could pray for me. I needed their prayers. Even more, I needed the prayers of the saints "in light". They were a welcome addition to the covenant family I already had, and I could no longer ignore them. We were all in this together. "For we are God's fellow workers; you are God's field, God's building" (1 Cor 3:9).

* * * * *

It has been said that the ceiling of the Sistine Chapel is "an artistic vision without precedent". But before 1980 you might have been disappointed to find the pictures so discolored after years of rising candle smoke that they appeared to be almost monochrome. When at last the filter of grime was removed and the ceiling restored, the pictures came alive with color—sky blue, apple green, vivid yellow, and soft pink against a warm background of pearl gray. People always knew Michelangelo was amazing, but now they were even more impressed. For me, discovering the cult of the saints had a similar effect. I always knew that God was amazing, but when the misconceptions about Mary and the saints were finally cleared away, I was even more impressed.

There was something about the way things fit together, a kind of music. The way Mary and the saints all dovetailed in Christ, the way they brought glory to the Father in the loving bond of the Holy Spirit, was not only right, but elegant. The edges of where earth touched eternity, like the edges of clouds, seemed to disappear. The communion of saints was more than mood lighting. We all depend on one another, quite literally, for dear life. As Saint Paul said, "The eye cannot say to the hand, 'I have no need of you'" (1 Cor 12:21).

My beard grew. Every week began with seeking Mary's intercession and ended with seeking the intercession of my fellow Christian brothers in prison. We often had the Society over to our home. We drank wine and installed ribbons into our Bibles. We hosted a "shower of roses" tea party for the feast of Saint Thérèse, and made crepes for the feast of Saint Bernadette. We listened to the Cistercian Monks of Stift Heiligenkreuz's *Chant*, Bach's *Christmas Oratorio*, and the Benedictines of Mary Queen of Apostles' *Angels and Saints at Ephesus*. We had readings from J. R. R. Tolkien and Maximilian Kolbe and Saint Louis de Montfort. They were warm, laughter-filled days, days of peace under Marian-blue skies. The dividing line between now and eternity became smeared. Death was not the end but the beginning. For Christ has made saving earth the business of heaven.

Candles among Gunpowder

Why do you call me, "Lord, Lord," and not do what I tell you?

—Jesus (Lk 6:46)

What is truth?

—Pontius Pilate (Jn 18:38)

Imagine standing before an enormous mountain. Between you and the summit stands not only weeks of hard climbing, but also innumerable dangers—dehydration, poisonous berries, sudden drop-offs, forests as dark as Mirkwood, wild bears and snakes, and high above, a fog thicker than wood smoke. To survive the journey, you'll need to pack for all kinds of weather—hot afternoons, biting night winds, freezing rains; but more than appropriate gear, you need a map. Thankfully, there are thousands. But as you plan your route, you can't make sense of the tangle of trails. It's nearly impossible to retrace an identifiable route, and what's worse is that the maps actually contradict one another. One map marks a path as reliable, another posts a warning, "Do Not Enter: Bear Cave Ahead". One calls a route "Old Reliable", and another calls it "Road to Hell". The travel guides are even worse. Some say a certain weed is a valuable source of energy, and others say it's poisonous. Some recommend visiting the old inn, and others say it is run by cannibals. And then one particularly inviting brochure claims that the way up the mountain is actually easy and so wide it's impossible to miss; everyone makes it to the summit. What would you do?

You are standing on the brink of what the earliest Christians called "the Way" (Acts 9:2). But what first looked like a fun climbing adventure has changed into something else—something more like *survival*. It was at first comforting that everyone seemed to agree that Jesus is "the way". He said himself, "I am *the way*, and the truth, and the life; no one comes to the Father, but by me" (Jn 14:6). But Jesus also said: "The gate is narrow and the way is hard, that leads to life, and those who find it are few" (Mt 7:14), and, "Not everyone who says to me, 'Lord, Lord,' shall enter the kingdom of heaven, but he who does the will of my Father who is in heaven" (Mt 7:21). This raises the question, How can we *do* the will of the Father if we do not *know* what his will is? How can you climb the mountain if you do not know the way? It's one thing to step out into the black, to risk climbing a foreign face of rock, or to enter a complicated labyrinth of paths knowing that you are retracing a tested, trustworthy route of ascent—it's quite another simply to guess and wish for the best!

I was at a crossroads. I was finally pulling out all the self-contradictory maps and travel guides to "the way", the Christian life, and wanting to know once and for all which one was trustworthy. When I left Nashotah House at the conclusion of my first year, I had believed in sleeping saints and women priests. I had contended that Christians had "freedom of conscience" when it came to moral issues, and a "right to their own opinion" when it came to dogma. I protested anything having to do with Mary and found the idea of purgatory intolerable. Even more, having never solemnly sworn to be true to one woman forever, forsaking all others, I couldn't help but to see the world through the eyes of a bachelor. So you can imagine just a few months into the fall semester of my second year—fingering the beads of a rosary and praying for the holy souls in purgatory, convinced that only pagan religions had priestesses and that Christians did not have a right to their own opinions about matters of faith and morals—my classmates and professors did not recognize the strange new creature in their midst.

"But the Holy Spirit is doing a new thing," Sven said one night in the pub, shocked that I had gone to the dark side.

"He did a new thing in Christ two thousand years ago," I said.

"But the Church does not have the authority to—"

"It's not the priesthood that concerns me," said Guy. "What I want to know is, why do you suddenly believe in praying to dead people?"

"For the Nicene Fathers, the communion of saints included those on earth *and* in heaven."

"Want to know what the Fathers *didn't* believe?" said Sven. "They didn't believe in worshiping Mary."

I blinked.

Guy sighed. "I don't get it, Tyler, what's gotten into you?"

A silence filled the room. We had been brothers. Just the summer before, Guy and Sven had stood in my wedding. But now they didn't recognize me, and I had to admit: I didn't really recognize myself either.

They understood that I could no longer stay up until 2 A.M. in the pub or in the library, but soon enough it became clear that I was, as Saint Paul once described married men, "distracted" (1 Cor 7:34). Even more, it was difficult to appreciate that I could do a theological one-eighty in just a handful of months. We mourned the unexpected rift in our friendship, each in his own way. And slowly, the sadness mixed with anger. Then the arguments began, hot, foamy arguments that left us red in the face. And the kind of martial metaphor that pervades argument—"He *demolished* his argument", "Your position is *indefensible*", "The idea was *shot down*"—seemed only to doom our debates from the outset. I was perhaps overzealous for the communion of saints, and my take-no-prisoners polemic certainly didn't help matters. There seemed no way out of the fog. But then, after a particularly nasty fight, Guy began an effort of peacemaking. Perhaps our disparate views could be less incompatible and more happily complementary? He had an idea that seemed to allow for us to disagree without either of us necessarily being right or wrong.

"It's just for fun," Guy smiled.

"What is?" I asked.

"The Virgin Mary," he said. "All this Catholic stuff. We'll never really know for sure whether it's right or wrong; the Bible isn't clear one way or the other, but if it helps you love Jesus, I see no harm."

"Really?"

"It might not be dogma, but it is a valid tradition and I respect that," Guy said, shrugging. "It's just for fun."

"Oh," I said, uncertain of whether I agreed.

But as the months rolled on, the theological category "just for fun" proved to be very helpful in maintaining a sense of equilibrium in our friendship. This way, Guy and Sven were able to tolerate my new "obsession with Mary" without having to agree. For a while it seemed that we had found a way out of the impasse.

Now, it would be impossible to appreciate the significance of Guy's idea without some backstory. By "tradition" Guy was referring to a popular theological nuance made at Nashotah House. In the first week of class, all freshmen were introduced to a distinction between dogma, doctrine, and tradition. This was usually illustrated by a series of concentric circles, with dogma at the center, then doctrine, and finally tradition. The center was "necessary", but the circumference was "supplemental". The further one moved away from the center of the circle, the further one moved into the realm  of speculation. *Dogma* was that which had been laid out by the Church as incontrovertibly true and no longer able to be disputed (e.g., the Trinity). *Doctrine* was true enough to be taught by the Church, but remained open to debate (e.g., for Anglicans, the Sacrament of Confession). *Tradition* was helpful, but not necessarily true (e.g., for Anglicans like Guy, the Rosary). In other words, tradition was "just for fun".

These theological notes were especially helpful in articulating where we felt Roman Catholicism "went too far". Rome's problem was that it put too many traditions and doctrines in the dogma category. It made necessary that which was not necessary. It wasn't that transubstantiation was "wrong", for example, we just didn't believe it was dogma. We pointed to the Eastern Orthodox and said, "It's a mystery." And mysteries shouldn't be made de fide. At the risk of oversimplification, and admitting that there were nearly as many versions as there were students, there was a general suspicion on campus that dogma was divisive, especially Roman dogma. The solution to divisive dogma was to move as many things as possible out of the "necessary" category and into the spectrum between the "almost necessary" and "just for fun" categories. The smaller the dogma circle, the more inclusive the Church. For the sake of unity, sometimes it was better simply to agree to disagree.

When it came to agreeing to disagree, Nashotah House was a shining city on a hill. We had our *Pax Nashotah*. So even though Anglicans disagreed about a wide variety of issues (women priests, homosexuality, Mary's intercession, purgatory, the number and nature of the sacraments, and so on), they could come to Nashotah House to live in peace. For example, some Anglicans believed in the Sacrament of Reconciliation, and others did not. Perhaps both views were right, but not all the time? To make seemingly dissonant views harmonize, it was said of Confession: "All may, some should, none must." In other words, while some found it helpful to confess to a priest and receive absolution, this sacrament was not necessary for the forgiveness of postbaptismal sin. The tidy phrase was applied to almost any contentious issue. This way, no matter what your views, if you had been baptized and confessed Jesus as your Savior, you could receive the Eucharist. Agreeing to disagree, we could be one.

However well-intentioned, the sad reality was that the *Pax Nashotah* was little more than a temporary truce between warring camps. The fact of the matter was that students came to Nashotah House from dioceses in open schism with one another and had no choice but to put up with one another until they could return. Occasional skirmishes were unfortunate but perhaps not surprising. Sometimes, they were almost humorous.

For example, as I've said before, the Saint Michael bell rang three times a day, and everyone stood to say the Angelus. Normally a community says the Angelus out loud, but for the sake of unity we said it in silence. An inaudible Angelus allowed for a plurality of beliefs. There is no living voice of authority in Anglicanism, and so when it came to the Blessed Virgin we were literally reduced to silence. This silence, together with calls for more dialogue, was held up as a kind of modus operandi for how people who don't agree can somehow be "more Catholic than the Catholics".

Agreeing to disagree, students mostly kept their opinions about Mary's intercession to themselves, but every now and then a student sighed angrily or simply refused to stand. They knew for whom the bell tolled. On Marian feast days, the Society of Mary wore medallions on bright blue ribbon necklaces in chapel. For those who disagreed, the practice was annoying at best. And when I joined the Society, Guy and Sven could sit idly by no longer. They started a new society, the Society of the Bible, and on the Feast of Our Lady of Lourdes they came to chapel wearing Bibles attached to bright red ribbon necklaces. When everyone stood for the silent Angelus, those wearing the red ribbons shook their Bibles while those wearing the blue ribbons crossed themselves more than usual, and after much pious coughing all around, everyone received the eucharist, both the idolaters and iconoclasts alike, all under the white flag of the *Pax Nashotah*.

As time rolled on, I became increasingly uncomfortable with the idea that the communion of saints was a fun but ultimately unnecessary supplement to the Christian life. As I grew closer to the Blessed Mother, especially, I began to feel just how tragic and divisive it was that so many Christians lived as if she didn't exist. I *wanted* to agree to disagree; compromise looked like the more loving thing to do, but I could find no neutral ground. The communion of saints was either true or false; their intercession, real or fake; invoking them, saving or damning. Whatever consecrating oneself to the Blessed Mother was, it was certainly not "just for fun".

And the more I thought about it, the more problematic was the phrase "all may, some should, none must." It seemed not only to relativize the Sacrament of Confession, but also to relativize the priesthood itself. Jesus was the high priest who forgives sins, and he shared that authority with his clergy, the apostles: "He breathed on them, and said to them, 'Receive the Holy Spirit. If you forgive the sins of any, they are forgiven; if you retain the sins of any, they are retained" (Jn 20:22–23). In the Old Testament, the priests could judge someone to be in communion with God's people or cut off from the covenant. In the New Testament, Jesus gave his new priests, the Twelve, an even greater power: "Whatever you bind on earth shall be bound in heaven, and whatever you loose on earth shall be loosed in heaven" (Mt 18:18). Saint James, perhaps knowing that the Church could forgive sins in God's name, and that it was a matter of heaven or hell, urged Christians to call for a priest and to confess their sins (Jas 5:14–16). Likewise, Saint Paul urged Christians to confess, presumably to a priest, and considered his own ministry to be one "of reconciliation" (2 Cor 5:18). The *Didache* demanded that Christians receive the Sacrament of Reconciliation before receiving the Eucharist, "that your sacrifice may be pure" (14:1). I could grant that it was within the realm of possibility that Jesus, in his mercy, could still forgive someone who abstained from the means of grace in his

New Covenant, but just because God is not bound to the sacraments it did not follow that "all may, some should, none must." Either the Sacrament of Confession was true or it was false, either absolution was real or it was fake, but if it was real, it could not be "just for fun".

For me, as I've said, it was a matter firstly of love—better to receive God's love and better to love him back. But what does it look like to *love* God? "If you love me, you will keep my commandments" (Jn 14:15). When someone loves God, he obeys him. And "his service is perfect freedom".[1] But how could I obey his commandments if I didn't know what they were? The Christian travel guides contradicted each other. Some said there were many commandments, others that there were really only one or two, others that there were none at all. If obedience is how you *love* God, I needed to know: How many sacraments were there? To be obedient to bishops, the successors of the apostles, is to be obedient to Christ: But which bishops? What did holy obedience entail?

* * * * *

When I was in high school, classmates talked about how world religions are basically the same, and only superficially different.

"Different religions have different opinions about the small stuff," a student would say, "but when it comes down to the essential beliefs, every religion is the same."

Let's call this the Unknowable God perspective. Using the mountain metaphor one more time, God (or whatever you call god) is at the top of a mountain, hiding in the clouds. We are all at the bottom of the mountain. You may take one path up the mountain, I may take another, and in the end we all end up at the same place. To think that one religion could possibly be the sole and exclusive source of truth is to be arrogant and close-minded. To be humble and open-minded, we must admit that, when all is said and done, different religions are really just different forms of the same thing: a path up the mountain to God.

A problem with the Unknowable God perspective is that it didn't account for Jesus. Christianity claims that God is not hiding up on a mountain waiting for us to find our own way to him. In the Person of Jesus Christ, God came down the mountain, as it were, and showed us *the way* back up to God. Jesus *is* the way to the Father. And after he ascended back up to the Father, he left behind his apostolic Church to hand out maps, to teach "the faith which was once for all delivered" (Jude 1:3).

The popular idea that all religions are foundationally the same and only superficially different has rightly been called *religious pluralism*, but I was beginning to feel like my spirituality had created what might be called *Christian pluralism*. A Christian pluralist does not necessarily disagree with Catholic dogma; he simply disagrees with the fact that it is dogma at all. For him, truth should not be so exclusive. Why give an answer to what could remain a never-ending question? The powerful play goes on, and everyone should get to add a verse! Christian pluralism (Christian agnosticism or indifferentism) is the conviction that all Christian denominations are foundationally the same and only superficially different "pieties" or "spiritualities". The visible disunity, the disagreement over the means of grace, the contradictions of how the faith is to be lived, the clashing of Church orders, the disparity of stories—all of this, Christian pluralism suggests, is exactly what Jesus intended when he intended his Church. "Just believe in Jesus, or whatever you call Jesus. He's up there on the mountain. How you get to him is your own business."

And yet, I was beginning to see that there was a dark side to such a nice-sounding message. Held up as "mere Christianity", it was in fact a major contributor to moral plasticity and doctrinal confusion. I could see all around me that it led to schism, broken relationships, pain, and ambiguity. I had to admit that what had first drawn me to Anglicanism was that it had liturgy and sacraments and bishops without being dogmatic about it. I could have tradition, but still pretty much believe whatever I wanted. To me, it was all part of the "poetry", and Jesus loved the "beautiful mess". But now I was not so sure.

I felt like one life was dying and another was yet to be born. I could not doubt this as I looked about to see the radical changes in my life, from marriage to preparing for the priesthood. And behind all the nice talk about "agreeing to disagree" was the threat of actually being wrong, of having somewhere along the way made a terrible mistake, a threat that receded into the distance yet never disappeared—no matter how small I made the dogma circle.

A choice confronted me. Would I, as I felt my foundations shaking, pull back to the old high ground of inclusiveness? Frightened by the loss of my familiar mooring places, would I become paralyzed and cover my inaction with nice-sounding slogans about grace and compromise? And if I did, would I surrender my chance to participate in something less gassy and more real? Would I forfeit the distinctive characteristic of Christianity—namely, that there are not multiple paths up the mountain to God, because God has come down the mountain? Or would I seize the courage necessary to face the terrifying possibility that the *way* up the mountain was in fact "narrow" (Mt 7:14)?

My growing unease about doctrinal relativism was perhaps especially acute because after my diocese left AMiA (the Anglican Mission in America) to join ACNA (the Anglican Church in North America), I was in the awkward position of pursuing Holy Orders without a bishop. I needed to find a bishop, but which bishop? As I asked around, I discovered that switching bishops was common practice for postulants, and students would often interview bishops until they found one with whom they could agree. It was not uncommon for students to enter the seminary as members of, say, ACA (the Anglican Church in America) and leave as priests in TEC (The Episcopal Church), or vice versa. While I was grateful that I could look for a bishop with whom I could get along, the whole idea of bishop shopping seemed to defeat the very purpose of bishops in the one, holy, catholic, and apostolic Church.

It didn't seem to stop at the seminary level, either. Later that year I began an internship at an Anglican "church plant" in Milwaukee whose leadership thought women could be priests. Because the local bishop of their diocese did not think women could be priests, they searched for a new bishop and a new diocese that would accommodate their convictions. Eventually, they would join C4So (Churches for the Sake of Others), a new diocese that like-minded congregations could join regardless of geographical location. But in the meantime, I was in the awkward position of interning at a parish that was looking for a bishop that would let them have women priests while my entire diocese was looking for a bishop that would be against women priests, all while trying to find a bishop who would temporarily take me under his wing so I could just get ordained. Thankfully, after only a few short months I found a very kindhearted bishop in ACNA from the diocese of Pittsburgh, and he was able to help me get on with my postulancy.

Although I had found a bishop and it looked like the dust would someday settle, I was no longer comfortable with some of the practices of my sending parish back in the suburbs of Minneapolis. For example, my parish offered infant Baptism as an option for the "Catholic Anglicans" and baby dedications for the "Evangelical Anglicans", and both grape juice and wine were consecrated in order to satisfy parishioners' disparate views about alcohol. The Sacraments of Confirmation and Confession were not even offered. I prayed about it and eventually worked up the courage to call my priest on the phone and talk about it.

"Why do we have infant Baptism and baby dedications?" I asked.

"A lot of our parishioners think it's wrong to baptize a baby," my priest explained.

"But if Baptism is necessary for salvation, how can it be optional?"

"We need to be compassionate," he said.

"Why do you consecrate wine and grape juice?" I asked, deciding to change the subject.

"Some of our parishioners are not comfortable drinking wine," my priest explained.

"But the *matter* of the sacrament is bread and wine."

He sighed. "Look, we don't want to be fundamentalists."

"Fundamentalists?"

"Yes," he said. "We're first Christians, then Anglicans."

I contemplated my priest's answer for a very long time. At first glance, to be Christian first and Anglican second seemed harmless enough. Yet something seemed to be lurking behind the open-armed message of compassion. By saying that we were "first Christians, then Anglicans", my priest seemed to be saying, in so many words, that Anglicanism was just one of the many optional paths up the mountain we call Christianity. Beneath all the talk of liturgy and sacraments and tradition, beneath the bishops and the altars and the stoles, there seemed to be a fundamental conviction that none of it was actually necessary. In an effort to avoid fundamentalism, he had in fact reduced Christianity to a few fundamentals, a short list of "essentials". It struck me then that Guy's theological category, however crude, put the fun in fundamentalism: at the end of the day, anything in addition to the basic fundamentals of Christianity, even Anglicanism itself, was "just for fun".

I was not trying to point fingers or find fault with my sending parish or with Anglicanism in general. My growing concern with Anglicanism was deeply personal. I thought these things through as one might look into a mirror. If I was going to be an Anglican priest, my priesthood would mean something—but what? As a priest, I would have to preach the truth—but what truth? I would have to administer the sacraments—but which sacraments? Why become an Anglican priest if both Anglicanism and the priesthood were not necessary?

As the year went on, I was increasingly aware that this "fundamentalism" wasn't limited to my sending parish or my diocese. Wasn't this the same principle behind an inaudible Angelus or an optional Sacrament of Reconciliation? By being "first Christians, then Anglican", we were able to embrace a wide variety of self-contradictory morals and doctrines as long as we held to a really basic short list of essentials: *Just believe in Jesus; everything else is footnotes.* The short list varied, depending sometimes on who you talked to, but the fact remained that as long as one accepted a list of *fundamentals*, everything from the intercession of the saints to the Anointing of the Sick to bishops themselves, was, to use Guy's category, "just for fun".

It was difficult to resolve the dilemma because the practice of ditching a bishop you disagreed with and finding another one, leaving one denomination and starting a new one, had been Anglicanism's modus operandi from the start. Ever since England broke camp with Rome, her bishops have been breaking off from one other in a seemingly endless pattern of dissolution. So ruined, the only way these fractions were able to consider themselves a "communion" was to agree to disagree—not enough actually to unite TEC with ACNA with AMiA, but just enough to cover the vague, floating sense of dislocation and disinheritance.

In the meantime, the waffling, erratic declarations of Anglicanism left it to be seen where the Church really stood on grave matters. In an effort to be inclusive, we made the dogma circle as small as possible. The vexed questions of sexuality, a female priesthood, the number or necessity of the sacraments, the communion of saints, and so on, were pushed out from the central circle of dogma and placed in the outer rings of speculation. This way, the current controversies of faith and morals would not be so divisive, would be more loving. But was it really loving?

Again, how can we *do* the will of the Father if we do not *know* what his will is? *Of course* the Church may permit divergent views on purely speculative points, but when it came to the means of grace, shouldn't she teach the truth? If Mary were *in fact* the Spouse of the Holy Spirit (and as such the Mediatrix of All *Graces*), wouldn't her role in the family of God be indispensable? And if Christ left behind his apostolic priesthood to forgive sins in his name, wouldn't it be presumptuous if not dangerous to relativize his commands? "You take that path, I'll take another. In the end, everyone gets there."

All of this is to say that I was beginning to experience firsthand that to "agree to disagree" was colossally bad advice. Agreeing to disagree was not a means to Christian unity, at least not the kind of unity "in spirit and truth" (Jn 4:24) where "those who believed were of one heart and soul" (Acts 4:32). The High Priestly Prayer was clear: Christ's vision of a unified Church included an *agreement* on the truth. Jesus said the Holy Spirit would lead his Church "into *all* the truth", not just a few really basic essentials (Jn 16:13). And even the most cursory reading of the Gospels makes one wonder if agreeing to disagree was what Jesus had in mind when he established what he called "my Church" (Mt 16:18).

God came down the mountain in the Person of Jesus Christ and showed us the way to the Father. He left behind his apostolic Church to make that way known. This path, "the way", is not meant to be many paths or many ways—alternative ethical stances, optional moral imperatives, contradicting dogmas, uncertain means of grace, division and contradiction and schism. Jesus came to earth to make known the means of grace so that we could have the hope of glory. He said, "The truth will make you free" (Jn 8:32). Yet the practice of agreeing to disagree seemed to be premised on the suspicion that the truth will *not* set you free. He told the Twelve on the night of their ordination: "When the Spirit of truth comes, he will guide you into all the truth" (Jn 16:13). Yet the impulse to make the dogma circle as small as possible seemed to be based on the assumption that the Holy Spirit leads the Church only into some truth: "Keep debating, don't decide; no matter your maps, no matter your gear, no matter what you do, you'll get to the top of the mountain."

I took solace in the fact that at least I was an Anglo-Catholic. I belonged to a small remnant that did not think things like the communion of saints or Confession were up for perennial debate, or that bishops and sacraments were fun add-ons to a more basic, truer Gospel. And it was sometime before the spring of 2013 that I concluded that the bigger the dogma circle, the better. The truth really does set you free. Some things really are black and white.

I held these new convictions as candles among gunpowder, for they seemed to threaten the very reason for the Church of England's existence. Even more, they threatened my personal vocation, for if there was any hope of establishing a church in Minneapolis, or even continuing my internship in Milwaukee, I would have to speak as one who didn't really know the way up the mountain.

* * * * *

Listening to Gillian Welch's *Revival*, Brittany and I traveled back to Minneapolis to meet with our core team. The idea was to pray and read the Scriptures as we honed the mission, vision, and values of the church we would start together. This way, we would all be on the same page. When everyone arrived at the parish basement, we drank tea and talked enthusiastically, agreeing that this new parish would use only the best hymns with the best of contemporary worship. We all wanted a traditional building, but agreed that kneelers would be off-putting for most visitors. Ethnic diversity and social justice were key to any urban ministry. One service would be Rite 2, in normal English, and another would be Rite 1, replete with "thees" and "thous". No one really lit up when I hinted that I would wear traditional vestments instead of a cassock alb and wanted to celebrate the Mass *ad orientem*. And then I confessed that I would not be able in good conscience to dedicate babies in lieu of Baptism, nor would I be able to consecrate grape juice for the eucharist. My team looked at me with a kind of horror.

"Tyler, some people are alcoholics," my friend said. "They can't have even a drop of alcohol."

"Pasteurization wasn't even invented until the late 1800s," I said. "What did alcoholics do before then?"

"That doesn't sound loving," he replied.

"Jesus loves alcoholics more than we do, and wine was his idea, not mine," I said. "Isn't the eucharistic blood of Christ the *remedy* for sin?"

"I'm just saying we would be putting an alcoholic in a difficult situation," he said.

"But to receive the eucharist he wouldn't even need to drink the wine. The Body and Blood of Christ are each present in both the bread and the wine," I said, referring to the doctrine of concomitance. "Besides, no one comes to the altar as an *alcoholic* or a *homosexual* or any identity because our deepest identity is *Christ*. We do not receive the eucharist as alcoholics, but as the baptized."

"Speaking of Baptism," interjected another core team member, "I just want to make sure we won't be forcing parents to baptize their children."

"But Anglicanism *believes* in infant Baptism," I said. "It's what we do."

"Wasn't Jesus all about grace?" she asked.

"If Jesus was all about grace, would he have revealed contradicting means of grace?" I replied, a little too boldly.

"Jesus wasn't a legalist," she said, growing angry. "Look, if we're going to plant a church with you, it needs to be a safe place where all are welcome."

I could see that launching an Anglo-Catholic church was going to be an uphill battle. Clearly I would have to introduce my Anglo-Catholic beliefs slowly, in chapters, perhaps over a lifetime. As Anglicans we had lots of good taste when it came to hymns and liturgy, but we were clearly not on the same page about the means of grace. I remember returning to Wisconsin driving well below the speed limit and feeling very deflated.

That same semester, I began teaching catechism classes at the Anglican church plant in Milwaukee. They were biweekly informational meetings for people of a variety of ages, some seeking the Sacrament of Baptism and others Confirmation. Very quickly, I learned that almost no one appreciated what I had to say. In fact, after several of the parishioners discovered the Anglican teaching on baptismal regeneration or the empowering of the Holy Spirit, they withdrew their children from the program. I was finding that it was very difficult to get Anglicans to be Anglican, and this only reinforced the growing sense of just how challenging it would be to plant an Anglo-Catholic church in Minneapolis. It was one thing to gather the hipsters; it was quite another for them to commit to any of it. The Milwaukee parish had amazing music and met in a beautiful building. The bearded pastor had tattoos and a man bun, and the altar was made out of reclaimed timbers. Even the liturgy from the Book of Common Prayer was printed on rustic card stock. Everything was as it should be. But while teaching catechism classes, I found that if certain Anglican doctrines, especially the "Catholic stuff", moved from the "cool" category to the "necessary" category, people either checked out or simply disagreed. They believed in the sacraments the way one might believe in meditation or icons: a cool tradition, but ultimately not necessary.

I quickly learned to teach as one not entirely certain if anything were really true, in the dogmatic sense of the word. Although this method worked well in getting parishioners to warm to an idea, what good was it if they took coolness' optional quality as permission to carry on as before? It is all very well to relieve someone of the responsibility of accepting or rejecting a real truth, by presenting, say, the sacraments in a noncompulsory way, but what is that solace worth if he never avails himself of Confirmation or Confession? And by presenting faith and morals in a speculative way, wasn't I practicing the very principle of Christian pluralism I found to be harmful? I brought this concern to my spiritual director, Father Willard. The topic was the Milwaukee church's hunt for a bishop that would approve of women priests. The matter was sensitive because a woman in leadership was pursuing Holy Orders, and the matter came up often in my class on the sacraments.

"But if I told them that women cannot be priests, wouldn't they be hurt?" I asked.

"Yes," said Father Willard. "So what?"

"Well, I don't want to hurt anyone!"

"What does that have to do with it?" he asked. "The truth will not *harm* them." He stood and reached for a book from his shelf. "If anything, the hurt might help them," he continued, handing me a copy of Henry Cloud and John Townsted's *Boundaries*. "Did the dentist hurt you when he drilled out your cavity?"

"Yes," I said, taking the book.

"Did he harm you?"

"No," I said.

"When you ate the sugar that gave you the cavity, did that hurt?"

"No."

"Did it harm you?"

"Yes," I said, beginning to see.

"Truth hurts," Father Willard said, smiling. "But truth never harms anyone."

"But they'll hate me!" I said.

"*Not many of you should become teachers*," he said, quoting James 3:1, "*because those who teach will be judged more strictly*. Don't worry about what people think about you, worry about what God thinks about you. And read *Boundaries*. That book helped me enormously."

I looked out the window.

"I hear you, but it's one thing to talk and it's another to be heard," I said. "I want to communicate. I don't want to hit people over the head with dogmas. I want to woo them."

"Good," he said. "And let your gentleness be evident to all. But remember that Jesus did not seek the favor of the world. He did not make the truth attractive by conforming it to the values of the present age."

Father Willard pointed to a sign above his doorway. It read: "His disciples turned back and no longer followed him. —John 6:66".

"No matter how compassionate you are or how well you communicate, sometimes people just walk away," he said, gently, "like when Jesus' disciples refused to accept his teaching about the Eucharist."

Although I took Father Willard's advice to heart, I'm afraid to say it would be some time before I would have the courage to act on it. The simple fact of the matter was that if I even hinted that any of the sacraments might be imperative, I was either publicly rebuffed or privately advised not to be so "mean" or "uptight". I began to feel quite frustrated by the fact that there was no universal authority to which I could appeal. If Anglicanism were the true church, why was it not able to hold an ecumenical council to decree what was dogma and what was heresy?

Every Sunday, we recited the Creed. To believe in the Creed is to believe in ecumenical councils; that is, it is to believe that one way the Holy Spirit guarantees authentic development of dogma is through the gathering of bishops to define dogma, condemn heresies, and issue decrees that serve as clear "maps" for the faithful. For the first several centuries of the Church's life, that's exactly what happened. But, in my mind, somewhere along the way the Holy Spirit decided the Church would no longer have universal teaching authority, at least through ecumenical councils.

But I was beginning to wonder if what *sola scriptura* does to the Bible, Anglicanism did to tradition. Without a *living* voice of authority, "tradition" (the Fathers, the early councils, the creeds) was in effect reduced to a dead letter, a grab bag. Even with regard to the authority of the first four councils, which we believed proclaimed the foundational truths of Christianity, if a certain decree did not seem to us to be biblical, we could reject it. Without a living voice of authority, what passed the threefold test of Catholicity laid down by Saint Vincent of Lérins—namely, "what has been believed everywhere, always, and by all"[2]—was left to the individual's discretion.

A lot has happened since 1054, when the Eastern churches and Rome went their separate ways. The Church has been hit with the gusts of the Reformation, doubts about the number and nature of the sacraments, Protestant theories of atonement and justification, various contradictory Mariologies, technological advances in birth control and abortion, the novel idea of women priests, faulty anthropologies, and especially Modernism, the "synthesis of all heresies", as Saint Pius X called it.[3] In the face of new heresies, doctrinal confusion, and urgent moral questions, shouldn't the Church be able to speak with the universal authority of Christ? In other words, since the Church exists in history, shouldn't dogma develop? Empowered by the Holy Spirit as the Church is, how can successors of the apostles *not* speak truth to every generation? The Church must be able to speak yesterday and today; she must speak with a *living* voice. Yet according to Anglicanism, the Church has been unable to speak officially and with universal authority to these urgent matters, for we believed that there hasn't been an ecumenical council for at least one thousand years!

I had always considered Rome's claim to hold ecumenical councils to be arrogant because their "ecumenical" councils didn't include everybody. But a tiny part of me was beginning to find it frightfully compelling. Here was a Church that claimed to speak officially and with universal authority in *every* generation. Against Rome, desperately, I held to what was left of my "poetry" and "beautiful mess" theory, and I'm afraid I mistook 1 Corinthians 11:19, "there must be factions among you", as divine favor of schism. Divisions were inevitable, and Rome was for perfectionists struggling with an over-realized eschatology. Ecumenical councils were simply a thing of the past, or perhaps something to be hoped for "someday".

But surely it was worth some earnest reflection that Roman Catholics claim ecumenical councils *still* happen, visible and recognizable apostolic authority *still* voices universal and identifiable dogma. If Roman Catholicism were true, her ecumenical councils would have the same binding authority that they did in the early centuries. And I remember thinking, *It's one thing to believe that once upon a time the Church held ecumenical councils; it's quite another to believe she still does.*

I had nowhere to go with these questions, these troubling doubts about my own vocation, but I couldn't ignore them. As I lifted everything up in prayer, I saw that I could not change my sending parish or my fellow seminarians. I could not change Anglicanism or Eastern Orthodoxy. Even as a priest, I might not even be able to change much about my own parish. But I could change myself. And I asked myself: *What must I do to be saved?* There was no short list, no "one thing" to get off the hook.

* * * * *

My professors were sharp and kind and bright-eyed. They joined students for lunch every day and surrendered countless office hours to answering all the biblical and theological questions we had. My respect for my teachers ran almost as deep as my respect for the many bishops who came and went from Nashotah, visiting from far-flung corners of the Anglican Communion. They were gentlemen, brave men, and genuinely loving. I remember when I got the news that my old college professor, Dr. Breyers, had passed away. Stunned, I ran out into the snow wearing nothing but my cassock. The sky was sleeting ice. I climbed onto a hill that overlooked the surrounding fields and wept. Just then, Bishop Salmon drove by.

"Now, you come with me," he said, rolling down his window.

Embarrassed, I wiped my eyes and got into his car. I told him about the Guild and Dr. Breyers and my grief to learn of his death.

"Come with me," he said, pulling up to his office. "You look cold and I want to give you something."

After entering his office, he opened his closet and handed me his black wool cope, the kind that one wears over one's cassock. He put it over my shoulders and it was warm.

"There," said Bishop Salmon. "Remember, you are a child of God."

"Thank you, your grace," I said.

Snow seems to invite contemplation. It encourages one to travel back and think about one's life. Something about the way it hides the dirt, covering the mess with a blank slate, makes room for reflection. The winter of my second year in Wisconsin was painful and yet also invigorating. I was often found sprawled on the library floor, moaning. Books lay open, as if speaking to one another: Basil's *On the Holy Spirit*, Athanasius' *On the Incarnation*, Irenaeus of Lyons' *On the Apostolic Preaching*, John of Damascus' *On the Divine Images*. I was plodding through Gregory the Great's *Pastoral Rule* and Augustine's *On Christian Teaching*. I was busy compiling notes, dog-earing pages in books, writing essays. Having continued with Greek and begun studies in Hebrew, I seemed always to be holding flash cards. And all the while I was distracted by the simple question, What must I do to be saved?

What is truth, and what is our part in it? All Christians must climb. Along "the way" all are safe, and yet none are safe. What faith can stir a soul to step forward, and whence is the answer, the bottom line, to the unanswered questions? I did not yet know, but I had a hunch. Perhaps he is free who accedes to authority and, in surrendering, rises above himself and climbs the mountain. When all else fails, look at the map. Read the instructions. If such advice exists for building electric train sets and backyard swing sets, does it exist for picking up your cross and following Christ?

The Church has a job to do. Christ commanded her to "go therefore and make disciples of all nations, baptizing them in the name of the Father and of the Son and of the Holy Spirit, *teaching* them to observe all that I have commanded you" (Mt 28:19). Like her King, the Church is called "to bear witness to the truth" so that "every one who is *of the truth* hears [Christ's] voice" (Jn 18:37). The apostolic Church is meant to be a light along the way: "*You* [the Church] are the light of the world.... Let *your* light so shine before men, that they may see *your* good works and give glorify to your Father who is in heaven" (Mt 5:14, 16). Bishops and sacraments point to a paradox in our experience of the Kingdom: to be free in Christ entails also being a slave to Christ, a personal relationship with Jesus entails also a social relationship with his Church, the kingdom of heaven is on earth, salvation involves the soul and the body, and we live in the "already/not yet". Our ecclesiology must be adequate to our agency in the mission of Christ, being both personal and social, embodied and spiritual, liberating and religious. We must know "the way" up the mountain—which berries are poisonous, which guides are trustworthy, which trails are dead ends, and so on.

It's like learning to play guitar. The years of practice may engender discipline and, prospectively, a little dexterity and enjoyment. Learning to play the guitar invites students into a tradition that has preceded them and will endure long after they are gone. Like religion, it takes work. You can't just sit down and play; it is an apprenticeship that takes years, even a lifetime.

The guitarist's power of expression springs from a prior obedience. His musical agency is built up from an ongoing submission—to what? To his teacher, yes, but also from subjecting his fingers to the discipline of the frets, to the physical realities of the guitar, and to the necessities of music that can be expressed in notation. These "rules" cannot be altered, only broken or ignored. Ignoring that the guitar needs tuning might afford the thrill of transgression, but it will not change the fact that the music will be out of tune. Breaking the rules of tempo might occasion a feeling of rocking out, but it will not change the fact that we live in time and therefore experience music in time. The Church lives in time, and the Christian's power of expression, the degree to which he reflects the glory of God, is built on an ongoing submission to bishops, subjecting one's body and soul to the discipline of the sacraments, surrendering to a truth he cannot qualify.

In other words, we do not climb to God on our own terms. God has come to us. And the Son of God did not become obedient unto death in order to reveal uncertain means of grace. The God of Israel does not reveal contradictory truths. God came down the mountain so that we could truly know "the way". Jesus himself says it is not a plurality of ways, the wide way, but a difficult way, a way with a "narrow gate" (Mt 7:13–14).

Where do ideas land? Where do ideas as seemingly small as snow-flakes land? By the end of that winter, I had come to the conclusion that Christian pluralism was not the message of grace it was pretending to be. Open-armed and compassionate on the outside, divisive and damning on the inside, Christian pluralism has worked its way into Christian circles, wreaking havoc in every conceivable way. In the name of love, agreeing to disagree obfuscated the truth and thereby failed to love truly. As the social continuity of the Incarnation, the Church must be the living voice of Christ. *Ubi Christus, ibi Ecclesia.* How could it be loving to push the means of grace out of the dogma category and into the realm of "mystery"?

By *mystery* we often mean something like an interesting uncertainty, but Gerard Manley Hopkins said that a mystery is an incomprehensible certainty.[4] Though we cannot wrap our minds around it, a mystery does not reduce the sentence of God's revelation to a scribble. Dogma develops, and the *mystery* of a dogma, whether it be transubstantiation or Mary as mediatrix, does not reduce it to an everlasting question mark. Again, how can we do the will of the Father if we do not know what his will is? If the journey will end, ultimately, in heaven or in hell, who would dare to follow a map of scribbles and question marks? "A man will give his life for a mystery," Edwin F. Cardinal O'Brien once observed, "but not for a question mark."[5]

13

Awesome Family Planning

$$Ana\text{-}\begin{Bmatrix} MARY \\ ARMY \end{Bmatrix} gram.$$

How well her name an *Army* doth present,
In whom the *Lord of hosts* did pitch his tent!

—George Herbert[1]

How can it be a large career to tell other
people about the Rule of Three,
and a small career to tell one's own children about the universe?
How can it be broad to be the same thing to everyone and
narrow to be everything to someone?
No, a woman's function is laborious, but because it is gigantic,
not because it is minute.

—G. K. Chesterton[2]

Fall is bright and full of colors. But winter, like an old prophet, has a way of making things black and white again. Bare branches scratch against a blank sky, and the snow is freaked with jet. My first winter as a married man had a way of bringing the normally blurred picture of myself into focus, and the image was anything but flattering. Marriage had a way of taking me down a notch. One by one, my faults inevitably revealed themselves, faults I hardly knew I had, and always Brittany was gracious. That winter certainly helped me see my faith in a more realistic light. Jesus seemed to be asking me, "Do you love me?" And I saw quite clearly that there were only two answers: either Amen, or *Non serviam* ("I will not serve"). While the Yes was simple enough, the No was infinitely subtle, at times so nuanced it even looked like a Yes. But God is never fooled. Love is all or nothing.

Our first Christmas together was simple but intentional. Through the lectionary and the slow, long view of liturgical time, we wanted somehow to live it, at least a little. On the days just before the birth of Jesus, during Advent, we reflected on the old prophecies, the angel's troubling news, and Mary's Yes. We imagined the difficult journey from Galilee to Bethlehem or from Bethlehem to Egypt. We meditated on the birth, the shepherds' wonder, the angels' singing, the star. We made our first Advent wreath of fresh evergreens, three penitential candles, and one rose-colored candle. We added a white center candle to represent Jesus. One by one, each candle was lit. We wanted somehow to enter the story, to make it our own, to feel the truth of Christ's plan for all creation, to make all things new.

One night, I read a story about an Algonquin woman and her starving baby. They were stranded in the Arctic. At an abandoned camp she found one small fishhook and a line, but she had no bait. The baby cried, but there was no bait. So she took a knife and cut a strip of flesh from her own thigh. She fished with the worm of her own flesh, and she and her baby survived into the spring. Ernest Thomson Seton first told the story, but I read it in Annie Dillard. Apparently a man from northern Ontario had seen the scar on her thigh. I remember putting down the book and thinking that this was not unlike the Christmas story, the story of God taking *flesh*. "For God so loved the world that he *gave* his only-begotten Son" (Jn 3:16). For God, love is self-gift. On Christmas we remember that out of love, God gave nothing less than *himself*.

Brittany had set up a small Nativity crèche in our living room. I looked over at the tiny figurines surrounding the Christ child, and asked myself: *What can I give Jesus? What can anyone give to God?* Still thinking of the Algonquin woman, I realized that I would have to give him *myself*. A love that is not self-giving is no love at all. In love, God gave *himself* to the world, in the Person of Jesus. And during Advent we remember that Mary received God's radical love and showed us how we can love God back: she gave God *herself*.

It was black or white, Amen or *Non serviam*. If my life was to tell the Christmas story, I would have to be like Mary, who, when her very life was on the line, held nothing back, saying: "Be it done unto me according to thy word." In all things, I would have to say Yes.

* * * * *

In those days, Brittany came home from work around the same time I returned from Evensong. I hung my black cassock on a peg, she changed out of her uniform, and we scampered into the kitchen to turn up the stovetop burners and sauté vegetables or boil pasta. We listened to Patsy Cline and Tammy Wynette. These hours together were golden, a slow spin on a hot spit. Marriage yielded a sweetness I had never known before, a splendor that brightened what would have otherwise been a dark winter.

We often talked late into the night, settling into the old Victorian loveseat we found at the thrift store. We talked about the future, our ministry, and especially Brittany's career. Should she go to grad school? Should she get licensed so she could go back into high-need schools, where her heart was? Although she loved to teach, it was beginning to feel like something was off. Whether they were in poverty-stricken, rural Mississippi or in the well-heeled, cloistered military academy, the students were remarkably similar: too many were heartbroken, angry, lonely, afraid. Perhaps the school system had failed them? But the discipline issues, the disenchantment, the inability to focus or even to care—all of it seemed to be a symptom of a deeper problem. The simple fact of the matter was that more and more students came from empty houses, busy mothers, absent fathers. Was it any wonder that they stumbled into her classroom with a sense of homelessness?

"These kids don't need a smartboard or specialist," Brittany sighed. "They need a mother's love and a father's direction."

We were silent for a moment.

"The idea of becoming a mother terrifies me," Brittany continued, looking up at the ceiling.

"I know what you mean," I said.

"No, you don't," Brittany said. "Dads don't have to choose between their children and their careers, while women can't seem to win either way, and doing both is near impossible."

Over the next few months, Brittany began to change. We were both growing closer to the Virgin Mary, wanting to imitate her fiat, and our new friends in the Society encouraged us along the way. We were hungry to learn more about how to bear God into the world, how to grow in Mary's way of trust. Around this time, Brittany stumbled upon the only other women her age who wanted to talk about the Blessed Mother—Catholic mom bloggers. Drawn to their bravery and joy, Brittany forwarded links to me. As my high school civics teacher would say, women could have been lawyers, doctors, schoolteachers, presidents of the United States of America, and instead they were stay-at-home moms. They lifted the lids of their soup pots to share the aroma of holiness with a world that had lost its sense of smell. They punctuated their mornings and evenings with prayer, oriented their calendars to the liturgical year. They changed diapers and cleaned and cooked and disciplined and cried, and they were not afraid to share that in the midst of such grueling hours they had somehow found grace. And they spoke of Mary in the most ordinary of ways, as if she were a part of their daily lives. They spoke of her as the world's first and best Christian, a model of motherhood.

This new understanding of motherhood fascinated me. Because the Church's existence traces back to the moment when the divine Word took flesh from Mary's womb, Christian discipleship takes its cue from Mary, from her *motherhood*. Not only did Mary conceive Jesus in her womb, but she first conceived him in her heart. In her simple fiat, "Let it be done to me according to your word" (Lk 1:38), she modeled a trust that God wanted from everybody, even me. As I mentioned before, when a woman called out to Jesus, "Blessed is the womb that bore you!" Jesus replied, "Blessed rather are those who hear the word of God and keep it!" (Lk 11:27–28). He said this not to belittle the Incarnation or denigrate his own mother, but to highlight that God wants every Christian to follow the example of his mother.

It was as if Mary's burning taper of trust touched some charred filament in my chest. While Brittany read Catholic mom blogs, I scoured biblical commentaries and theological treatises on the Mother of God. And the more I grew to love the Mother of God, the more I grew to appreciate motherhood itself.

For class, I was assigned to write an essay about Mary as the Ark of the New Covenant. Quickly my research led me to Revelation 11 and 12, where, at last, the lost Ark of the Old Covenant has been found. Except now it's not a golden chest, but "a woman clothed with the sun" (12:1) and crowned with the stars, the very woman who gave birth to Jesus—Mary of Nazareth. As mother, Mary was the *place* where God chose to tabernacle with us.

This discovery led me to Stephen Ray's study[3] of Mary's visit with Elizabeth in the Gospel of Luke that draws from Old Testament stories about the ark to illustrate that Mary was the Ark of the New Testament. For example, in 2 Samuel, the Philistines had taken the ark and God's presence with it; when they finally get it back, six key things happen that Luke draws our attention to in his account of Mary visiting Elizabeth.

- As King David went out to the hill country of Judea to retrieve the ark that the Philistines had sent back to Israel (2 Sam 6:3), Mary went to the hill country of Judea (Lk 1:39).
- After Uzzah touched the ark and was struck dead (2 Sam 6:7), David fearfully wondered, "How can the ark of the LORD come to me?" (2 Sam 6:9); after Elizabeth sees Mary, she wondered, "Why is this granted me, that the mother of my Lord should come to me?" (Lk 1:43).
- David left the ark in the hill country of Judea for *three months* (2 Sam 6:11), and Mary stayed with Elizabeth for *three months* (Lk 1:56).
- As the house that had housed the ark in this interim was *blessed* (2 Sam 6:10–11), Elizabeth proclaimed Mary to be *blessed* (Lk 1:42).
- As David (wearing the priestly linen ephod) *danced* and *leaped* before the ark and everyone shouted for joy before the ark (2 Sam 6:14, 16), John the Baptist, who was from the priestly line of Aaron, *leaped* for joy in Elizabeth's womb upon Mary's arrival (Lk 1:41, 44).
- The ark was eventually brought to Jerusalem, where God's glory was revealed in the temple (2 Sam 6:12; 1 Kings 8:9–11); so also, Mary eventually presented Jesus in the Jerusalem temple (Lk 2:21–22).

In crafting his narrative this way, Saint Luke seemed to be saying that, like the old golden chest, Mary was a sacred vessel where the Lord's presence tabernacled with his people—except this time, it was God *in the flesh.*

The God who is everywhere was *in* Mary, his divine presence radiating out from her, the Light of the World waiting to be born. At her Yes, the Holy Spirit conceived in her womb the very Son of God. Jesus took his human nature from her human nature, his flesh from her flesh, dwelled in her womb, was born from her body, was nursed at her breast, was raised in her home, was launched into public ministry at her intercession, and was even crucified with her by his side. Mary was so much more than the Ark of the Old Covenant: she was the Theotokos, the *Mother of God*. So it was that like the Levitical singers of old, Elizabeth lifted up her worship song before the New Ark of the New Covenant. Dr. Gary Anderson put it this way: "If one could turn to the temple and say, 'how lovely is thy dwelling place,' and attend to its every architectural detail, why would one not do the same with the Theotokos?"[4]

I shared these discoveries with Brittany, and they worked their way into us, leading us not only to appreciate Mary but to appreciate the way her specific *motherhood* models Christian discipleship in general. Mary-as-ark reminded us that discipleship wasn't just a job. Christians are not called to "share" Christ. They are called to *be* Christ, to bear him out into the world. Mary-as-ark also reminded us that motherhood wasn't just a job either. A mother does not "make" a home. To be the mother is to *be* home. She is, as Robert Farrer Capon put it, *geography incarnate*.[5]

By accident, my study of Mary-as-ark led me into the thorny issue of head coverings. I had noticed that, perhaps strangely, some of the Catholic mom bloggers seemed to love chapel veils, or mantillas (*manta* means "mantle" or "cloak"). I knew that in the Old Testament, the ark was *veiled* because it carried the *living* God, but I had never noticed that in all her statues and icons, except for the ones where she is being crowned with stars, Mary was also *veiled*. Was it because she had carried in her womb the God who was "the way, and the truth, and the life" (Jn 14:6)? I had always assumed head coverings were a patriarchal leftover, perhaps intended to help prevent men from lusting, but if that were the case, why were chapel veils made of beautiful lace?

I started to notice veils everywhere. The chalice was veiled until the Consecration because it held the *living* Blood of Christ. The ciborium in the tabernacle was veiled between Masses because it held the *living* Body of Christ. The monstrance was covered in a canopy during procession because it held the *living* Christ. It didn't take long for me to connect the dots: life-bearing vessels are *veiled* because they are sacred. Perhaps these Catholic moms covered their heads when attending Mass or in the presence of the Blessed Sacrament because they knew that they were the liturgical symbol of a *life-bearing vessel?* In the context of the Mass, a chapel veil was a reminder that God was born of a woman, that God has betrothed himself to his Church, and that the Church is a sacred vessel. God can touch a woman in a way he cannot touch a man—he can fill her with *life*.

Saint Paul's command about head coverings in the context of the Mass really was culture-bound—to the culture of Christ (1 Cor 11:1–16). Men don't cover their heads during Mass, because they are a liturgical reminder of the One to whom all of us—men and women together—are united by Baptism: Christ the Bridegroom. Women cover their heads as a liturgical reminder of who all of us—men and women together—are by Baptism: Mother Church, the Bride of the Lamb. Together in the Mass, we tell the story of the wedding of heaven and earth, Christ and his Bride, the first thing. "The first things must be the very fountains of life, love and birth and babyhood," wrote G. K. Chesterton, "and these are always covered fountains, flowing in the quiet courts of the home."[6]

And it all came back to Mary. She was ground zero. She was *where* "the Word became flesh and dwelt among us" (Jn 1:14). Her motherhood was the pattern for all discipleship. "Blessed rather," Jesus says, "are those who hear the word of God and keep it!" In other words, if we *hear* and *keep* the Word within us, like Mary, we will be *blessed*. In addition to the only-once physical birth of Christ, there is another dimension of motherhood that brings Christ into the world again and again: it rests upon hearing, keeping, and doing the Word. Like Mary, we are to be rich soil for the seed of God to grow, to "birth" God to the world!

* * * * *

Brittany was stretching the limits of her faith, and when Lent arrived, we were ready for a kind of a spiritual spring-cleaning. As we plodded through winter, Brittany and I prepared for Easter through modest penances and fasts, hoping to rein in our selfishness and practice our dependence on God, if only a little. We wanted to make room in our hearts so that, as Gerard Manley Hopkins put it, God might "easter in us, be a dayspring to the dimness of us, be a crimson-cresseted east".[7] The period of self-denial certainly helped us to appreciate better all the good things in life that we so often took for granted—coffee, beer, meat, long summer days.

One thing we were not abstaining from, however, was the marriage act. Because Brittany was on the pill, we didn't have to worry about kids. It never crossed our minds, even for a second, that we would ever abstain from making love, not even for the sake of growing in discipline or love.

I always wanted children—I just didn't want too many, too soon. And I didn't want the stress of providing for them until we were financially stable. So it was not a good omen when the mailman dropped off a cardboard box on our front stoop. Thinking it was my new copy of N. T. Wright's *The New Testament and the People of God*, I ripped it open only to frown at a thick copy of Pope Saint John Paul II's *Theology of the Body* and a slim encyclical letter of his holiness Paul VI, *Humanae Vitae*.

"Every sperm is sacred?" I joked.

"Don't worry," Brittany said. "These mom blogs keep mentioning these books, and I just want to learn more. You're the one who said sex and marriage are sacred. What is sacred about using sex in a way that deliberately excludes its basic purpose?"

Her words made me flinch.

A week later, Pope Saint John Paul II's *Evangelium Vitae* arrived with *Mulieris Dignitatem*. Soon Brittany was reading Mary Eberstedt, Elizabeth Anscombe, and Gertud von le Fort.

When we sat down to dinner one night, Brittany brought her copy of *Humanae Vitae*. She told me contraception had been around for thousands of years, but the advent of the hormonal contraceptive pill in 1960 was a watershed moment. By making contraception easier to use than ever before, it kicked off the sexual revolution and fundamentally altered relations between the sexes. On a more personal level, she said the pill had changed her body. She said contraception was a violation of the design God built into us. She said the pleasure of sex was an additional blessing, but the *purpose* of sex was primarily procreation. I stared at her with bulging eyes.

"Here," Brittany said, and stuck her hand between the pages. "See, it's not a steel jaw trap."

I didn't move. *Humanae Vitae* lay on our dining-room table, the pages dog-eared and wrinkled.

"What's this even about?" I asked.

"It's about the life we are afraid to live," Brittany said. "It's about living like we mean it."

"I'm not so sure," I said.

"Look, it's short," she said. "It's full of hope and promise. If we let it, maybe it will be a gentle nudge to become something more."

"But a *pope* wrote it," I said, looking down at the encyclical like it had mold on it. I gingerly picked it up. "I'll read it," I said weakly, as if I were submitting myself to a week of grueling chores.

"Offer it up," Brittany said.

I had every intention of reading *Humanae Vitae*, but every time I reached for it a vision flashed before my eyes of me staring at a screaming baby, reeking of vomit, and not quite able to fit it into a cute onesie with ten thousand impossible buttons. Besides, I could smell nonsense, no matter how much incense Catholics used to mask it.

Days turned into weeks. Instead of reading *Humanae Vitae*, I thought I would do my own research into the history of the Anglican position on birth control. I quickly learned that artificial contraception was considered to be immoral by all Christians, Protestant and Catholics alike, in all places and at all times, until the Lambeth Conference of 1930. Martin Luther considered contraception an act "far more atrocious than incest or adultery".[8] Yet within a single generation a universal and unbroken Christian ethic was abandoned.

"Thank God," I thought.

And yet, there was the gnawing question of why Catholics hadn't truckled to the spirit of the age. I could put it off no longer. Picturing Pope Paul VI in his starched, unblemished robes, safe from the risk of pregnancy and the responsibility of children yet dooming the Catholic faithful to a life of diapers and laundry, on the eve of the Solemnity of the Annunciation, I went to bed with *Humanae Vitae*. It didn't take long. I was immediately struck by how sensible it was. The encyclical warned that artificial birth control would lower moral standards throughout society, give rise to infidelity, and lessen the respect for women, and that governments would use reproductive technologies as a means of coercion. I could see that the pope's words were frighteningly prophetic. By the time I finished, Brittany had fallen asleep next to me.

I lay in the stillness, and the only thing I could think of was how human life is a fearful and terrible thing. I wanted to dismiss the encyclical as a work of absolutely unsurpassed arrogance and imperial menace, but I had to hand it to the old pontiff: if God and the devil were battling, the battlefield would be here, quite literally on the frontlines of life and death.

I tiptoed down the stairs and stood by the sliding back door of our small apartment. Brittany had taped a picture of the Annunciation on the wall, in preparation for the next day's festivities with the Society. We were hosting friends to celebrate the solemnity, which happily coincided with the beginning of Holy Week. I stared at Botticelli's rendition of the scene, the angel Gabriel bent so low before the Virgin, as if in awe of the fact that she could do something no angel could ever do—conceive the eternal Son of God! I recalled a line from E. E. Cummings: *Here is the deepest secret nobody knows, here is the root of the root and the bud of the bud and the sky of the sky of a tree called life.* Life! No one asked to be born into this never-ending story. For better or worse, it never stops. I shivered in the blackness. Even after death, whether we choose heaven or hell, we are immortal. Like the angels, human beings will never stop existing. And there was something very human about *Humanae Vitae*, achingly human.

Looking out into the dark night, it struck me that *Humanae Vitae* was written for humans, not angels. And angels and humans are, of course, not the same. For example, every single angel was made by God, and no angel comes into being unless God makes it, but angels do not procreate. They do not get to join God in making more creatures to bring him glory. It's different for humans. Every single human being was made by God—and also by a mother and father. *Unlike* angels, men and women procreate. Fruitfulness seemed to be a defining feature of male-and-female creation. It's *why* God made us male and female in the first place. Even when conceding that some people never procreate and that some couples are infertile, the fact remained that every single one of us was born of a woman, begotten of a man. Infertility was the exception, not the norm. Pleasure and intimacy were desirable and attended, but sexual complementarity—fertility, procreation—was primary and essential. The simple fact of the matter was that if humans did not reproduce sexually, we would not have sexual organs. If humans did not reproduce sexually, we would argu-ably not even have marriage.

I shivered in the blackness, following this train of thought. How many people does it take to make a baby? The idea of marriage as the conjugal union of one husband and one wife seemed to emerge out of *human nature*, the fact that one man and one woman can become a *mated pair*, "one flesh". Although marriage has many other goods and purposes, and although not all marriages produce offspring, marriage was clearly different in *kind* from other relationships because humans reproduce sexually, and human offspring are raised best with both the biological mother and father. They also require an unquantifiable amount of nurturing and education. If humans did not reproduce sexually, and if children could simply swim away from their mothers after birth like baby sharks, then the institution of marriage would never have been established. Historically, marriage laws served to reinforce the bond between children and their parents, especially to link children to their fathers. Apart from its unique suitability to conceive and rear children, everything else about marriage seemed to be derivative. And all of this was God's idea.

The marriage act is *how* the sons of Adam and daughters of Eve get to join God in making more creatures to bring him glory! This is as much a privilege as a burden. It's no small thing to bring into existence a creature made in the image of God who will never cease to exist, "an immortal horror or everlasting splendor", as C. S. Lewis put it.[9] Not even the angels get to do this. Yet from the start, this unfathomable privilege was entrusted to us: "Be fruitful and multi-ply" (Gen 1:28).

Startled by the extravagance of it all, I tiptoed back up the stairs and climbed back into bed. Lying next to Brittany, I asked myself: *What are people for?* I had always considered Catholicism's vision of sexuality to be pseudo-realistic, even outlandish, but I could appreci-ate a defense of human life, of the family. It certainly wasn't shallow.

Few people will admit that they live for money, or work, or power, because it sounds shallow, and it is. "For home, for country!" soldiers say. "Save the women and children!" Human life is the most valuable thing on the planet. You could build the tallest buildings, find a cure for cancer, paint the most beautiful painting, establish the mightiest empire, or fly to the moon, and it would be nothing compared to what the most ordinary man and woman can do quite naturally: conceive a child. The buildings will crumble, the empires will fall, but the child will last forever. From the very beginning, out of the abundance of his love, God wanted to fill the world with men and women made in his image who would delight in him and bring him glory. Unlike the angels, the human vocation is not only to sing but also to create. The more people, the more praise. To say there are too many people in the world is like saying there is too much praise, too much love. Even so, is it always intrinsically wrong to use artificial contraception deliberately to prevent new human beings from coming into existence?

I sighed, and underneath the sigh was something dangerous, something that felt disloyal to the plans Brittany and I had made. Procreation was all fine and good, but didn't Brittany and I need a few years to establish our marriage? As we started the new parish, we would largely depend on Brittany's salary. What about our ministry? What about planning every pregnancy and spacing them out? What about being responsible? What about paying for college? Sex was intended for procreation, yes, but it was also intended for pleasure and intimacy. Shouldn't Christians welcome reliable birth control—just as they welcomed the discovery of penicillin—as one more step in human progress? The more I thought about it, the more the idea that artificial contraception was immoral seemed completely impractical. And although I believed in the apostolic succession and the authority of bishops, I did not believe in popes. Besides, "You no play-a the game, you no make-a the rules." No pope was going to fool me! With that, I fluffed up my pillow, rolled over, and fell asleep.

* * * * *

After dinner, Brittany and I liked to listen to records and talk. In those days, we listened to Sufjan Stevens' *Seven Swans*, Paul Simon's *Graceland*, and Yo Yo Ma's *Cello Suites*. Perhaps not surprisingly, being newlyweds, Brittany and I often talked about ourselves. We talked about how every marriage has the potential to be a great work of art, but great works of art don't happen by accident. You have to mean it. You also need a model, an example to follow.

Most couples strive to conform their love to some pattern or ideal, even if it's less than ideal. I'll never forget when a friend told me that he and his girlfriend were going to get married. They had only been dating for a little over a month.

"Do you love each other?" I asked, not knowing what else to say.

"We're gay for each other," he said.

"What?"

"The kids, the church, the house with a white picket fence—we reject all that," he explained. "We're gay for each other."

My friend didn't identify as gay, yet he considered homosexuality to be an *ideal*. As Brittany and I talked about it, it seemed plausible that a society that operates on the assumption that children are a lifestyle option, and therefore *values* contraceptive sex, could conceivably come to view homosexuality as an *ideal*. Before anyone dreamed of normalizing sodomy, people wanted to be able to have sex without conceiving a child. And latex, chemicals, and surgical procedures make it possible to believe that sex is firstly about recreation rather than procreation. Pornography shrewdly crops fertility from the scene, and it shapes what people expect from sex. The cultural acceptance of sodomy, so obviously unfruitful, would only legitimize the belief that sex was firstly about pleasure or intimacy. Besides, wouldn't claiming that homosexual behavior is wrong hold others to a moral standard to which one's own behavior does not conform?

"No one, not even my parents, ever once asked me if I wanted to be a mother," Brittany said. "The only questions were which college, which career, which city. But when it came to sex, everyone assumed I would have lots of it."

I coughed.

"It was simply taken for granted that I would sterilize myself," Brittany continued, "like having good hygiene."

When it came down to it, were Brittany and I "gay" for each other? So removed from its natural purpose, had we reduced our marriage bed to mutual masturbation? Every marriage has the potential to be a great work of art, and the more it corresponds to the heavenly pattern, the greater it will be. I agreed with Saint Paul that marriage was a great mystery, a sacrament, and that it ought to mirror the love Christ has for his people, the Church. Brittany and I were not called to "be gay" for each other; we were called to be *Christ* for each other (cf. Eph 5:32). But what did it look like to "be Christ" for each other?

* * * * *

Holy Week arrived, and it was as if the clock stopped ticking. Triduum, the three-in-one day that begins at sundown on Holy Thursday and concludes with the Easter Vigil, helped us to see things in perspective. The marriage bed is a parable of the Kingdom of God, and Triduum is when the Kingdom of God enters into our time. On Holy Thursday we remembered how before the Passover meal, Jesus bent low to wash his disciples' feet, following the old ordination rites for priests, and told them to do the same. On Good Friday, we traced Jesus' "Sorrowful Way" in penitential prayer. We revered Christ's passion and death on the Cross, that instrument of torture that has become the instrument of salvation. In the grief of Holy Saturday, we remembered Christ's descent to the dead, to the stink and rot of death. We started preparations for the Easter feast, chopping herbs and sifting flour for the cake. At the Easter Vigil, which began in darkness, we sang of God's faithfulness from Adam to Christ. We watched as those who had been praying and preparing to join in the sacraments were bathed in the waters of Baptism and anointed with oil, like brides before a wedding in days of yore. While keeping Triduum, I kept asking: What would it look like for Brittany and I to "be Christ" for each other?

It wasn't until sometime during the Octave of Easter, those eight days in which Christians ask, *How can I live my Baptism?*, that I saw the answer plainly: to "be Christ" looked like *dying to self*. It looked like imitating Jesus, who, even though he was God, "emptied himself ... and became obedient unto death, even death on a cross" (Phil 2:6–8). It looked like a *total self-gift*. "Husbands, love your wives, as Christ loved the Church and gave himself up for her" (Eph 5:25). It looked like stepping out in trust, saying, "Not my will, but yours" (Lk 22:42). It looked *fruitful*. As God's Trinitarian love is creative, Christ's love is the means of new birth, "a new creation" (2 Cor 5:17).

Clearly, our marriage bed did not conform to the pattern of Christ and his Church. We had been approaching our marriage bed as if pleasure and intimacy were the point, but in order to sustain the illusion we needed purchasable accessories or hormonal treatments, not to mention the unpleasant side effects for Brittany. Clearly, something was terribly wrong. The marriage act was intended to be a *total self-gift*, but we were measuring out our giving through such calculative self-interest. Confusing responsibility with "control", we were not giving ourselves to one another completely. We were not trusting God.

The decision to trust God with fertility might have been easy and inconsequential for someone else. For me, it was an arduous and invaluable form of obedience, of love. Wrestling through it forced me to reevaluate my priorities and learn to surrender, which I would need to practice again and again in the coming years. It pushed me to decide how much I would trust God to care for our family's needs, as we exchanged control for trust in Jesus. I knew that God wanted a radical trust, my willingness to trade my own dreams for his: sex is oriented toward procreation, joining God in making more immortal human beings made in the image of God.

The arguments made sense, but my heart needed to catch up. I was proud and it was difficult to admit that I could have been wrong about contraception. As John Henry Cardinal Newman says: "Quarry the granite rock with razors, or moor the vessel with a thread of silk; then may you hope with such keen and delicate instruments as human knowledge and human reason to contend against those giants, the passion and pride of man."[10] The idea of giving God *everything* sounded good in principle; living it was another matter. I did not know if I could give him that. But I sensed that if I didn't, if I did not say Yes, step by step, I would follow the path of the fallen angels who said, "I will not serve."

Brittany and I prayed together. We stayed up late into the night, talking. The fact of the matter was that Brittany and I were called to be holy as God is holy. And the holiness of God is pure love, a total self-gift, a complete surrender that holds nothing back. Was it possible to dedicate our marriage to God—to be holy, set apart—while holding back something as central to our humanity as our God-given fertility?

God loved the world so much that he gave his only Son. He gave himself completely, holding nothing back. In response, what did the Blessed Virgin Mary give God? She gave him her *fertility*. She gave God not only her heart but her *body*, a total self-donation.

Some things really are black or white. Loving God, we could not say, "This far, and no further." Like Mary, we had to *trust* God with our fertility, our plans, our future. We needed to take a step in the right direction, even if it was just a small step. There was no other way. For us, the secret to being Christ for each other, the secret to giving God everything, was to start small. When it came to our fertility, we had to "offer it up".

* * * * *

"Is it safe?" someone said.

"Safe?" I said. "Of course it isn't safe. But it's good."

"What about your career?" someone asked Brittany.

She laughed. "Do I really want to give the best years of my life to a career?"

Spring is soft and melty, and you can almost smell the colors. Springtime is love time, the time for sowing and planting. In spring, we are reminded that the land is not a blank slate, but an ecosystem. If a farmer walked away, the fields would eventually turn back into their natural ecosystem. Spring reminds us that we ought not simply to impose our will upon the land, force-feeding it chemicals and poisons to make it do what we want it to do. Rather, we should work with it. If we do not listen to the land, we will destroy it. Nature matters.

Our bodies are bearers of truth. They are instruments of love, carriages of grace. God shares his divine life with us, enabling us to create with him. Whatever else we may be, as men and women we are sexually complementary and mutually involved in generation. This is no social construct. This is the permanent and irreducible truth of biology and human nature. This is our heritage and our future. This is our doom. In motherhood and fatherhood, Brittany and I could collaborate with God to create and sustain life. We could see that throughout human history, the song of praise spreads out, the choir increases, the chorus grows louder. This is why God made marriage, why he made us male and female in the first place: unlike the angels, the human vocation is not only to sing but also to *create*.

"Next you'll tell me not to fight cancer or to avoid aspirin when I have a headache," one friend said.

But being a man or a woman is not a headache, and it certainly is not like having cancer. Sexual differentiation is one of our greatest natural resources. As with any natural resource, a good thing can be squandered. Minerals, forests, water, fertile land, and other natural goods can be exploited, poisoned, or destroyed. Sexuality is no exception. True, we could clear-cut and bulldoze this ecosystem. We could force-feed it chemicals and poisons. We could make this ecosystem do whatever we want it to do. But in the end, we would only destroy it. But sex was not meant to be exploited, polluted, or commercialized. It was intended for human flourishing, for the procreation of children, for our mutual society, help, and comfort. We had been given this gift in trust. In order to be responsible, we need to listen to the land. What does it want to be? How could we work with it, naturally? "Sow for yourselves righteousness, reap the fruit of mercy; break up your fallow ground, for it is time to seek the LORD, that he may come and rain salvation upon you" (Hos 10:12).

A woman is not an appliance. The fruitfulness of her body reminds us that she ought not to be used and then discarded. Her breasts and womb remind us that human life—not robotic or aquatic or alien life, but *human* life—means children and commitment. These things, like all sacred vessels, are veiled. In the Sacrament of Matrimony, man and wife come together to make their bodies extraordinary, irreplaceable, fruitful. We tell the story of Christ and his Church. Of course, we do not deserve Christ's self-donation, his total, cruciform gift; but we must follow his example. We must love without limits. "And what does he desire? Godly offspring" (Mal 2:15).

It took time, but Brittany and I were learning to listen to the land. We wanted to work with it, not against it. We did not want to live our marriage *in spite* of being sexual, but *through* our natural fertility. We realized that people would look at us like we were dinosaurs who had not yet heard that our kind were supposed to be extinct. But, in fact, we would simply be one man and one woman coming together in marriage. We started practicing what one Catholic mom blogger, Haley Stewart, called "Awesome Family Planning". Standing side by side, complicit, we wanted to do what we were made to do—glorify God and revel in him with the most basic gift: our bodies. It's a command: "Glorify God in your body" (1 Cor 6:20).

It wasn't long before Brittany told me she had news. Her eyes were damp and bright. I had just gulped down a mouthful of cereal and milk came out my nose. We held each other in the Bible-black predawn, hearts racing—just the thought of it was terrifying—but our cheeks were streaked with happy tears when the sun broke through a cloud of white chalk, and filled our small apartment with the utter east.

14

My Kingdom for a Horse!

The God-Man did not establish ephemeral institutions.

—Vladimir Solovyov[1]

Jesus Christ did or did not mean that there
should be built up in the world,
after his departure, a visible and organized
society bearing his name.

—William Reed Huntington[2]

The thing is, when you write about your life you are tempted to make things appear better than they seem. You want to craft a more acceptable version of the story or present only the carefully edited edition of the person you wish you were. But words are revealing. Like looking in a mirror, writing has a way of exposing the least tidy version of yourself. You have to avoid the temptation to suck in your stomach. You have to lean in and take a good look at your own story with gut-honest vulnerability, and this almost always hurts.

In a way, Awesome Family Planning was the most religious thing Brittany and I had ever done. Sex was no longer on our terms. We were no longer in control. We were trying to love God with our hearts *and* our bodies, not only with our words but with our lives, and holding nothing back—not even our fertility. And as we tried to honor the natural cycles of Brittany's feminine body and God's designs for the marriage bed, we were surprised to feel like we were beginning to live a story much bigger than ourselves. Unexpectedly, more than the liturgical year or the long sacred view of time of the Benedictine monastics, more than our growing appreciation for liturgy or discipline, beautiful vestments or soaring cathedrals, it was the Sacrament of Matrimony that forced us to address head-on the fact that Christianity was never meant to be "spiritual but not religious". In particular, discovering the truth about Awesome Family Planning forced us to reconsider the papacy—when so many got this wrong, how did the popes get it right?

People tend to search for and favor information that confirms their preexisting beliefs, Christianity as it was first presented to them. It's difficult to accept that those who first told us about Jesus, who first showed us the way, could have been wrong on a few key points: *Christianity is not a religion; it's a relationship.* It's difficult to admit that there might be more to the story than we had ever imagined, more to the Kingdom and more to the cost of discipleship. In my heart, I knew what I was wrestling with—the very sovereignty of my God and my King.

Things were getting real, and fast. With my ordination in the works and a baby on the way, a crisis began brewing. The thought of being a father and a priest was as rousing as a burning brand, but it brought a deep sense of anxiety. I was beginning to sense that *fatherhood* and the *priesthood* were not just beautiful ideas but very real responsibilities, and, frankly, I felt ill-equipped. How were we going to afford this? Would I be a good dad? In what ways would this change our starting an Anglican church in Minneapolis? Even more, as the new life Brittany carried under her heart began to grow, I began to wonder to what church our child would belong, or his children and grandchildren. This was no longer mere theological speculation. It was becoming a matter of covenant faithfulness.

Over the years I had come to see that in Scripture, God's divine covenants were family bonds. When Christ formed the New Covenant with us, it was more than a social contract or legal exchange in which he took our sin and gave us his righteousness. This was part of the truth, but it was not the whole truth. Just as the Old Covenant was how God fathered Israel as his own family, so also the New Covenant is how Jesus gathered together a worldwide family in which he shares his divine sonship with us, making us children of God. To be baptized is to be born again into this family, the Church. To be justified is to share in the family graces, as "sons in the Son". To be sanctified is to share in the family life of the Holy Spirit. To celebrate the eucharist is to feast at the family table. For the sake of my growing family, I longed for the unity and truth of God's family. But which family? Which table? Which truth?

The joy of August had blown out like a candle, ushering in a dark and interrogating September. I sold my painter's truck, a red Ford Ranger, so that we could buy a four-door Honda with room for a baby car seat. We sent out our fundraising letters, as usual, and I networked with bishops and priests and parishioners to prepare for starting a parish in Minneapolis. I continued leading the weekly prison Bible study, and with the beginning of my senior year also began a chaplaincy internship at a Congregationalist nursing home. My jobs included counseling the elderly, helping out with chapel, and comforting the dying. Their hands felt small and cold in mine, like the claw of a bird. I was very aware that I was a guest visiting at the end of a long journey, and from the outside it was heartbreaking to watch people grow old without the sacraments, with no hope of Viaticum, no possibility of purgatory, no communion of the saints.

Pregnancy was changing Brittany, and her "nesting instinct" was strong. Unfortunately, with the due date just one week before my graduation from seminary, it was almost impossible. We could pack the overnight bag for the night at the birth center, we could pick the color of the car seat and study the pros and cons of vaccinations, but we couldn't paint the baby's nursery or buy a crib—we didn't know where we would live, or if I would have a job. I could tell that it was hard for her to have our future be "up in the air", and I tried my best to remain positive.

As autumn blew in, I continued my internship at the Anglican church in Milwaukee, teaching classes, assisting in the liturgy, preaching, counseling, helping out wherever I was needed. The parish was everything Brittany and I thought we wanted—urban, hip, liturgical, biblical, social justice–oriented, great worship music. So why did we dread going each Sunday? To make matters worse, outside of the Society of Mary, Brittany was having a hard time finding other Anglican mothers who were open to life or believed in the sacraments the way we did. Unexpectedly, pregnancy exposed just how lonely we felt in the Midwest Anglican subculture.

Not only were my classes at the Milwaukee parish criticized for being "too Catholic", but our launch team back in Minneapolis did not approve of my views on women's ordination, the necessity of the sacraments as a means of grace, my prayers for the holy souls in purgatory, or the value I put in having a relationship with those saints who have passed through death and are with God in heaven. They said that it was standoffish for a priest to look liturgically East, that refusing to consecrate grape juice was unpastoral. Expecting parishioners to baptize their newborn babies was insensitive. Requiring parishioners in a state of mortal sin to go to Confession before receiving the holy eucharist was simply out of the question. And still, we all agreed that we were "more catholic than the Catholics". We valued liturgy and disapproved of projector screens, but after much discussion it became clear that everyone basically wanted an Evangelical church with a touch of "historic Christianity".

To make matters worse, my canonicals were sent back again and again because my answers were "too Catholic". For example, I was assigned to write an essay about the question of stealing in terms of Anglican ethical thought. I appealed to Thomas Aquinas. To correct my errors, I was assigned to write a book review of Rowan Williams' *Crisis and Recovery* which was held up as a model of Anglican ethics. What troubled me wasn't just that Williams' book was obscure and an inadequate resource for Anglican ethics but that the whole process of correcting my "Catholic answers" seemed only to expose that Anglicans didn't have any. The problem was, of course, that I was a postulant for Holy Orders in a church that, as they say in England, didn't seem to do what is said on the tin. Anglican doctrine seemed to be as thin and malleable as a coat-hanger wire. Its episcopal authority seemed to be an always breaking slab of real estate. In the meantime, what would I preach? What sacraments would my parish be able to offer?

My canonical supervisor noted that I was "obviously coming from a particular strain of Anglicanism", but these "strains" were actually flat-out contradictions. As an Anglican priest, I would have to submit to my bishop—but his particular "strain" of Anglicanism was totally arbitrary, at least on the ground. In theory, we believed that bishops were the bond of unity, the guardians of the truth, and the instrument of grace. "The order of bishops exists as a safeguard from schism and division," wrote Anglican theologian Vernon Staley. "To separate from the bishops is to separate from the Church of which the bishops are rulers ... an act of disloyalty to Jesus Christ, whose representatives they are.... By this means the true faith is preserved in the world."[3] I began to wonder how this could be if Anglicanism was premised on the idea that bishops could be in schism with one another, teach contradictory truths, and disagree on the means of grace. I felt as though someone was pulling the carpet out from under my feet.

Schism is, by definition, *diabolic* ("to tear apart," "to scatter"). Yet I was soon to be priested in a diocese (ACNA) that had split off from a splinter group (AMiA), which had in turn separated from another division (TEC), which had its origin in another division, the Church of England. Each splintering, like the Reformation itself, was considered tragic but necessary. But was this what Jesus had in mind when he established his Church? And didn't the defense of Anglicanism reduce Anglicanism itself to a *necessary evil*? Christ prayed so fervently that his covenant family would be one (Jn 17:21). Was this just wishful thinking, or did Jesus provide the *means* for unity?

Now, this might not seem like much of a crisis to many, but for someone about to become a priest, knowing his denomination was predicated on the idea that schism was an unfortunate but necessary reality, it meant the world. And fatherhood was changing me. Brittany was pregnant, and her growing bookshelf of baby books told her what to expect; my job was to learn what I could do to make the next nine months safe and holy. But would an Anglican church plant be a safe place for us to start a family?

Little did we know that between the stick turning blue and the drive to the delivery room God would call us further than we had ever gone before. By "offering up" something as physical and personal as our marriage bed, Brittany and I began to see not only our *marriage covenant* but also the *New Covenant* in a fresh way. Things that were once fun ideas were becoming painful realities. And with my final year of seminary, we began to wonder if there was more to Church—more to the New Covenant and more to the Kingdom of God—than we had ever imagined. In the end, it was the Kingdom that would force us forever to leave the sands of spirituality and to accept the rock on which Christ built his Church.

* * * * *

When I used to say, "I'm spiritual but not religious," the Kingdom of God was always out there, not here. It was "at hand", but insubstantial.

Divorced from the past, from the human body, the world of people, images, sacred space, time, tradition, obligations, and especially apostolic authority, such a kingdom was certainly "purer". It also wasn't anything like a kingdom.

Religion, on the other hand, is *in* the world but not *of* it. The Kingdom of God is undeniably *here*. The eternal Son of God took on flesh. He became a man. He entered our world through the family, sanctifying a home in Nazareth. He did not abolish the law, but fulfilled it (Mt 5:17). He established what he called "my Church" (Mt 16:18), "the new covenant" (Lk 22:20; 1 Cor 11:25), "the kingdom of God" (Lk 4:43).

The Church Fathers identified three dimensions of the "Kingdom of God". First, the Kingdom is Christ himself. He is the pearl and the treasure, which one will give everything to possess (Mt 13:44–46). Second, the Kingdom is present in the heart of the believer. Through the Holy Spirit, Christ the King reigns in the heart of every disciple (Eph 3:16–17). Third, the Kingdom is the Church. The Church is the Mystical Body of Christ, who is himself the King, and also the assembly of those in whom Christ dwells. It is a real "kingdom", a covenant family under the reign of Christ, governed according to his constitution and in accordance with his laws. This third, ecclesiological dimension reminds us that Christianity is not a private spirituality, but a public religion, a real Kingdom with a real King.

In an effort to reduce Christianity into a spirituality, it is sometimes suggested that the first two dimensions of the Kingdom somehow make the ecclesiological dimension impossible. But Jesus did not write a book to encourage people's private spiritualities; as far as we know, he never told the apostles to write anything at all. Instead, seeing that the people were *scattered* like sheep without a shepherd, he *gathered* the Twelve and sent them not only to preach the "kingdom of heaven" but also to baptize, and to make disciples (Mt 9:35–10:8; 28:19). At their ordination, he told them to preside over the Eucharistic liturgy because he knew that if we do not eat his flesh and drink his blood, there could be no life in us (Lk 22:19; Jn 6:53). Jesus did not write a book; he established a Kingdom. The Church on earth is, of course, a mixed reality, with both weeds and wheat, good fish and bad, but this does not change the fact that she is the Body of Christ (cf. Mt 13; Col 1:18). The Church in heaven is the fullest realization of this Kingdom, but in the meantime the Church on earth makes this Kingdom truly present in mystery. So what did Jesus want it to look like?

The Bible tells one story, and it rhymes. The New Testament Church was the fulfilment, rather than the destruction, of the Old Testament Church. Raymond Brown put it this way: "The kingdom established by David was a political institution to be sure, but one with enormous religious attachments (priesthood, temple, sacrifice, prophecy).... *It is the closest Old Testament parallel to the Church.*"[4] God had promised that David's would be an everlasting dynasty: "Your house and your kingdom shall be made sure for ever before me; your throne shall be established for ever" (2 Sam 7:16). In Jesus, that promise was kept.

I had already come to see that the apostolic ministry of the Church ran deep into Israel's history, to Jerusalem and her kings, and to the ministers of the kingdom. Jesus was the new King David, the "son of David", the "king", the "Christ"—which means "anointed one", a title given to a Davidic king anointed at his coronation (Mt 1:1, 6; 16). What's more, the Davidic kings did not rule alone. They appointed ministers to help them. As King Solomon appointed *twelve* officers to rule his kingdom, so also Jesus appointed *twelve* apostles to rule his Kingdom after his Ascension (1 Kings 4:7; Mt 19:28). By calling the Twelve, Jesus was establishing the hierarchy of his Kingdom on earth. This was why Anglicans believed in bishops—the Church is *apostolic*. By choosing *twelve* men to be his apostles, Jesus, "the root and the offspring of David" (Rev 22:16), was symbolically gathering the twelve tribes of Israel; the Twelve correspond to the twelve princes of the tribes of Israel in the wilderness (Num 1:4–16).

Christianity is not just another spirituality, because Jesus *gathered the tribes*, established a *Kingdom*. The Twelve were his royal cabinet, entrusted with viceroyal authority to represent him in his New Israel, the Church: "As the Father has sent me, even so I send you.... If you forgive the sins of any, they are forgiven" (Jn 20:21, 23); "He who hears you hears me, and he who rejects you rejects me" (Lk 10:16). King Christ had appointed them to an office, and an office left vacant must be filled (Acts 1:20). Thus, the apostles appointed presbyters in each church (Acts 14:23). Paul reminded Timothy that the office of bishop was conferred on him through the laying on of hands (1 Tim 1:6; 4:14; 5:22). As *King,* Jesus was the ultimate foundation stone (1 Cor 3:10; 1 Pet 2:6–8); because he was establishing a *Kingdom,* he appointed ministers as foundation stones as well (Mt 16:18; Eph 2:20; Gal 2:9; Rev 21:14). Even after Christ's Ascension, the Kingdom was to remain a social reality, with apostolic succession and authority. In other words, the Kingdom of God is not only spiritual but also religious.

So why did Anglicanism exist? Our very ecclesiology *depended* on the idea of a Kingdom divided, bishops torn asunder, an endless tearing and scattering. In our defense, we tended either to reduce the Kingdom of God to a spirituality or simply to admit that our existence was a necessary evil. Had Henry VIII lifted the Church out of the ground only to plant it firmly in midair?

Was I experiencing my own kind of "nesting instinct"? I was certainly having something like a crisis of fatherhood. I had become a biological father, and I was soon to become a spiritual father. The more Anglicanism began to feel like a melting ice floe, the more I longed for a lifeboat. At my ordination, I would swear obedience to my bishop, who was the spiritual father of all the priests in our diocese—but to whom did all these quarreling, divided bishops swear obedience? Was there a father for the fathers?

"It sounds like you're looking for the Catholic Church," Old Hickory said over the phone, when I shared my apprehensions about Brittany's pregnancy and my pending priesthood.

"But the pope is a tyrant, not a father," I said.

"But 'pope' means 'father'."

I sighed.

And then one cold Sunday in January, feeling woozy and disoriented, Brittany and I snuck over to a neighboring Catholic parish, just to see. Everything was going fine until the elevation of the Host. Brittany leaned over as if in pain, but her eyes were fixed upon the altar. I had to remind her that we were not in full communion with the Catholic Church and so we could not receive the Eucharist. Afterward, we decided to walk to a nearby diner; our collars turned up against the biting wind. Our coats flapped like sails. The snow was so cold it squeaked. The sun broke out between a rift of clouds, and the wind seemed to sweep the words from her mouth. She said that during Mass she heard a voice clearly say, "Love him!" She knew she needed God's life to get inside of her, into the child in her womb. It was like her body was yelling, "Eat that! I need it!"

A shiver of fear rushed through me, as if I had just witnessed a kind of omen I had been looking for without realizing it.

I cannot say that I was happy. But for the sake of my growing family, for the sake of my calling to the priesthood, I prayed that God would help me to be open to the truth, no matter the cost. That night, after hours of study, I stepped in the living room and announced to Brittany that I was going to look into the papacy. Learning about the Kingdom and the Twelve, I needed to go back to that horrible passage in Scripture where Jesus announced the establishment of his Church, to the line that stopped me cold: "You are Peter, and on this rock I will build my Church" (Mt 16:18).

* * * * *

It was a hard winter. The peaked rooftops of the seminary were laden with snow. Every day the postman delivered more books about the biblical roots of the papacy—and Brittany reminded me about the budget. Among others, I read Scott Butler's *Jesus, Peter, and the Keys*, Stephen Ray's *Upon this Rock*, and John Salza's *The Biblical Basis for the Papacy*. On most mornings I wore my old favorite bathrobe, the one that made me feel like C. S. Lewis, and brewed coffee. Day after day, steaming cup in hand, I opened my Bible to the famous passage in Matthew 16:13–20, and got to work. I was trembling slightly, with both fear of the unknown and a deep childlike excitement.

First, it struck me that when Simon said, "You are the Christ, the Son of the living God" (v. 16), he probably didn't mean "You are the Second Person of the Trinity." In the Old Testament, the title "Son of God" was descriptive of a *Davidic king* (Ps 2:7; 2 Sam 7:14). Being a Jew, Simon was revealing Jesus' *dynastic* identity.

This discovery was electric, bringing me fully awake and sentient. Our Lord's response to Peter's confession that he is the true Davidic King would be total gibberish if Jesus were not referring to something obviously related to *kings* and *kingdoms*, something that Simon and the other apostles standing nearby would recognize. It was unlikely that Jesus was pulling words and phrases of out of thin air:

Blessed are you, Simon Bar-Jona!
For flesh and blood has not revealed this to you,
but my Father who is in heaven.
And I tell you, you are Peter,
and on this rock I will build my Church,
and the gates of Hades shall not prevail against it.
I will give you the keys of the kingdom of heaven,
and whatever you bind on earth shall be bound in heaven,
and whatever you loose on earth shall be loosed in heaven.
(Mt 16:18–19)

"You are the Christ," Peter said. "And I tell you, you are Peter, and on this rock I will build my Church," said Jesus. The wordplay was clearly intended to underscore a point. What was it?

Grammatically, it was clear that "this rock" could not be Jesus himself—he was the one who was going to *build* his Church. Of course, Jesus was the foundation stone (1 Cor 3:10; 1 Pet 2:6–8), but the apostles are also identified as foundational (Eph 2:20; Rev 21:14; Gal 2:9). Nor could "this rock" be Peter's confession: the antecedent to the pronoun "this" was clearly the man *Simon*, whom Jesus had just renamed "Rock" (Peter). Because Jesus probably spoke Aramaic ("You are *kepha* and on this *kepha* I will build my Church") and also because "Rock" had not yet been used as a proper name in the Greek-speaking world, Saint Luke had to compensate by taking a feminine noun, *petra*, and making it masculine, *Petros*. Clearly Peter was the rock upon which King Christ would build his Church.

Why did Jesus rename Simon in the first place? Certainly not because of his stable character! The only other men God *personally* renames in salvation history are Abram and Jacob, and every new name represents covenant, fatherhood, and authority. As such, he was the leader and representative for the apostles who would open the door of the Gospel to Jews and Gentiles. But—and this was a big but!—the context seemed to say nothing about papal *succession*. Perhaps Peter's unique role was a *charism* that ended with his death?

Ah, what a relief—there was no biblical basis for the pope. The designation of Peter as "the rock" was temporary, not a permanent apostolic office. The Church had bishops, but it didn't have a pope.

Yet, perhaps strangely, over the years I had returned to the popes for answers. Again and again, I had found them to speak only the truth on matters of faith and morals, even when it wasn't popular. The popes were right about the filioque clause (that the Holy Spirit proceeds from the Father and the Son). Popes Pius IX and Pius XII were right about the Blessed Virgin Mary. Pope Paul VI was right about the marriage act, and Pope Saint John Paul II was right about the theology of the body. I had to ask myself honestly: *If the popes were right about sex, about Mary and the Mass and the other sacraments, about heaven and hell and purgatory, was the only thing they were wrong about the papacy itself?*

This led to another question: What did Jesus mean by the "keys of the kingdom"? Was this exchange an unsolvable problem, or did Peter and the disciples know what Jesus was doing?

To be fair, I wanted to hear what the Catholic scholars had to say. They suggested that Peter identified the *dynastic* identity of Jesus; so, in turn, Jesus revealed the *dynastic* office appointed to Peter. By renaming Simon "Rock" and handing him the "keys" to his kingdom, Jesus may have been paraphrasing the popular passage about a succession of royal stewards in Isaiah 22:19–23. During the reign of Hezekiah, a man named Shebna was the chief steward. But Shebna was no longer worthy of his office. So God sent Isaiah with news that he would be replaced by a more righteous man, Eliakim:

> Thus says the Lord GOD of hosts, "Come, go to this steward, to
> Shebna, who is over the household, and say to him: . . .
> I will thrust you from your office, and you will be cast down from
> your station.
> In that day I will call my servant Eliakim the son of Hilkiah,
> and I will clothe him with your robe, and will bind your belt on
> him, and will commit your authority to his hand;
> and he shall be a father to the inhabitants of Jerusalem and to the
> house of Judah.
> I will place on his shoulder the key of the house of David;
> he shall open, and none shall shut;
> and he shall shut, and none shall open.
> I will fasten him like a peg in a sure place,
> and he will become a throne of honor to his father's house."
>
> (Is 22:15, 19–23).

Straightaway, I noticed that the symbol of the chief steward's authority was the "keys" of the royal household, and that he had the power to "open" (loose) as well as to "shut" (bind). He wore special robes of honor and a belt, a traditional priestly garment. His office did not cease with his death, but was a *chair* ("throne") to be filled by one man succeeding another. He was a "father" to the inhabitants of Jerusalem.

Curious, I began looking into it. The Davidic kings appointed ministers to help them, and the royal steward was the highest-ranking official in the king's royal court, appointed to manage the day-to-day affairs of the kingdom. His office was second only to the king in authority. He was not the king himself, but he was the king's mouthpiece, the king's right-hand man. While many of the king's ministers had power to bind and loose, the chief steward could bind what the others had loosed and loose what the others had bound. Were the parallels mere coincidence? Peter revealed the dynastic identity of Jesus, so, in the presence of the other eleven apostles, Jesus revealed the dynastic identity of Peter—as the one "over the household".

The excitement I felt over this idea was startling. To be honest, for several days I wrote the whole thing off on the grounds that the passage from Isaiah was "obscure" and that the office of royal steward was even more "obscure", and therefore somehow irrelevant. But, alas, the succession of royal stewards appeared not only in Isaiah 22:19–23 but *throughout* the Old Testament.

In particular, my research led me to the famous story of when the Pharaoh gave this royal office to Joseph (Gen 41; 45:8). Pharaoh asked his stewards and Joseph a question that could be answered only by divine revelation. Only Joseph answered correctly. In response, Pharaoh appointed him to be the chief steward over his house, giving him his ring and changing his name to Zaphenath-paneah. Pharaoh said to Joseph, " 'Since God has shown you all this ... you shall be over my house, and all my people shall order themselves as you command; only as regards the throne will I be greater than you.... Without your consent no man shall lift up hand or foot in all the land of Egypt.' And Pharaoh called Joseph's name Zaphenath-paneah" (Gen 41:39–40, 44–45).

I had to admit, the parallels between Pharaoh's royal appointment of Joseph and Jesus' royal appointment of Peter were striking: both were asked a question by a king, both received a revelation from God, both answered the king with an infallible declaration, both were appointed to the office of royal steward by a king, both of their names were changed by a king, and both received signs of their royal assignment. These were hardly a pair of mismatched socks!

Being familiar with their own heritage, it seemed very plausible that Peter and the other apostles would have recognized that Jesus was referring to Isaiah 22 and Genesis 41. Although largely unknown today, the stories of Joseph and Eliakim would have been well known to any first-century Jew. Peter had just identified Jesus as the true King David, and in response Jesus identified Peter's role in his Kingdom. It made sense that Jesus would refer to a popular kingdom tradition because the Kingdom of God fulfilled and amplified the Davidic kingdom.

I bent over my books, taking notes furiously. Because the Davidic kingdom was the prefigurement of the Church, it made sense that while King Christ appointed *twelve* ministers, he would also appoint *one* to be the chief steward, giving Peter the symbols of this office and a new name. What Jesus gave to the apostolic college *as a whole* (Mt 18:18), he gave to Peter *individually* (Mt 16:19). As soon as Jesus told the Twelve that they will sit on thrones to judge the tribes of Israel, he immediately turned to Peter and told *him* to strengthen the others (Lk 22:28–32). As the chief steward, Peter was to feed his sheep, to rule over them (Jn 21:17). This was clearly not a personal charism but an office; and an office left vacant must have successors. Could it be that as in the Davidic kingdom of old, the pope is the King's premier representative and final court of appeal? Like the numerous Davidic royal stewards, who were each a "father to the inhabitants of Jerusalem" (Is 22:21), the pope leads as the "Holy Father" of the Church; like Joseph, who was "over [the] house" (Gen 41:40) of the Pharaoh, the pope is "over the Church".

It felt as if I were falling in slow motion, like a feather, or as if some great hand held me gently, guiding me down to *terra firma*. By what hermeneutic could I dismiss Petrine primacy and authority, while simultaneously retaining bishops? It was true that in Revelation 3:7–8 it's made clear that the keys belong to Jesus ("the holy one, the true one, who has the key of David" [v. 7]), but this only confirmed the Catholic Church's claim that Jesus gave *his* keys to his foremost apostle, Peter, *not unlike* how any Davidic king would have given his "keys" to his royal steward.

But once formed, prejudice is remarkably perseverant—especially anti-Catholic prejudice. Perhaps the New Testament did not give witness to Petrine authority in the Kingdom of God? I combed through the Gospels, looking for evidence of Peter's office that at all resembled that of the royal steward. First, and most emphatically, Jesus *prophesied* that he would rename Simon *Cephas*, "Rock" (Jn 1:42). The first disciple Jesus called was Simon Peter (Lk 5:1–11). Whenever the apostles were named, Peter headed the list (Mt 10:1–4; Mk 3:16–19; Lk 6:14–16; 9:32; Acts 1:13). In general, Peter spoke for the apostles (Mt 18:21; Mk 8:29; Lk 12:41; Jn 6:68–69), and he figured in many of the most dramatic scenes (Mt 14:28–32; 17:24–27; Mk 10:23–28). An angel was sent to announce the Resurrection to Peter, and the risen Christ first appeared to *Peter* before any other apostle (Mk 16:7; Lk 24:34). Mirroring Peter's threefold denial, Jesus asked Peter three times, "Do you love me?" (Jn 21:15–17). Then, as the "good shepherd" (Jn 10:11, 14), Jesus told Peter, "Feed my sheep" (Jn 21:17). It was Peter's faith that would "strengthen [his] brethren" (Lk 22:32).

Greatly discouraged by what a "plain reading" of these texts was suggesting, I turned to the book of Acts and the epistles. On Pentecost, Peter preached to the crowds (Acts 2:14–40). Peter worked the first healing miracle (Acts 3:6–7); even his shadow was healing (Acts 5). Peter headed the apostolic meeting that elected Matthias to replace Judas (Acts 1:13–26). Peter received the first converts (Acts 2:41), inflicted the first punishment (Acts 5:1–11), excommunicated the first heretic (Acts 8:18–23), led the first council in Jerusalem (Acts 15), and announced the first dogmatic decision (Acts 15:7–11). It was to *Peter* that God revealed that Gentiles were to be baptized and accepted as Christians (Acts 10:46–48). In Galatians, Paul validated his claim to be an apostle by invoking Peter (Cephas) twice. He went "to Jerusalem to visit Cephas" (1:18)—referring to him as *Cephas* ("Rock"), thus emphasizing his name change and apostolic vocation. Paul said that Christ "appeared to Cephas and *then* to the Twelve" (1 Cor 15:5). Clearly Peter had authority and primacy in the apostolic college. It wasn't that Saint Paul was second fiddle—he just wasn't the pope.

I got up and walked restlessly around the room. It's one thing to peck at the Catholic Church's argument; it's quite another to make one. And I had to admit, the Catholics had a strong biblical argument for the papacy. But my heart was as rooted as a turnip.

Somewhat desperately, I explored the Eastern Orthodox position on the matter. But the Orthodox churches were deeply divided among themselves, not unlike Anglicans. Their rejection of the pope was not so much biblical, but political. They claimed that Peter had only a "primacy of honor" among the apostles, not a primacy of *authority*. But the concept of a "primacy of honor" without a corresponding *authority* was not in the Bible. In fact, whenever Jesus speaks of Peter's relation to the other apostles, he seems to stress Peter's special mission to them and not his "honor". Of course, Christ's appointment of Peter's office came with honor, but the honor *followed* the authority of the office. Like brothers without a father, the Eastern churches were halved and quartered by their imperial politics and national ties—Greek, Russian, Ruthenian, Bulgarian, Hungarian, and so on.

The days seemed to move in a slow, almost drugged stupor. And then I read the great Orthodox convert to Catholicism Vladimir Solovyov. His comments on Jesus' words to Peter made sense:

> The God-Man did not establish ephemeral institutions.... In founding his visible Church, Jesus was thinking primarily of the struggle against evil; and in order to ensure for his creation that unity which is strength, he crowned the hierarchy with a single, central institution, absolutely indivisible and independent, possessing in its own right the fullness of authority and promise: "You are Peter, and on this rock I will build my church, and the gates of Hades shall not prevail against it" (Matt. 16:18).
>
> Our Lord expressly connected the permanence and stability of his Church in its future struggle against the powers of evil. If the power of binding and loosing conferred on the apostles is not a mere metaphor or a purely personal and temporary attribute, if it is, on the contrary, the actual living seed of a universal, permanent institution comprising the Church's whole existence, how can Peter's own special prerogatives, announced in such explicit and solemn terms, be regarded as barren metaphors or as personal and transitory privileges? Ought not they also to refer to some fundamental and permanent institution, of which the historic personality of Simon Bar-Jona is but the outstanding and typical representative?[5]

My heart snapped open. I didn't want to admit it, but if I considered it plain enough that there was New Testament evidence for apostolic succession in general, wasn't the authority of the Petrine office even more "plain"? Not even Paul's famous rebuke of Peter in Galatians 2:9–14 called into doubt "infallibility", because Paul rebuked Peter's failure to act on the truth, not an official proclamation that was false. Even today, bishops publicly rebuke popes. Catholic doctrine doesn't proclaim the pope's impeccability (absence of sin), only his infallibility (absence of error). The idea is that the Church is to speak the Word to the world. Is *Christ* infallible? The answer to that question is at the heart of the papacy's genius: "The truth will make you free" (Jn 8:32). Having been called "Satan" by Christ (Mk 8:33), having denied Christ three times (Mt 26:33–35; Mk 14:29–31; Lk 22:33–34; Jn 13:36–38), Peter was obviously not above reproach—yet *Jesus gave Peter the keys.*

I was not a Donatist. The validity of the sacraments does not rise or fall on the holiness (or sinfulness) of the priest. From the beginning, the apostolic Church had a lying Judas, a denying Peter, and a doubting Thomas. It was still apostolic. Was it still Petrine? Was the Catholic Church God's covenant family on earth?

I shared my findings with Brittany. To my surprise, she leaned back in our threadbare couch and smiled.

"You realize that if Catholicism is true, we're ruined," I said. "I won't be able to be a priest, we won't be able to start a church together, and after all this fundraising and talk, my reputation will be ruined."

Her smile slowly faded as this sank in. She stood and wrapped her arms around me, her growing belly pressed between us. "We need to pray."

* * * * *

Becoming a father had a way of making time speed up. I was learning, slowly, but life was now moving so quickly. I read the work of people who had converted to Catholicism—Gerard Manley Hopkins, Dorothy Day, Edith Stein, Thomas Merton, Robert Hugh Benson, John Saward, John Henry Newman, to name a few. I was greatly stirred by G.K. Chesterton's *The Catholic Church and Conversion*, and when

Brittany and I discovered Scott and Kimberly Hahn's conversion story, *Rome Sweet Home*, we could not put it down. I remember lying next to her as she read aloud passages from Stephen Ray's *Crossing the Tiber* from the neighboring pillow, and loving her—her countenance, her gentleness of spirit, her unaffected eagerness, her courage. Even though becoming Catholic would destroy all of our plans, and even though the timing couldn't have been worse with a baby on the way, somehow we were falling even more in love.

By mid-February, it was time to "talk shop" with the seminary friends I most respected. I shared the biblical case for the papacy with Sven.

"You just think the grass is greener on the other side," Sven said. "But Catholic bishops have nasty disagreements, and most of the laity don't even believe."

But a nasty disagreement is not the same as schism. Quarreling around the family table is a very different thing than running away from home altogether. *Of course* the sheep need a shepherd. And wasn't Jesus clear that Peter was to be the shepherd of the shepherds, a bishop to the bishops?

Next, I shared the biblical case for the papacy with Guy. He was convinced, but believed that ultimately Church history showed that the papacy was wrong.

"It's a good thing I don't believe in *sola scriptura!*" Guy said.

Next, I talked with another friend who conceded Jesus builds the Church on the rock that is Peter and his successors, the popes, but argued that he didn't need to be in communion with Rome because, in his view, the pope had exaggerated his office.

"So you thought you'd take matters into your own hands?" I asked.

"Yes," he said. "I mean, ultimately I submit only to the Bible."

I couldn't believe my ears.

But what exactly did Church history have to say about the papacy? What did the Church Fathers say about the bishop of Rome? I ordered more books. Not only was the patristic witness to the authority and primacy of Peter's successors in Rome overwhelming, but the later developments of this office were clearly in concert with the biblical witness. The papacy was the oldest dynasty in the world. Empires and kingdoms have come and gone, republican senates and brutal demagogies have risen up only to fall again, and the unbroken succession of popes has survived them all. The popes themselves have never been in doubt about their office as an institution established by Christ himself, destined to endure until the return of the King. Catholics form a fifth of the world's population; and the book of Acts ends, symbolically, with Peter and Paul in Rome because "Rome" symbolized the expanse of the reign of God "to the end of the earth" (1:8). Church history seemed only to strengthen the case for the papacy, not the other way around.

Then I asked a friend who was soon to be ordained a priest in the Episcopal Church why he wasn't Catholic.

"I think it's dangerous to search for a pure church instead of seeking the cross where we happen to find ourselves," he said. "Better to stay where you're planted."

Although this sounded quite brave, perhaps even noble, the more I thought about it, the more it raised problems. For example, what if a Nestorian priest refused to become Catholic because he felt it was better to stay where he was "planted"? It's one thing to believe God has called you to be a *missionary* to a schismatic, heretical sect; it's quite another to claim he's called you to become a *member*!

I shared the biblical basis of the papacy with my classmate Will. I knew he had been troubled by the papacy for some time and had almost converted at one point. As we walked through the Bible, he was wonderstruck. Together, we read John Henry Newman's *Development of Christian Doctrine*. Will was a faster reader than me, and he finished first.

"Can I come in?" he asked one night, knocking on my door.

We invited him into the living room.

"I believe," he said.

Will's eyes were bright with emotion though he looked worn, pale around the gills. He opened to the last page of Newman's book and read the invitation to convert to Catholicism:

> Time is short, eternity is long. Put not from you what you have found; regard it not as mere matter of present controversy; set not out resolved to refute it, and looking for the best way to do so; seduce not yourself with the imagination that it comes of disappointment, or disgust, or restlessness, or wounded feeling, or undue sensibility, or other weakness.

Wrap not yourself round in the associations of years past, nor determine that to be truth which you wish to be so, nor make an idol of cherished anticipations. Time is short, eternity is long.[6]

There was an awkward silence for a moment.

"I believe," Will said, tears streaming down his face. "I'm going to become Catholic."

The thought nearly stopped my heart. Because Will was to be priested in less than a month, we knew this decision would cost him everything. But John Henry Newman's words seemed to be written directly to us: "nor make an idol of cherished anticipations".

The next day, Will called his bishop to share the bad news. They spoke for several hours, and for several days after, Will didn't leave his apartment. At last, curious, I went to visit him.

"Look, Catholicism is not true," he said, somewhat testily.

I blinked.

"How so?" I asked.

"My bishop asked me if I was called to be married to my wife, and I said yes. He asked me if I was called to be a priest, and I said yes. And then my bishop reminded me that if God had called me to both marriage and the priesthood, and if Catholics don't allow priests to be married, then Catholicism cannot be true."

I nodded, and walked back to my apartment with a heavy heart. I was trembling slightly, with both fear of the unknown and a child-like wonder. Over the leafless trees the sky was crowded with clouds noted with a streak of blue watercolor. My breath vaporized on the bitter air. At first, it seemed Will had a point. But the more I thought about it, the more subjective his reasoning seemed. The truth of Catholicism does not rise or fall on an individual's sense of personal calling. It's either true or false—regardless of whether one feels called to be a priest and be married at the same time. As the implications of this realization began to settle, I realized that I had to make a decision. It was a matter of covenant faithfulness.

Just the thought of becoming Catholic made me break into a cold sweat. My scalp felt electrified. It was a matter firstly of love—better to receive God's love and better to love him back. What did it look like to *love* God? Again, "If you love me, you will keep my commandments" (Jn 14:15). When someone loves God, he obeys him.

If the Kingdom of God is nothing less than the gathered tribes of Israel, then I don't see how we can justify being out of communion with Christ's appointed "prime minister", the keeper of the keys, Peter and his successors. King Jesus deserved my total obedience. Schism was sin, no matter how eloquent my excuses. To those scattered national churches and independent provinces who remain out of communion with the pope, Saint Paul's question was a challenge: "Is Christ divided?" (1 Cor 1:13).

I tried not to panic over the mounting problems becoming Catholic would create. I sighed, suddenly miserable at the thought of what was happening to me, and how inauspicious the whole dreadful thing had been. But deep, deep down beneath the dread, I felt a smoldering hope.

When I arrived home, Brittany was reading in the living room. I walked down the hall and collapsed on the couch and told her that things weren't looking good. We would have no home. After so much preparation, people would understandably feel ill-used. My reputation was at stake. The truth shone out clearly, but the way forward was dark and foreboding.

Exhausted, I put my head in my hands. Brittany came and sat in my lap and kissed the top of my head and hugged me, wordless.

* * * * *

In hindsight it was inevitable, but at the time I couldn't think of anything more unexpected or more calamitous than becoming Catholic. And none came with greater swiftness. T. S. Eliot once spoke of "the awful daring of a moment's surrender".[7] Jesus was asking us to leave all that was familiar—our plans, home, families, friends. And the cost seemed unbearably high. Only the Holy Spirit could give us the strength to let go, to surrender. We couldn't do this alone.

We prayed like we had never prayed before. We sought Mary's intercession and entrusted ourselves to Saint Joseph. I felt a nudge to talk about Catholicism with Justin, one of my closest friends in the Society. I was shocked when he admitted that he too was discerning whether to be received into the Church. After class the next day, I mustered enough courage to tell another friend. To my wonderment, he confessed that he too believed in Catholicism.

Within a week, I discovered that five other seminarians were on this same path.

While the campus was in a tumult about the impending visit of a liberal female Episcopal presiding bishop, Katharine Jefferts Schori, we gathered to drink tea in Justin's small apartment. We prayed the Rosary together and then talked late into the evening as Justin refilled our mugs with chamomile tea and served plates of buttered toast and marmalade.

We discussed the *tu quoque* objection that someone becomes Catholic for the same reasons Protestants choose denominations, because it conforms to one's interpretation of Scripture. The objection seemed to be a form of despair. It was like saying that a child choosing to obey his mother is the same as another child choosing to disobey his mother, because they are both making a choice. It precluded the possibility of a real Church to which one could submit in the first place.

No, the Church is an objective fact. She is heavy and in the way and annoying—like rocks, or dinner tables, or good mothers. There must therefore be some other way of locating her, apart from one's private interpretation of Scripture, and the only other way was by a succession of apostolic authority going all the way back to King Christ. The fact of the matter was that no denomination dared make the claims Rome made for herself—to be the one and only true Church founded by Jesus himself with an unbroken line of magisterial authority in union with the infallible vicar of Christ and handed down in apostolic succession all the way back to Peter. The difference between Protestantism and the Catholic Church was the difference between an idea and its realization.

In this light, *Extra ecclesiam nulla salus* (outside the Church there is no salvation) made a lot of sense. We also discussed *Apostolicae Curae*, the 1896 papal bull of Pope Leo XIII that declared Anglican orders to be invalid, meaning Anglican "priests" are not, in fact, priests. The argument made a lot of sense, especially when we considered why Orthodox orders were considered valid, even though they were out of full communion with Rome. The vocation of the Church had to come before our personal sense of vocation to the priesthood. It couldn't be the other way around. And, of course, if Anglican orders weren't valid, neither was their eucharist. We sat for a long while as the gravity of it settled in. The clock in Justin's living room ticked loudly. But in the end, we all knew the truth. It was no longer a question of *if* but *when* we would be received into the Church. I was so thankful for the courage and faith of these brothers during such a difficult time.

My bishop visited Nashotah House to express his disapproval of presiding Bishop Schori's impending visit. The school was "too liberal". We went out for coffee and I told him that I was considering becoming Catholic. He tried to understand why I would give up the priesthood for Catholicism, arguing that the GAFCON (Global Anglican Future Conference) movement was the *real* Catholic Church, all the while blaming Nashotah House for being "too Catholic". It was a painful visit, and losing his respect knocked the wind out of me, like a punch to the solar plexus.

Word soon spread that I was becoming "a papist". People questioned my motives. I felt misunderstood and was discouraged by how many classmates felt like I was rejecting them personally, though it was certainly understandable. In their view, by saying Yes to Catholicism, I was saying No to everyone else (while true in one sense, this is not the whole truth in that Catholics can and do recognize appropriate things to say Yes to in every other faith or philosophy). Many Anglican bishops rejected my overtures of friendship, and nearly everyone let me know one way or another that I was converting for some subjective reason—because I was a perfectionist, an idealist, or had some other personal problem. It felt like we were living through Luke 14:26: "If any one comes to me and does not hate his own father and mother and wife and children and brothers and sisters, yes, and even his own life, he cannot be my disciple." Never before had Matthew 10:34 hit so close to home: "I have not come to bring peace, but a sword." It was a very lonely time in my life.

Meanwhile, a storm was brewing. The more conservative Anglicans were bullying the student responsible for Bishop Schori's visit, mostly online. Campus assemblies were held so that students and priests could voice their concern about the head of the Episcopal Church visiting—after all, Nashotah House was "Anglican", not Episcopalian. It was countered that Nashotah was actually Episcopalian, and Episcopalians *were* Anglican. Bishops from all over America weighed in. And then, on the eve of Ash Wednesday, the student who invited Bishop Schori died alone in his room. It was later discovered to be from complications with heart disease.

"How much happier you would be, how much more of you there would be," G. K. Chesterton once said, "if the hammer of a higher God could smash your small cosmos."[8] Heartbroken and afraid, I knew then that my quarrel was not with Anglicanism. It was with my own heart. There was no time for dithering. Brittany and I were bone tired, and our child was on the way. Though this simple act of obedience seemed so impossible, I knew that we needed to become Catholic. I called the priest of a nearby Catholic parish. He was kind enough to meet with Brittany and me, and together we talked and prayed. Though it was late in the year, because of our unusual formation and catechesis, by the grace of God we were allowed into the RCIA (Rite of Christian Initiation of Adults) process. The hammer of a higher God had fallen.

And just like that, the future that Brittany and I had imagined evaporated.

* * * * *

At first, when Brittany told me the good news—"We're going to have a baby!"—nothing seemed to change. I didn't need to *do* anything. But with every passing month, the weight of fatherhood grew heavier and my responsibilities multiplied. What was at first just news became life-changing news, news I had to live. As I discovered the truth of Catholicism, I was forced to question the very roots and foundation of my Christian faith, what I had always called "the good news".

I went back and listened to the contemporary Christian music that had so shaped my early faith in the '90s. I listened to Burlap for Cashmere, Rich Mullins, Chris Rice, Switchfoot, and Jars of Clay's self-titled debut album. Most of all, I listened to the self-titled album of Caedmon's Call. I flipped through my old Trapper Keepers and journals, my extensively highlighted Teen NIV Study Bible, and read the books that had been the spiritual classics of my youth—books by Charles Swindoll, J. I. Packer, John Piper, and A. W. Tozer—all the while wondering if this was the entire story. It all came back to this question: What is the Gospel?

In my youth, I thought the Gospel was the *good news* of what God has done for us in the Person of Jesus Christ. I remembered that fateful night I accepted Jesus as my Lord and Savior at church camp. "Salvation is easy," the speaker in the Hawaiian T-shirt said. "You don't need to *do* anything." The only problem was that after I asked Jesus into my heart, I still had a life to live. Did it matter? When it came to heaven or hell, would my *life* produce any real outcome?

Of course it mattered. When it comes to salvation, God had already done his part; the question was, Would I do mine? Christianity is not *only* news. It's the kind of news you have to live. But how do you live it?

One answer is, you must have a personal relationship with Jesus. After all, God is the Gospel. "Redemption means that God, acting as God truly does, gives us nothing less than himself," said Pope Emeritus Benedict XVI. "The gift of God is God."[9] But after Christ's Ascension into heaven, how does God give himself to us? How are we brought into right relationship with Jesus? The answer is, of course, the Church. To live the Gospel, you must have a *social* relationship with Jesus.

When the Greeks won the battles of Marathon and Solnus, they sent heralds (or "evangelists") to the surrounding cities to proclaim the Gospel: "You are no longer slaves; you are free!" One ancient Roman inscription from around the same time as Jesus proclaimed the "Gospel" of the birth and coronation of the Roman emperor, stating, "The beginning of the gospel of Caesar Augustus". Thus, Saint Mark begins his Gospel, "The beginning of the gospel of Jesus Christ, the Son of God" (1:1). And again, the term "Son of God" was a Davidic term for a king. For Mark, the Gospel is that Jesus is King—and every king has a *kingdom*. "Jesus came into Galilee, preaching the gospel of God, and saying, 'The time is fulfilled, and the kingdom of God is at hand; repent, and believe in the gospel'" (Mk 1:14–15).

It is perhaps no coincidence, then, that Jesus explicitly linked his Kingdom to his Church when he "came into the district of *Caesarea Philippi*" (Mt 16:13), a city named in honor of Caesar Augustus. It was situated on an enormous rock wall about two hundred feet high and five hundred feet long at the foot of Mount Hermon. From the base of this rock burst springs that fed the Jordan, a symbolic river in

Judaism. On this rock pagan temples and sacrifices were made to Pan and *Caesar was worshiped*. Beneath it there was the "Cave of Pan", and inside this cave there was a seemingly bottomless pit that was considered to be the very gates of hell. The scene is conspicuous. Far out in unclean Gentile lands, on a rock dedicated to the worship of Caesar, Jesus pointed to Simon and said, "You are Peter, and on this rock I will build my Church, and the gates of hades shall not prevail against it. I will give you the keys of the kingdom" (Mt 16:18–19). The reign of Christ had begun. Jesus is the one true King, not Caesar, and he said he would build his Church on the rock that is Peter.

Is it any wonder that the Catholic Church alone, filled with the Holy Spirit and the promise of Christ to Peter, is capable of perpetual unity and renewal? Is there any peace apart from the peace of Christ in the Kingdom of Christ? *Pax Christi in Regno Christi.* The Catholic can truly say, "I am no longer a slave; I am a child of God!" (cf. Gal 4:7). *Romanus civis sum*: "I am a citizen of Rome."

Growing up, I thought the good news was that I could have a personal relationship with Jesus—without religion. I wanted the King but not the Kingdom, the head but not the body, the vine but not the branches, a culture but not the cult. But like the Incarnation of Christ himself, the Church is a historic fact. She is the *social* continuity of the Incarnation. She is, as Saint Ignatius of Antioch said, the *thusiasterion*, the "place of sacrifice".[10] Here, a once scattered people are gathered into one covenant family, the family of God participating in the family life of the Trinity. God aims at a paradox: things are to be many, yet somehow one. "About Jesus Christ and the Church," said Saint Joan of Arc, "I simply know they're just one thing, and we shouldn't complicate the matter."[11] Christ and his Church are one flesh—the Head and the Body; *totus Christus caput et corpus est.*

I could feel a change in the weather. I could feel a change in me. At last, I was brave enough to ask why I had been so afraid. All these years I had been packing ice around my heart, trying not to feel the truth of the Church. I submitted to the authority of Scripture, but submitting to Scripture had been inevitably to submit to an *interpretation* of Scripture—my interpretation. The fact of the matter was that I had wanted Christianity, but I had wanted Christianity on my terms. In the process, I had diminished the Church to a picturesque ruin. And it occurred to me then that a Catholic is someone who sees the Church not as he wishes her to be, but as she is. And in spite of attempts to destroy her, refute her, revile her, she stands immovable, teaching what has always been taught, doing what she has always done. Jesus established one, holy, catholic, and apostolic Church— and this was good news. This was life-changing news, the kind of news I needed to *live*.

A lump was stuck in my throat, a homesickness, and I could no longer hold it back. Life outside of the Catholic Church felt unbearably tentative and abstract. John Henry Newman saw it:

> Turn away from the Catholic Church, and to whom will you go? It is your only chance of peace and assurance in this turbulent, changing world. There is nothing between it and skepticism, when men exert their reason freely. Private creeds, fancy religions, may be showy and imposing to the many in their day; national religions may lie huge and lifeless, and cumber the ground for centuries, and distract the attention or confuse the judgment of the learned; but on the long run it will be found that either the Catholic Religion is verily and indeed the coming in of the unseen world into this, or that there is nothing positive, nothing dogmatic, nothing real in any one of our notions as to whence we come and whither we are going. Unlearn Catholicism, and you become Protestant, Unitarian, Deist, Pantheist, Sceptic, in a dreadful, but infallible succession.[12]

Not being Catholic seemed to vaporize the "Kingdom" into something ethereal—obviously not yet fulfilled, but also not yet inaugurated. "Catholicism" was warped into a cafeteria of cool traditions. "Apostolic" was skewed to mean only that the Church has a mission. "Church" was reduced to a proposition—not *of* this world, but not *in* it either. As this "invisible church" scattered into a thousand quarreling fractions proclaiming a thousand contradictory truths, I had always thought I had no choice but to grip my Bible tighter and leave one denomination for yet another. Out of full communion with the Catholic Church, Christianity became by degrees just another spirituality. But there were more things in heaven and on earth than were dreamt of in my philosophy, more to the story than I had ever imagined, more to the Kingdom and more to the cost.

* * * * *

Winter gave way to spring. My heart felt like a flower in early bloom trembling in a gusting wind. We attended RCIA, met with Catholic priests to pray and talk, and I was considering getting a job at a nearby bread factory, anything that would pay the bills. At night we would escape to the Mater Dei adoration chapel at a nearby parish to kneel side by side before our Savior. And now that the weather was warm, we drove to the Shrine at Holy Hill as often as we could to pray with the Carmelite friars. We needed prayer. In just weeks Brittany would give birth to our firstborn son, and soon after that we would be received into the Church. It was late April and summer was coming on and, after that, a future we could not see.

"My navel looks like an Eskimo built an igloo on the moon," Brittany sighed.

The windows were down, and we could almost smell the greens and yellows that dotted the rolling hills. I glanced over at her as she pulled a loose strand of red hair behind her ear.

"You're beautiful," I said, reaching to take her hand.

When we arrived at Holy Hill, Brittany insisted on taking the stairs. At thirty-six weeks pregnant, she said it would help the baby get into position. We climbed the stairs slowly, pausing often so that Brittany could catch her breath. Her high cheek bones were freckled by the springtime sun. At last, we reached the outcropping basilica with its stunning high altar and twin belfries overlooking Wisconsin. The heavy doors swept against the floor behind us, shutting out the sound of visitors loitering outside.

The pungent aroma of incense still clung to the air when we entered the nave and filled the sun-bathed transepts, moving upward through the heaven-yearning Gothic forms. Crutches lined the entryway to the side chapel dedicated to our Lady from the many people who had been healed there. Upon entering, we dipped a finger in the holy water font, pausing, even though we knew each pause broadened the distance between us and our quarry. I would say we were looking for clarity, but in truth we were searching for a more elusive prey. Thankfully, the crowded chapel was cold, cold enough to keep us honest.

And that was why we had come—and why we lingered still, almost wishing we could turn back. We were searching for something that can only be found through the help of prayer.

We were looking for trust.

We were looking for the kind of love that *does*.

Genuflecting, we crossed ourselves before the Presence. We were drawn to it, like a moth to flame. Though we had never felt so vulnerable and alone, Brittany and I knew that we were not alone. We were made for God, for his Kingdom. And we longed to come home—to the family we had always desired, the Catholic Church and the Holy Trinity. And in the silence that filled those hours I could feel my heart beat in time, as if emptied of all pride, but not emptied of longing.

EPILOGUE

The Culture of Christ

The kingdom of heaven may be compared to a king
who gave a marriage feast.

—Matthew 22:2

For today the new oblation of the new King's
revelation bids us feast in glad array.

—Saint Thomas Aquinas[1]

If this book could have smells, it would have the wet smell of cold
stone. It would have the sour smell of stale incense, the dusty smell
of grandmothers in old coats, and the springtime smell of flowers.
It would have the smell of lemons and ginger from the polished
wooden pews.

If this book could have light, it would have the soft light that crashes
through the stained-glass windows with dust floating in it. It would
have the warm light of the candle burning by the tabernacle, fueled by
oil or wax, the light that honors the Presence. It would have the electric light from the renovations, and the new light of Sunday mornings.

And if this book could have sound, it would have the high, pealing
sound of bells calling the faithful. It would have the clicking sound
of mothers and their rosaries and the piercing screams of babies, the
hushed sound of the altar boys lighting candles, and the angelic sound
of the choir. It would have the murmuring sound of the priest vest-
ing as he prays, and the men in the back confirming that, yes, there
will be a second collection, and, no, the vestry will not be meeting
tomorrow. This book would have the thumping sound of kneelers

and the grunting of old men kneeling as they do their penance after making a good Confession.

And I suppose that if this book could have tastes, it would have the taste of bread breaking in your mouth, sticking to your teeth, dry and hard to swallow. The taste of transubstantiation and nourishment and life.

It would have all these and more because love *does*. Jesus could have saved the world with a simple nod or word. Instead, he *did* something—he became man and died on the Cross. Before Jesus ascended to heaven, he told his apostles to *do* something—to preach, baptize, and make disciples. When he established the New Covenant of his blood, he ordained clergy to preside over the Eucharistic liturgy, saying: "*Do* this in remembrance of me" (Lk 22:19; 1 Cor 11:24). Why? Certainly not because he had to! He knew human nature, and he knew that human nature needs to *do* something. He knew that love is more than a feeling, and it starts and ends with the once-for-all Sacrifice of the Mass.

It would have all these and more because Jesus is King. He has gathered the tribes into one visible and identifiable covenant people. We owe him our allegiance. We owe him our lives. When Christ inaugurated his Kingdom he inaugurated a culture, a culture rooted in cult—and by their parties ye shall know them.

In every succeeding age, the beating heart of the Church is *eucharistia*, thanksgiving, festival. Jesus established the New Covenant in his own flesh and blood and renews it through the Holy Mass. Whenever Christ's sacrifice is renewed at the altar, we are in communion with God and one another. Made one in the Holy Spirit, we feast at the family table with the Father, the Son, the Blessed Mother, and all the company of heaven. We sit at the Supper of the Lamb, together with the family of God on earth—the pope and all the bishops united to him, together with all the saints in whom God has been glorified. "Behold, I stand at the door and knock; if any one hears my voice and opens the door, I will come in to him and eat with him, and he with me" (Rev 3:20).

It would have all these and more because this is the heart of the matter: Christ and his Church, the marriage of heaven and earth, an immortal match, an immovable feast.

* * * * *

Because of my obligations at the seminary during the Triduum, we were not able to be received into the Church during the Easter Vigil by the bishop, surrounded by the happy faithful. Instead, we first received the sacraments on the same day our newborn son was baptized, on a bright morning in June, on the Feast of Saints Peter and Paul. Our new parish priest had been granted the faculty to perform our Confirmations, laying his hands on our heads and invoking the outpouring of the Holy Spirit and anointing our heads with the oil of Sacred Chrism. The service was plain. We did not yet know many Catholics, so those in attendance were mostly friends and family who were understandably less than enthusiastic about this unexpected turn of events. The priest dedicated our newly baptized son to Our Lady of Perpetual Help, and my father recited "God's Grandeur" by Gerard Manley Hopkins, and late that night we held each other in bed and wept.

We knew that those closest to us were confused and hurt by our becoming Catholic; and honestly, we found the experience of becoming Catholic deeply, almost shockingly, painful. Yet despite the tears we were grateful. Mercy had led us home. We were not the first to convert to Catholicism nor the last. Within just a few years, by the grace of God, nine seminarians from Nashotah House alone became Catholic.

Catholicism is a thing that gets hold of you and does not let you go. Before all else, it is a life. And as we began to bring the sacred into the midst of the everyday, our apartment was soon crowded with the trappings of any Catholic home—crucifixes, holy water, candles, statues, and icons. In the Church year, we reenacted the life of Christ. In the sacraments, we participated in the life of the Holy Spirit. In the bishops in union with the pope we heard the living voice of Christ. In the works of mercy, we brought Christ's healing and hope to a hurting world and to one another. We knew we were not yet worthy of heaven, and so we ran to Jesus, "the mediator of a new covenant, and to the sprinkled blood that speaks more graciously than the blood of Abel" (Heb 12:24). At the Sacrifice of the Mass, we consumed our Lord's very flesh and blood and received every grace necessary for becoming saints. Living the Christian liturgy, we wanted not only to recall the events of salvation but to actualize them, to make them present. The idea was that as Christians we were not only to believe in Christ, but to *become* Christ.

Ah, but we had arrived so late! Like travelers from a ruined land, we found it surprisingly difficult to adapt to the foreign customs of Catholicism. We were only just beginning to learn the self-denial of fasting and mortification, how to do penance, how to make a total consecration to Jesus through Mary, how to pray novenas, the miraculous medal, the Rosary, nonliturgical blessings, and prayers for the faithful departed. Catholic parlance, liturgical rites, the veneration of relics, indulgences, holy water and holy oils, keeping the Friday fast, the Lord's Day—there were so many new practices to learn, new habits to develop. What was sinful had to be uprooted, what was painful had to be joined to the Cross, and what was not yet holy had to become holy. We did not want to waste our sufferings, yes, but we also didn't want to waste our good works. For we were quickly learning that salvation is a Catholic's "unfinished business".

Religion is a long job. The goal is eternity, the family life of the Trinity, but we needed to live this mystery now. And at last, we had moved from a hypothetical union to a truly organic oneness with God in his covenant family, the Catholic Church.

Now, although the *work* of the Catholic religion was challenging, we knew it was necessary. When I was young, I had believed that good works only "proved" that I was *already* going to heaven—but this led to an endless cycle of worrying whether or not I was really going to heaven based on my good works. Because I was saved by faith and not by works, my modus operandi was "Let go and let God." Thus, wanting to be "authentic", I followed the path of least resistance—we're not saved by years of straining to develop holy habits and dispositions! Looking back, I see that I had, of course, simply confused "works of the Law" with "good works". They are not the same, and the axe was already at the root of the trees. As Brittany and I began to live the Catholic year, we began to *feel* that faith without works is dead (Jas 2:17).

Of course, it would be a mistake to say that I can do anything good—much less become holy—without the power of the Holy Spirit. But it is equally mistaken to say that God does not work through creaturely means. Just because I can't become a saint without God's help doesn't mean I don't need to become a saint. After all, God is an artist. "The command *Be ye perfect* is not idealistic gas," said C. S. Lewis. "Nor is it a command to do the impossible. He is going to make us into creatures that can obey that command."[2] For Jesus, good isn't good enough. Lewis put it this way:

> If we let Him—for we can prevent Him, if we choose—He will make the feeblest and filthiest of us into a god or goddess, a dazzling, radiant, immortal creature, pulsating all through with such energy and joy and wisdom and love as we cannot now imagine, a bright stainless mirror which reflects back to God perfectly (though, of course, on a smaller scale) His own boundless power and delight and goodness. The process will be long and in parts very painful, but that is what we are in for. Nothing less. He meant what He said.[3]

Jesus does not want one conversion story—he wants ten thousand conversion stories. And what is a conversion but the daily turning away from sin and toward God? It's easier said than done, but Jesus gives me the divine life so that I can in turn *live* it.

But how do you love God? How do you live the divine life? The more Brittany and I struggled with the seemingly impossible vocation of sainthood, the more we realized that we could never become truly ourselves, truly Christlike, without doing the work. We had to start where we were, and we had to start small. Even the little things mean a lot. Little by little, one travels far.

* * * * *

"The Mass is ended, go in peace."

"Thanks be to God!" we said, and meant it.

Perhaps some couples transition to parenthood easily, but we were not one of them. It would be months before we learned that our son had a painful dairy allergy, and so we were awake with eyes as wide as saucers, desperate to sooth our newborn baby as he writhed in our arms, for countless hapless nights. To continue nursing, Brittany had to change her diet, which meant that I had to change my diet, and unbeknownst to us nearly everything we once enjoyed somehow had dairy in it. And still, it wasn't the exhaustion or the hunger or even cleaning the cloth diapers that left us looking as frazzled as a bad perm; it was the fact that the baby never went away. The central activities of our marriage—the hours of conversation, the long walks, the cooking and reading together—all of it seemed to have been snatched away from us only to be replaced with an all-consuming yet mind-numbing responsibility. We would eventually learn how to be parents without going insane, but for months there seemed to be this one vexing thought, this one vocation, this one cute, adorable, never-ending nightmare: baby.

It felt like being at the State Fair only to get sick. We couldn't ride any of the rides or eat any of the food served in the concession stands. We could only sit on the bench. As newbies, we were excited to go to daily Mass, to pray the Stations of the Cross, to go on pilgrimage, to sign up for a weekly hour of Eucharistic Adoration, to join the Divine Mercy Cenacle or the Jeff Cavins Bible Study Group. Instead, if we weren't home tending to the needs of a completely loveable but utterly helpless human being, we were so fried we could only sit in our pajamas and pour a glass of wine. But we pressed on.

We couldn't do Catholicism the way we wanted to, but we did what we could. We were especially disheartened to admit that Sundays mornings had become a long grueling exercise in patience—our son squirming, drooling, banging books, screaming, Brittany nursing him as he tugged at her mantilla, the lady behind us sighing loudly, me carrying him to the men's room to clean up his blowout and change his clothes. Well-meaning parishioners grabbed our hands and lifted them up into the orans position, an exclusively priestly gesture during the Mass, and in general the liturgical liberties were so numerous I was forced to set my eyes on the crucifix in a desperate attempt to pray. The Holy Mass felt more an act of obedience than an intense spiritual experience. All in all, it's safe to say that I didn't feel anything at all—and that was okay.

This was new for me. For as long as I can remember I have had a personal relationship with Jesus. When I was younger, this relationship was most easily identified by the intensity of its emotional fulfilment and didn't necessarily point beyond me and Jesus. Ironically, foregoing the obligations of organized religion for the supposed freedom of spirituality left me little wiggle room, for I was enslaved by my whims and passions. I was trapped on a small parcel of real estate and felt at a gut level that I was missing out on the abundant life Jesus offers. Yet I demanded self-rule, like a trained seal barking for another herring. Although my spirituality took a definite shape (makeshift sacraments, yoga pants, political bumper stickers, scented candles, certain catch phrases, organic food, and so on), the fact of the matter was that I had no creed, no calendar, no strictures, no ritual observance of dietary rules, no culture—and that was the point: I was spiritual, not religious.

Like so many born in the Reagan-and-Rubik's-Cube era, I did not understand or respect the objective norms of religion; and to the extent that I misunderstood religion, it became harder for me to see the point of Jesus' commands, to live by them and to urge others to do the same. Understandably, I did not accommodate myself to the cross, but accommodated the cross to the life I was living anyway. "God doesn't want a big fake show," I said in the name of love and went on living as before.

But what if a husband did not come home to his wife on the nights when his heart just wasn't in it? Would she appreciate his "authenticity"? No, real love is not identified by its feelings, but by its habits and practices. Real love does not worry whether one is simply "going through the motions", because real love does.

Religion is the kind of love that doesn't stop at thoughts and feelings. It's a love that takes action. Before all else religion is a love that does. "Do whatever he tells you" (Jn 2:5), Mary said at the wedding feast.

Like all love, religion is prodigal—flowing out into lifelong fidelity to Jesus and his Kingdom and the sharing of the family life of the Trinity. Religion is a bodily as well as an emotional and spiritual union, a corporate as well as a personal relationship with Jesus and his Church. As such, religion can be distinguished from spirituality by its comprehensiveness: Baptism unites persons to Jesus and to the saints in all-encompassing ways that call for permanent and exclusive allegiance. *Filii in Filio, ex Patre et ad Patrem.*

Being so joined to the Trinity, the baptized are invited to grow into the full stature of Christ through a common life of religious abundance—making their Confessions, saying certain prayers at certain times of the day, fasting during Lent and feasting during Easter, tithing, feeding the hungry and healing the sick, wearing the religious medal or the brown scapular, going to Mass on Sundays and holy days of obligation, and so on. Though Catholics might fall short of the Church's strictures, the fact remains that they profess a creed, live a festal calendar, share a common meal, and submit to religious obligations that spring from the cultic rites of the Kingdom of God—and the obligation is the point: love does.

Even when I chafed at organized religion, I would have readily admitted the necessity of, say, traffic laws. If people just did as they pleased, some stopping only at red lights and others only at green, there would be chaos. To ensure a minimum of safe and orderly travel there needs to be legal coordination—an authoritative body that can pronounce traffic laws that people are obliged to obey. Is the Christian life, "the way", so different?

It was such a relief for Brittany to join a local Catholic mom's group. For the first time, she didn't have to tiptoe around every single matter of faith and morals, "agreeing to disagree". The other moms were thoughtful and questioning, to be sure, but there was a *consensus*, a shared sense of humility under the teaching authority of the Church and how the faith was to be lived. Their self-sacrifice and bravery, their devotion to our Lady and joyful obedience to Mother Church, their ambition for their homes and parishes, the pattern of their days and weeks, motivated Brittany in her own walk. Their wisdom about parenting and experience with catechizing, reading, cooking, nursing, cleaning, gardening, mending, budgeting, and the general management of the most human thing in the world—the home—empowered Brittany. She grew stronger and more confident. These women gave something to Brittany that I could never give: the gift of female friendship. It was a taste of what the culture of Christ can look like, a life of *formation*.

My experience has been that the logic of rejecting religion leads, by way of formlessness, toward chaos: it proposes a Kingdom of God for which it can hardly explain the point. But the eternal Son of God became man, and man is a social and sacramental creature who cannot deny his own nature. What is necessary for salvation? What are the means of grace? Which interpretation of the Bible is correct? What is the truth? Which church is the real church? For me to follow Christ I must "know how one ought to behave in the household of God, which is the Church of the living God, the pillar and bulwark of the truth" (1 Tim 3:15). Brittany and I had experienced firsthand that there must be an authoritative body that can proclaim the Gospel in its entirety and articulate the unifying activities, goods, and commitments necessary to see the Great Commission through to its eschatological end. Having been buried with Christ in Baptism, our old nature having been crucified, we are called to join the Son in his fidelity to the Father in the love of the Holy Spirit—and I am coming to see that this kind of covenant faithfulness has a definite *form*.

I have been wrestling with religion ever since I became Catholic. For me, religion has been a difficult, almost impossible renunciation. John Henry Newman saw it, reflecting on how we must live out our justification: "O easy and indulgent doctrine, to have the bloody Cross reared within us, and our hearts transfixed and our arms stretched out upon it, and our original nature slaughtered and cast out!"[4] But I have also come to see that the cruciform shape of Catholic culture is precisely why she is a living festival. Without the Cross, there is no Easter. Without sacrifice, there can be no feast. For a true festivity is seen only where there is still some living relationship with religious "cult"—the libation, the giving of the first fruits of the earth, the slaughtering of the best lambs, the seventh day's rest, the sharing of the Paschal meal, the Sunday Eucharist. Joseph Pieper has observed that in voluntarily keeping a feast day, men renounce the yield of the day's labor. "This renunciation has from time immemorial been regarded as an essential element of festivity."[5] We do not renounce things except for love. *Ubi caritas gaudet, ibi est festivitas*, says Chrysostom: "Where love rejoices, there is festivity."[6]

And has not Christ shown us that love is a cross? To repent, to give alms, to do penance, to participate in the Sacrifice of the Mass, to worship, and then to "go forth" rejoicing—is this not to join the festival of the Trinity? Such an affirmation of the world, like Mary's fiat, is more than the premise of festivity—it is festivity's heartbeat. Only love can say in the face of suffering, "Not my will but yours be done." Only the heart that says, "Amen," will receive the true fruit of the festival.

Perhaps we are saved not so much by "faith alone" but by fidelity to Jesus and his Kingdom? It seems that the perfect union of the divine and the human, which has been achieved in the Person of Jesus Christ, must find its *social realization* in the Church, which is his Mystical Body. The Church is unlike any other community on earth: she is the international, hell-breaking, heaven-touching Kingdom of Christ. And perhaps this is why Jesus came—that we might have life, and life abundantly. God has given us his own Body and Blood as food, his own family as our family. "The marriage feast is waiting, the gates wide open stand; Rise up, ye heirs of glory, the Bridegroom is at hand!"[7]

Religion, like salvation itself, will cost you everything. But in return, God will give you nothing less than *himself*. In the words of an old hymn:

> At the Lamb's high feast we sing
> Praise to our victorious King,
> Who hath washed us in the tide
> Flowing from his pierced side;
> Praise we him, whose love divine
> Gives his sacred Blood for wine,
> Gives his Body for the feast,
> Christ the victim, Christ the priest.[8]

* * * * *

There is a story my past needs to tell my present. I'm tempted to rip out old memories and replace them with new ones, but then I might miss the thread that ties the chapters together, which is love. God loves me, and even though I still fall short of loving him back, every day is a chance to renew my vows, to unite myself with the affections of Our Lady of Sorrows on Calvary and offer to the Father the sacrifice that his Son made of himself on the Cross, the same sacrifice he now renews on the altar. Though I am no longer early in my story, I still have a long way to go. I'm still learning how to love and be loved. I'm still learning how to do this thing we call religion.

I wonder if the New Testament is not so much a collection of books as it is a sacrament, a ritual Jesus commanded us to "do" (1 Cor 11:25)? At the Last Supper, Jesus gave his Body to be broken and his Blood to be poured out on the "altar" of the Cross. He was identifying himself not only as the high priest but as the unblemished Paschal victim, the offering of the New Covenant. In this cultic setting, he told his apostles to *do* this in remembrance of him (Lk 22:19; 1 Cor 11:24), thereby establishing the Christian priesthood and the Church's liturgy. When he rose from the dead, the Lord confected this very sacrament: "When he was at table with them, he took the bread and blessed and broke it, and gave it to them.... He was known to them in the breaking of the bread" (Lk 24:30, 35). Without the Eucharist, I would have no life: "Unless you eat the flesh of the Son of man and drink his blood, you have no life in you" (Jn 6:53).

What is the culture of Christ? It all comes back to family and faith and the meal that brings us together, the love story of the ages. God himself established these rites for our good, and they are ordered to his praise. And so from the start, the apostles repeated the Eucharistic sacrificial rite, making Christ known to the world. "They held steadfastly to the apostles' teaching and fellowship, to the breaking of the bread and to the prayers" (Acts 2:42; see Acts 20:6–7). Saint Paul continued the Paschal feast: "For I received from the Lord what I also delivered to you, that the Lord Jesus on the night when he was betrayed took bread ..." (1 Cor 11:23). He compared the Eucharistic banquet with the sacrifices of the temple; he even contrasted it with pagan sacrifices (1 Cor 10:8–21). It is a tale of two *cultures*: the pagan offering brought about communion with demons, but the Christian sacrifice brought about communion with the Body and Blood of Jesus. All sacrifice, Paul said, brings about communion ("participation" [1 Cor 10:16]). In the loving bond of the Holy Spirit, we join the Son in his self-gift to the Father. Just "as Christ loved us and gave himself up for us, a fragrant offering and sacrifice to God" (Eph 5:2), so also Saint Paul told the Church, "present your bodies as a living sacrifice, holy and acceptable to God, which is your spiritual worship" (Rom 12:1). Christians are many, but our sacrifice is one. In the words of John Senior, "What is Christian culture? It is essentially the Mass."9

In a sense, there is nothing special about religion. It is ordinary life in an ordinary parish. The people you live and pray with are just regular people. And the priests are just plain old priests. But sometimes something as ordinary as the Catholic religion can become a little less ordinary. For me, it was a revolution (in the sense of a circle coming back to its beginning, its right place).

The days passed, one very much like the other, in their slow orbit around the Sunday feast. We often walked to Mass, pushing our son in the stroller around a lake crowded with sailboats and down a bustling main street, passing the steeples of several Lutheran churches before crossing over the train tracks to our parish home. Brittany's eyes were as blue as water when the sun breaks out after a storm. We were hardly saints, but we were Catholic. Though my heart wasn't always in it, I was in a place where God could work on my heart.

I struggle with Saint Paul's words: "Christ, our Passover Lamb, has been sacrificed. Let us, therefore, celebrate the festival" (1 Cor 5:7–8). This is no ordinary banquet. "We do not approach a temporal feast, my beloved, but an eternal and heavenly," wrote Saint Athanasius in his *Festal Letter.* "We come to it in truth."[10] I struggle because the Holy Mass *participates* in Christ's once-for-all sacrifice on the Cross, because this is the physical expression of the Son's eternal self-gift to the Father, bringing heaven down to earth and lifting earth up into heaven in chevron formation "with innumerable angels in festal gathering" (Heb 12:22). I struggle because I am not worthy. In this Messianic banquet of the Kingdom—offered in the liturgy of the Last Supper—Jesus gives to his Bride his very life, his Body and Blood, Soul and Divinity, everything. In every Mass, God renews his covenant, a covenant ratified in his own blood, giving us all the graces we need, the very life of the Trinity, a common life of religious abundance.

Once we have dined on fare as rich as this, how can we settle for the thin gruel of spirituality? Once our tongues have been so purpled with the Precious Blood, how can we keep quiet? What happens in the sanctuary does not stop there. It's spreading out, even now, from the heart of the Church to the ends of the earth. Religion is not dead, because it is not mortal: it is the liturgy of heaven—on earth.

What is the Catholic Church if not the family of God? What is the Mass if not the Marriage Supper of the Lamb? I remember talking with Brittany about how when I was young, I ran away from home. But I didn't know where to go or what to do, so I ended up sitting on the curb across the street. I told her how lonely I felt when I saw through the window my family sit down to dinner without me. I told her how I swallowed my pride, and when I entered the dining room my mother cried and my father laughed, and I sat down to a feast.

> "Look upon Zion, the city of our appointed feasts!
> Your eyes will see Jerusalem, a quiet habitation, an
>   immovable tent,
> whose stakes will never be plucked up, nor will any of
>   its cords be broken."
>   —Isaiah 33:20

ENDNOTES

1

MCMLXXXIV

[1] *John Henry Newman: Heart Speaks to Heart; Selected Spiritual Writings*, ed. Lawrence S. Cunningham (Hyde Park, N.Y.: New City Press, 2004), 47.

2

Makeshift Sacraments

[1] Thomas Aquinas, quoted in Jacquelyn Lindsey, ed., *Catholic Prayers for All Occasions* (Huntington, Ind.: Our Sunday Visitor, 2017), 120.

[2] Richard Foster, *Celebration of Discipline* (Grand Rapids, Mich.: Zondervan, 1988), 1.

[3] *Letters of Emily Dickinson*, ed. Mabel Loomis Todd (Boston: Roberts Brothers, 1894), 315.

[4] Henry David Thoreau, *Walden* (Boston: Houghton Mifflin, 1906), 364.

3

By Their Parties Ye Shall Know Them

[1] C. S. Lewis, "Alliterative Metre", in *Selected Literary Essays*, ed. Walter Hooper (Cambridge: Cambridge University Press, 2003), 24.

[2] Horatius Bonar, *Hymns of Faith and Hope* (London: James Nisbet, 1858), 164.

[3] Russel Kirk, "Civilization without Religion", in *The Essential Russell Kirk: Selected Essays*, ed. George A. Panichas (New York: Open Road Media, 2014), 107.

[4] Ibid., 107–8.

[5] Charles Péguy, *Lettre du Provincial*, December 21, 1899.

[6] *Selected Prose of T. S. Eliot* (New York: Harcourt Brace, 1975), 130.

[7] John Henry Newman, *The Idea of a University* (New York: Longmans, Green, 1905), 101.

279

[8] A. G. Sertillanges, *The Intellectual Life: Its Spirit, Conditions, Methods* (Washington, D.C.: Catholic University of America, 1946), 55.

[9] William Shakespeare, *Macbeth*, act 3, scene 2.

[10] Joseph Pieper, *In Tune with the World* (South Bend, Ind.: St. Augustine's Press, 1999), 62.

[11] *Autobiography of Benjamin Franklin* (New York: Houghton Mifflin, 1906), 84.

[12] Ibid.

[13] Alexis de Tocqueville, *Democracy in America*, trans. Henry Reeve (New York: Longman, Green, and Roberts, 1862), 31–32.

[14] T. S. Eliot, *Christianity and Culture* (New York: Harcourt Brace, 1939), 87.

[15] Hilaire Belloc, "The Catholic Sun".

[16] Hilaire Belloc, *The Path to Rome* (New York: Dover Publications, 2013), 86.

4

The Beautiful Mess

[1] Dante, *Inferno*, canto 8, line 1, in *The Divine Comedy*, trans. Henry Wadsworth Longfellow, ILT's Digital Dante Project, August 12, 2009, project Gutenberg, https://www.gutenberg.org/files/1001/1001-h/1001-h.htm.

[2] George MacDonald, *Diary of an Old Soul* (London: Longmans, Green, 1885), 37.

[3] William Shakespeare, Sonnet 87, *Poems and Sonnets of William Shakespeare* (London: Kegan, Paul, Trench and Co., 1881), 156.

[4] Joshua Harris, *I Kissed Dating Goodbye* (Sisters, Ore.: Multnomah Books, 1997).

[5] E. E. Cummings, "Since Feeling Is First", *100 Selected Poems* (New York: Grove City Press, 1954), 34.

[6] Ignatius of Antioch, Epistle to the Symyrneans, 7:1.

[7] *Autobiography of Benjamin Franklin* (New York: Houghton Mifflin, 1906), 273.

5

A Parliament of Owls

[1] "Mortification", in *The Poetical Works of George Herbert* (London: James Nisbet, 1857), 99.

[2] Geoffrey Chaucer, "The Somnours Tale", *The Canterbury Tales and Other Poems of Geoffrey Chaucer*, David Laing Purves, ed. (Edinburgh: William P. Nimmo, 1874), 8.

[3] Pius X, encyclical *Pascendi dominici gregis* (September 8, 1907), no. 39, http://w2.vatican.va/content/pius-x/en/encyclicals/documents/hf_p-x_enc_19070908_pascendi-dominici-gregis.html.

4 Homily of His Holiness John Paul II (Palafox Major Seminary, Puebla de Los Angeles, Mexico, January 28, 1979), http://w2.vatican.va/content/john-paul-ii/en /homilies/1979/documents/hf_jp-ii_hom_19790128_messico-puebla-seminario .html.

5 G. K. Chesterton, *Platitudes Undone* (San Francisco, Cal.: Ignatius Press, 1997), 38.

6 G. K. Chesterton, quoted in Dale Ahlquist, *G. K. Chesterton: The Apostle of Common Sense* (San Francisco: Ignatius Press, 2003), 160.

7 Procopius, quoted in Morsi Saad El-bin, *Sinai: The Site and the History* (New York: New York University Press, 1998), 88.

6

The Spell to Break the Spell

1 Gerard Manley Hopkins, "Starlight Night" in *God's Grandeur and Other Poems*, Stanley Applebaum, ed. (New York: Dover Publications, 1995), 8.

2 Peter Berger, quoted in Krista Tippett, *Einstein's God: Conversations about Science and the Human Spirit* (New York: Penguin, 2010), 2.

3 C. S. Lewis, "Myth Became Fact", *God in the Dock* (Grand Rapids, Mich.: Eerdmans, 2014), 59.

4 Martin Luther, quoted in Elizabeth Vandiver, Ralph Keen, and Thomas Frazel, *Luther's Lives: Two Contemporary Accounts of Martin Luther* (Manchester: Manchester University Press, 2004), 102.

7

A Vision Glorious

1 TEC (The Episcopal Church); ACNA (the Anglican Church in North America); ACiA (the Anglican Mission in the Americas); AMiA (Anglican Mission in North America); GAFCON (Global Anglican Future Conference).

2 John Keble, *Sermons, Occasional and Parochial* (Oxford and London, 1868), quoted in Geoffrey Rowell, *A Vision Glorious: Themes and Personalities of the Catholic Revival in Anglicanism* (Oxford: Oxford University Press, 1983), 8.

3 *Catechism of the Catholic Church*, no. 129; cf. Augustine, *Quaest. in Hept.* 2.73; cf. *DV* [*Dei Verbum*] 16; cf. also the *Catechism of the Catholic Church*, nos. 121–30.

4 Unless otherwise noted, emphasis has been added for all quotations.

5 Irenaeus of Lyons, *Against Heresies* 3.22, quoted in William A. Jurgens, *The Faith of the Early Fathers: Pre-Nicene and Nicene Eras* (Collegeville, Minn.: Liturgical Press, 1970), 93.

8

Don't Waste Your Suffering

[1] Augustine, *Sermon* 169.13, quoted in *Navarre Bible: The Letters of Saint Paul* (New York: Scepter Publishers, 2005), 269.

[2] John Henry Newman, *Sermons 1824–1843*, vol. 4 of *The Church and Miscellaneous Sermons at St. Mary's and Littlemore*, ed. Francis J. McGrath (Oxford: Clarendon Press, 2011), 262.

[3] Augustine, *Sermon* 272 (*On the Day of Pentecost—To the Catechumens, concerning the Sacrament*), quoted in *Augustine Through the Ages: An Encyclopedia*, Allan Fitzgerald and John C. Cavadini, eds. (Grand Rapids, Mich.: Eerdmans, 1999), 332.

[4] Ibid.

[5] *Hymns of Worship and Service* (New York: The Century Company, 1988), 137.

[6] Joseph Ratzinger, *Collected Works: Theology of Liturgy* (San Francisco: Ignatius Press, 2014), 356.

[7] Scott Hahn, "The Fourth Cup", Lighthouse Talks (Greenwood, Col.: Augustine Institute, 2015).

[8] *Basil of Caesarea, Christian, Humanist, Ascetic* (Toronto: Pontifical Institute of Medieval Studies, 1981), 615.

[9] John Paul II, apostolic letter *Salvifici Doloris* (February 11, 1984), no. 19, emphasis in original, https://w2.vatican.va/content/john-paul-ii/en/apost_letters/1984/documents/hf_jp-ii_apl_11021984_salvifici-doloris.html.

9

In Chevron Formation

[1] Cyprian, *The Lapsed/The Unity of the Church*, trans. Maurice Bevenot (Long Prairie, Minn.: Newman, 1956), 13.

[2] Augustine, *A Sermon to Catechumens on the Creed* 16, quoted in Michael Ferrebee Sadler, *The Second Adam and the New Birth* (London: Bell and Baldy, 1862), 277.

[3] Augustine, *City of God* 10.20, http://www.americancatholictruthsociety.com/articles/augustinecatholic.htm.

[4] C. S. Lewis, *The Weight of Glory* (New York: HarperOne, 1949), 45.

[5] Homily of His Holiness John Paul II (Palafox Major Seminary, Puebla de Los Angeles, Mexico, January 28, 1979), http://w2.vatican.va/content/john-paul-ii/en/homilies/1979/documents/hf_jp-ii_hom_19790128_messico-puebla-seminario.html.

[6] George MacDonald, *Unspoken Sermons*, 3rd series (New York: George Rutledge and Sons, 1873), 11–12.

[7] Rite 1 comes from the *1979 Book of Common Prayer* (New York: Church Publishing, 1979).

10

Priestcraft

[1] Hans Urs von Balthasar, *Priestly Spirituality*, trans. Frank Davidson (San Francisco: Ignatius Press, 2013), 65.

[2] R. T. France, *Women in the Church's Ministry* (Eugene, Ore.: Wipf and Stock, 2004), 78.

[3] Kenneth Bailey, "Women in the New Testament: A Middle Eastern Cultural View", *Anvil* 11 (1994): 7–24.

[4] Ibid.

[5] William J. Martin, "Women Priests? E. L. Mascall", *Anglican Way Magazine*, February 15, 2015, https://anglicanway.org/2015/02/15/women-priests-e-l-mascall/.

[6] Columba Marmion, *Christ the Ideal Priest*, trans. Don Matthew Dillon (Herefordshire: Gracewing, 2006), 331.

[7] Ignatius of Antioch, *Epistle to Smyrnaeans* 8.2, quoted in Vernon Staley, *The Catholic Religion* (London: Mowbray, 1893), 33.

[8] Thomas Aquinas, *Summa theologiae* I.1.82, *Summa Theologiae: Volume 30, The Gospel of Grace*, Cornelius Ernst, O.P., ed. (Cambridge: Cambridge University Press, 2006), 233.

[9] Quoted in Robert Barron, *Catholicism* (New York: Image Books, 2011), 174.

[10] Monsignor Robert Hugh Benson, *Confessions of a Convert* (London: Longmans, Green, 1913), 92.

[11] *Book of Common Prayer* (New York: Church Publishing, 1979), 530.

[12] "AMiA" was the Anglican Mission in North America, a cluster of churches that broke away from the Episcopal Church in response to increased theological liberalism and was under the oversight of the Church of the Province of Rwanda.

[13] TEC (The Episcopal Church).

11

God Is an Artist

[1] *The Maxims and Sayings of Philip Neri* (Potosi, Wisc.: St. Athanasius Press, 2009), 19.

[2] C. S. Lewis, quoted in Sheldon Vanauken, *A Severe Mercy* (New York: HarperCollins, 2011), 125.

[3] Ibid., 94.

[4] C. S. Lewis, *The Screwtape Letters* (New York: HarperOne, 1942), 94.

[5] C. S. Lewis, *The Weight of Glory* (New York: HarperOne, 1949), 46.

[6] Edith Stein, *The Science of the Cross*, trans. Josephine Koeppel, O.C.D. (Washington, D.C.: ICS Publications, 2002), 14.

12

Candles among Gunpowder

[1] Collect in the *Book of Common Prayer* (New York: Church Publishing, 1979), 57.

[2] Vincent of Lérins, *Commonitorium Primum* 2.6 (*PL* 50:640).

[3] Pius X, encyclical *Pascendi dominici gregis* (September 8, 1907), no. 39, http://w2.vatican.va/content/pius-x/en/encyclicals/documents/hf_p-x_enc_19070908_pascendi-dominici-gregis.html.

[4] Gerard Manley Hopkins, *The Letters of Gerard Manley Hopkins*, ed. Claude Colleer Abbott (London: Oxford University Press, 1973), 40, 148, 186–87.

[5] Edwin F. Cardinal O'Brien, quoted in George Weigel, *Witness to Hope: The Biography of Pope John Paul II* (New York: Harper Perennial, 2009), 658.

13

Awesome Family Planning

[1] *The Complete Works in Verse and Prose of George Herbert*, ed. Alexander Grosart (London: Robson and Sons, 1874), 87.

[2] Quoted in Dale Ahlquist, *G. K. Chesterton: The Apostle of Common Sense* (San Francisco: Ignatius Press, 2016), 50.

[3] Steve Ray, "Mary, the Ark of the New Covenant", *Catholic Answers Magazine*, May 1, 2009, https://www.catholic.com/magazine/print-edition/mary-the-ark-of-the-new-covenant.

[4] Gary Anderson, *Pro Ecclesia: A Journal of Catholic and Evangelical Theology* 16-N1 (2007): 50.

[5] Robert Farrar Capon, *Bed and Board* (New York: Simon and Schuster, 1965), 62.

[6] Quoted in Ahlquist, *Apostle of Common Sense*, 160.

[7] Gerard Manley Hopkins, "The Wreck of Deutschland", line 277, quoted in *God's Grandeur and Other Poems*, Stanley Appelbaum, ed. (New York: Dover Publications, 1995), 4.

[8] Martin Luther, *Luther's Works*, vol. 7 (St. Louis: Concordia Publishing, 1968), 20–21.

⁹ C. S. Lewis, *The Weight of Glory* (New York: HarperOne, 1949), 46.

¹⁰ John Henry Newman, *The Idea of a University* (London: Longmans, Green, 1905), 121.

14

My Kingdom for a Horse!

¹ Vladimir Sergeyevich Solovyov, *The Russian Church and the Papacy*, Ray Ryland abridged edition (San Diego: Catholic Answers, 2002), 126.

² William Reed Huntington, *The Church Idea* (New York: E. P. Dutton, 1884), 26.

³ Vernon Staley, *The Catholic Religion: A Manual of Instruction for Members of the English Church* (London: A. R. Mowbray, 1901), 33.

⁴ Raymond Brown, "Communicating the Divine and Human in Scripture", *Origens* 22, no. 1 (May 14, 1992): 5–6.

⁵ Solovyov, *Russian Church and the Papacy*, 112.

⁶ John Henry Newman, *The Development of Christian Doctrine* (London: Basil Mantagu Pickering, 1878), 443.

⁷ T. S. Eliot, "The Waste Land", line 403, quoted in *Collected Poems, 1909–1962* (New York: Houghton Mifflin Harcourt, 1963), 52.

⁸ G. K. Chesterton, *Orthodoxy* (New York: Dover Publications, 2012), 13.

⁹ Joseph Cardinal Ratzinger and Hans Urs von Balthasar, *Mary: The Church at the Source* (San Francisco: Ignatius Press, 2016), 70.

¹⁰ Ignatius of Antioch, quoted in Mike Aquilina, *The Fathers of the Church*, 3rd ed. (Huntington, Ind.: Our Sunday Visitor, 2013), 119.

¹¹ Joan of Arc, Acts of the Trial of Joan of Arc, quoted in the *Catechism of the Catholic Church*, no. 795.

¹² John Henry Newman, *Discourses Addressed to Mixed Congregations* (London: Longmans, Green, 1891), 282.

Epilogue

The Culture of Christ

¹ Thoms Aquinas, quoted in *Poems of Grace: Texts from the 1982 Hymnal* (New York: Church Publishing, 1998), 260.

² C. S. Lewis, *Mere Christianity* (New York: HarperCollins, 2001), 205.

³ Ibid.

⁴ John Henry Newman, *Lectures on the Doctrine of Justification* (London: Rivingtons, 1874), 177.

[5] Joseph Pieper, *In Tune with the World: A Theory of Festivity* (South Bend, Ind.: Saint Augustine Press, 1999), 18.

[6] John Chrysostom, quoted in ibid., 23.

[7] Thomas Aquinas, quoted in *Poems of Grace*, 68.

[8] Ibid., 136.

[9] John Senior, *The Restoration of Christian Culture* (San Francisco: Ignatius Press, 1983), 126.

[10] Athanasius, *Festal Letter* 4.332, www.newadvent.org/fathrs/2806004.htm.

ACKNOWLEDGMENTS

I thank Brittany, for her love and courage and perseverance and joy and hope. I thank her for the thousand late-night conversations and the hours spent editing these chapters. I love and adore her. I must thank my children, Timothy and June, for sharing valuable daddy time with this project. I love them and thank God for them. My hope is that they love God and remember me at the altar when I die.

An inadequate thank you must go to my parents, who love my siblings and me. They showed us the love of the Father and worked hard to make a home in a world all too familiar with homelessness. I am so grateful to my dear friends Michael Ward and Holly Ordway and Anne Simonis; and Brother Hildebrand Maria Houser, OSBn, at the Benedictine Monks of Perpetual Adoration, Silverstream Priory in County Meath, Ireland; for their gift of time and attention to detail as they read the manuscript and offered feedback. A thank you goes to my good friend Sam Guzman, for his strength and foresight. Thank you Dale Ahlquist. And I must thank Peter Kreeft and Thomas Howard for their encouragement.

I am so grateful to Mark Brumley, Laura Perudo, Vivian Dudro, Diane Eriksen, and the great team at Ignatius Press. I also thank John M. Vella and Michael J. Lichens. I must thank my professors at Hillsdale College for turning on the light, and my professors at Nashotah House for their wisdom, counsel, and holy zeal. To all my friends who have shared in this journey—Bryce, Judson, Davey, Petrie, Ivan, Emrys, Patrick, Matthew, Nate, Ben, Lars, Tyler, Forrest, Justin, Stephen, Gabriel, Noah, Evan, Tim and Heather, Katy, John, and so many more—I am honored to be their friend and thank God for them. To all those at Church of the Cross, I cannot thank them enough for their love and kindness.

A thank you goes to Father John Yockey for shepherding my family into the Catholic Church, and to Father Tom Brundage for taking me on as a pastoral associate. A thank you also goes to all the parish-ioners at Saint Jerome Catholic Parish for their charity and witness to the truth. I thank the Blessed Virgin Mary and Saint Joseph the Worker and Pope Saint John Paul II for their intercession. Finally, all thanks and praise must go to the Holy Trinity, the one true God known in the Person of Jesus Christ.